INSTITUTIONS OF ART

INSTITUTIONS OF ART

Reconsiderations of George Dickie's Philosophy

Edited by Robert J. Yanal

The Pennsylvania State University Press
University Park, Pennsylvania

Library of Congress Cataloging-in-Publication Data

Institutions of art : reconsiderations of George Dickie's philosophy / edited by Robert J. Yanal.
p. cm.
Includes bibliographical references and index.
ISBN 0-271-01077-0 (cloth : alk. paper)
ISBN 0-271-01078-9 (pbk. : alk. paper)
1. Dickie, George, 1926- . 2. Aesthetics—History. I. Yanal, Robert J.
BH221.U54D535 1994
111'.85'092—dc20 93-18540
CIP

Printed in the United States of America

Published by The Pennsylvania State University Press,
Barbara Building, Suite C, University Park, PA 16802-1003

It is the policy of The Pennsylvania State University Press to use acid-free paper for the first printing of all clothbound books. Publications on uncoated stock satisfy the minimum requirements of American National Standard for Information Sciences—Permanence of Paper for Printed Library Materials, ANSI Z39.48-1984.

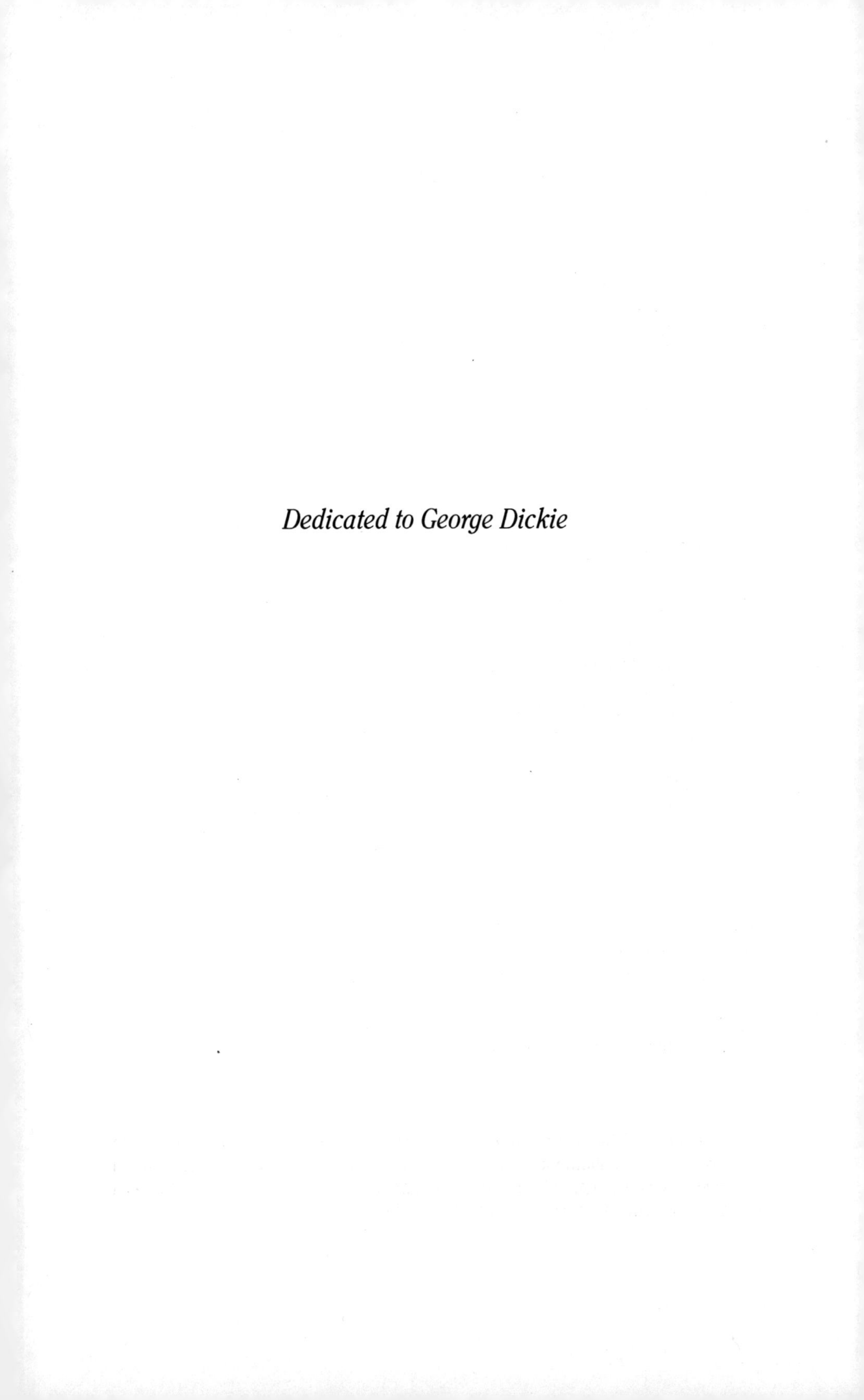

Dedicated to George Dickie

Contents

Preface

A considerable amount of philosophical aesthetics during the past twenty-five-plus years has been stimulated by ideas of George Dickie.

Dickie's first major piece, often reprinted, "The Myth of the Aesthetic Attitude," along with a number of companion essays, argued that there was no such distinct mental category as the aesthetic attitude or aesthetic attention, all putative instances being reducible to paying close attention.[1] These arguments against the existence of a distinct, autonomous aesthetic mental state, theories and descriptions of which were, until Dickie, the very stuff of aesthetics, left the field we continue to call "aesthetics" without a foundation. Although Dickie's arguments were and continue to be contentious— what important philosophical view of persisting significance isn't?—they permanently altered the landscape of modern analytic aesthetics.[2]

Dickie's next major work in aesthetics, the institutional theory of art, de-aestheticized the definition of art.[3] The best-known version of the institutional theory said that a work of art is an artifact upon which some-

1. "The Myth of the Aesthetic Attitude," *American Philosophical Quarterly* 1 (1964): 56–64; "Is Psychology Relevant to Aesthetics?" *Philosophical Review* 71 (1962): 297–300; "Beardsley's Phantom Aesthetic Experience," *The Journal of Philosophy* 62 (1965): 129–36; chaps. 4, 5, 6, and 8 of *Art and the Aesthetic* (Ithaca: Cornell University Press, 1974).

2. Important responses to Dickie's arguments include Allan Casebier, "The Concept of Aesthetic Distance," *The Personalist* 52 (1971): 70–91, and Monroe C. Beardsley, "Aesthetic Experience Regained," *The Journal of Aesthetics and Art Criticism* 28 (1969): 3–11.

3. The institutional theory of art first appeared as "Defining Art," in *American Philosophical Quarterly* 6 (1969): 253–56, though what is taken as its canonical version is found in *Art and the Aesthetic,* chap. 1. Dickie has since revised the theory: *The Art Circle* (New York: Haven Publications,

one acting on behalf of the artworld has conferred the status of candidate for appreciation. At the outset, the institutional theory was the principal counter to the art-as-open-concept theories of the 1960s, of which Morris Weitz's essay is the best-known instance.[4] The institutional theory was the most discussed proposal in aesthetics during the 1970s, inspiring supporters who produced variations on the theory as well as detractors who thought the theory thoroughly wrongheaded.[5] The legacy of the institutional theory is considerable. Besides an enormous literature pro and con, the theory has entrenched at least one of its theses. Today nearly everyone would agree that an object cannot be identified as an artwork merely on the basis of its "formal" or "aesthetic" properties (however these are to be construed). Even such competitors to the institutional theory as the meaning theories of Arthur Danto and Richard Wollheim[6] and the historicist theories of Jerrold Levinson[7] and Noël Carroll (in the present volume), theories which reject much of the institutional theory, still accept that theory's anti-aestheticism. Despite criticism and the appearance of new, competing theories, the institutional theory survives, both as an anthologized classic and in a recent book by Stephen Davies, *Definitions of Art,* which defends aspects of it.[8]

Dickie's most recently published book to date, *Evaluating Art,* supplies

---

1984). An important influence on the institutional theory was Arthur Danto's "The Artworld," *The Journal of Philosophy* 63 (1964): 571–84, though I should note that Danto has disentangled his views from the institutional theory. See Danto, *The Transfiguration of the Commonplace* (Cambridge: Harvard University Press, 1981), p. viii.

4. Morris Weitz, "The Role of Theory in Aesthetics," *The Journal of Aesthetics and Art Criticism* 14 (1956): 27–35, often reprinted; but see also the earlier (and better) essay by Paul Ziff, "The Task of Defining a Work of Art," *Philosophical Review* 62 (1953): 58–78.

5. Major critical pieces on the theory include Ted Cohen's "The Possibility of Art: Remarks on a Proposal by Dickie," *Philosophical Review* 82 (1973): 69–82; Richard Wollheim's "The Institutional Theory of Art," a supplementary essay to his *Art and Its Objects,* 2nd ed. (Cambridge: Cambridge University Press, 1980); and Anita Silvers, "The Artworld Discarded," *The Journal of Aesthetics and Art Criticism* 34 (1976): 441–54. *Culture and Art,* ed. Lars Aagaard-Mogensen (Atlantic Highlands, N.J.: Humanities Press, 1976), is an anthology devoted to the institutional theory. Non-Dickiean institutional theories of art are given by Timothy Binkley, "Piece: Contra Aesthetics," *The Journal of Aesthetics and Art Criticism* 35 (1977): 265–77, and by Marcia Eaton, *Art and Nonart* (Cranbury, N.J.: Associated University Presses, 1983), pp. 96–122.

6. See Danto, *The Transfiguration of the Commonplace,* and Richard Wollheim, *Painting as an Art* (Princeton: Princeton University Press, 1987), both of which propose *having a meaning* as an art-conferring property.

7. Jerrold Levinson, "Defining Art Historically" and "Refining Art Historically," in his *Music, Art, and Metaphysics* (Ithaca: Cornell University Press, 1990).

8. Stephen Davies, *Definitions of Art* (Ithaca: Cornell University Press, 1991).

(as Peg Brand puts it in her essay) an evaluative part two to the classificatory part one of the institutional theory.[9] *Evaluating Art* not only comes to terms with the great theoreticians of art appraisal of the second half of the twentieth century (including Beardsley, Ziff, Sibley, and Goodman), capturing what is best in their theories and avoiding their mistakes; it caps a growing tendency in recent literature to see aesthetic evaluation as only a *partial* evaluator of art.[10] For the thesis of the book is that the *artistic* value of a work of art consists not only in its aesthetic value but in its moral and cognitive values as well. The matrix system presented in Dickie's book as a way of exhibiting the aesthetic/moral/cognitive dimensions of artistic evaluation has generated further discussion, some of which is contained herein.

Dickie has always been interested in the history of aesthetics, and he has published papers and book chapters on selected topics and figures.[11] His current book-in-progress, *The Century of Taste,* explicates the theories of Hutcheson, Gerard, Alison, Kant, and Hume. Dickie argues that the middle three take theories of taste into a blind alley and that Hume's theory is both a successful continuation of Hutcheson's and the most plausible theory of taste. Dickie's criticisms of Kant, standardly regarded as the most profound theorist of taste, are sure to arouse controversy.

Consistently, Dickie's writing has been a paradigm of philosophical carefulness and clarity. His work ranks among the best examples of analytic aesthetics. As will be seen from this collection, the philosophy of George Dickie continues to provoke reaction and reflection.

We begin with a trio of essays reconsidering the institutional theory and its implications. Noël Carroll, in "Identifying Art," argues that none of Dickie's institutional theories, including his most recent theory in *The Art Circle,* has answered the challenge of Weitz. The institutional theory of art

9. George Dickie, *Evaluating Art* (Philadelphia: Temple University Press, 1988), which is preceded by, among other pieces by Dickie, "Evaluating Art," *British Journal of Aesthetics* 25 (1985): 3–16, and "Beardsley, Sibley, and Critical Principles," *The Journal of Aesthetics and Art Criticism* 46 (1987): 229–37.

10. This body of literature includes Carolyn Korsmeyer, "On Distinguishing 'Aesthetic' from 'Artistic,'" *The Journal of Aesthetic Education* 11 (1977): 45–57; Tomasz Kulka, "The Artistic and Aesthetic Value of Art," *British Journal of Aesthetics* 21 (1981): 336–50; Robert J. Yanal, "Aesthetic Value and Genius," in *The Reasons of Art,* ed. Peter McCormick (Ottawa: University of Ottawa Press, 1985); and Noël Carroll, "Art and Interaction," *The Journal of Aesthetics and Art Criticism* 45 (1986): 57–68. See Bohdan Dziemidok's essay in the present volume for a history of this trend.

11. See, for example, the historical chapters in his *Aesthetics: An Introduction* (Indianapolis: Bobbs-Merrill, 1971); "Taste and Attitude: The Origin of the Aesthetic," *Theoria* 39 (1973): 153–70; and "Hume's Way: The Path Not Taken," in *The Reasons of Art.*

does not, according to Carroll, tell us what a work of art is; it tells us only that a work of art (whatever it is) fits into a certain network of social practices. Carroll develops a method of historical narration for identifying a work of art, a method which is intended to be nondefinitional though indebted to the contextual aspects of the institutional theory. Jeffrey Wieand's "Perceptually Indistinguishable Objects" reexamines the role such cases—a pair of objects that appear identical, yet one and only one of which is a work of art—have played in the institutional theory. Wieand denies that the existence of perceptually indistinguishable objects forces an institutional (or relational) theory of art, as both Dickie and Danto have supposed. Susan Feagin, in "Valuing the Artworld," holds that it is desirable that the artworld not be the neutral entity of the institutional theory whose sole task is to confer art status: the artworld should, often enough, sponsor artworks that lead us to "explore and expand new regions of the human imagination."

The second trio delves into issues raised in *Evaluating Art.* Bohdan Dziemidok's "On the Need to Distinguish Between Aesthetic and Artistic Evaluations of Art" presents a history of recent aesthetics in which he traces some of the antecedents of Dickie's view that the value of a work of art is not reducible to its aesthetic value. Peg Brand's "Evaluating Art: A Feminist Case for Dickie's Matrix System" seeks to expand the role of cognitive value in evaluating art, pressing the case that this will allow for a less attenuated evaluation of works by female artists. In "Evaluating More Than Art" Marcia Eaton is interested in the public assessment of such things as the aesthetic impact of a dam on a landscape or funding decisions regarding the arts. Focusing on evaluative ranking (which of three novels, say, is the best, second best, third best?) Eaton shows, through an application of Kenneth Arrow's results, that aggregating individual rankings ("votings") via Dickie's matrix system will not yield a true group preference. Dickie's matrices, while nonrelativistic, turn out to be nonaggregatable.

The third trio tunes into Dickie's continued interest in the history of aesthetics. Peter Kivy's essay, "From Literature as Imagination to Literature as Memory," provides us with a historical account of modern thought regarding the source of the poet's ideas. Francis Bacon's philosophy located them in the imagination, an active, creative faculty which "may at pleasure join that which Nature hath severed, and sever that which Nature hath joined." As determinism came in (via Spinoza, Hume, and others) it infiltrated the imagination which, accordingly, could not be as "free" as it may have seemed. Thomas Reid, in an apparently unrelated development, managed to argue that the initiation of memory is a free act. If creativity requires freedom, then, the source of poetic ideas came to be located in memory, a move culminating in William Wordsworth's famous definition of poetry as "emotion recollected in tranquillity." Ted Cohen spins out "Partial Enchantments" of the central parable in Hume's wonderful essay on taste. Cohen shows how Hume's "ideal creature" theory trades a question of value (Is this object beautiful?) for a question of fact (Is there a joint verdict pronouncing it beautiful from persons who are good judges of beauty?). A footnote well worth reading defends Hume against certain Marxist criticisms. My own essay, concerning Kant on beauty and aesthetic ideas, deals mainly with a kind of apparent inconsistency in Kant's third *Critique:* namely, how the beautiful, which seems initially to concern "form" exclusively, can in that work's theory of fine art be said to apply to the expression of aesthetic ideas. Near the end I question Dickie's assumption in *Evaluating Art*—though this assumption is fairly common—that Kant is *entirely* in the school of those who want to provide only a narrowly construed aesthetic evaluation of art.

As editor, I want to thank the contributors for their excellent essays, and for their efforts in bringing their work to bear on George Dickie's philosophy, thereby achieving a unity unusual in collections of this sort. I also am grateful to the contributors for their encouragement and suggestions. Marcia Eaton was especially supportive. Peter Kivy and Noël Carroll suggested publication options. Ted Cohen, the best phrasemaker I know, proposed the main title of this volume. All the essayists are indebted to the two reviewers of this volume who wish to remain anonymous, though their suggestions have improved every paper. I would also like to thank Sandy Thatcher of Penn State Press for his support of the project, and Chuck Purrenhage for his meticulous copyediting of manuscripts in nine different styles and states of readiness.

The contributors dedicate this collection to George Dickie, whose influence and example we all warmly acknowledge.

1

RECONSIDERING THE INSTITUTIONAL THEORY

Noël Carroll

Identifying Art

As a student of George Dickie's, I have been profoundly influenced by his contributions to the philosophy of art. I believe that his criticisms of the notions of aesthetic perception, aesthetic attitudes, aesthetic experience, and so on remain fundamentally sound. And, as well, they place important constraints on theories of art. Notably, they preclude the possibility of sustaining what are currently called aesthetic theories of art: that is, theories of art which propose to define art in terms of the engendering of aesthetic experience. George Dickie's rejection of aesthetic experience, of course, set the stage for the proposal of his own variations on the institutional theory of art by effectively removing one sort of rival—aesthetic theories of art—from the playing field. And I am convinced that this move is still decisive.

George Dickie also successfully undermined the open concept/family resemblance approach to identifying art as a way of dialectically arguing in favor of institutional-type theories of art. In this matter, too, I believe Dickie's arguments are still powerful.

In challenging the viability of aesthetic theories of art and the open concept/family resemblance approach, George Dickie showed the importance of social context for the prospects of identifying art. His own variations on the institutional theory of art are contested, but his emphasis upon the relevance of social context represents a major contribution to the philosophy of art. In my own work, I have become suspicious of the plausibility of institutional theories of art, including its most recent reincarnation. I have argued that art is not identified by definitions, institutional or otherwise, but by narratives. The essay that follows is an attempt to provide further clarification of the narrative approach, which I advocate, to the problem of identifying art.[1]

Nevertheless, though I have departed from the letter of George Dickie's approach, I am still touched by its spirit, especially by its emphasis on the centrality of context. And, as well, my conception of the structure of the dialectical field on which debates about identifying art are staged is deeply indebted to Dickie's always careful and clear way of setting up the problem.

Identification, Essence, and Definition

One of the central questions of analytic philosophy in the twentieth century—notably in the second half of the twentieth century—has been "What is art?" Whether it was an issue of much urgency earlier is a matter of genuine historical dispute. And even in the second half of the twentieth century, there have been distinguished theorists—like Nelson Goodman[2] and Kendall Walton[3]—who have wondered whether there is much profit to be found in this issue. Indeed, in his landmark treatise *Aesthetics,* Monroe Beardsley did not bother to address the question in its canonical form.[4] Nevertheless, the sheer statistical evidence seems enough to warrant the claim that it has been *a* central question of analytic philosophy even if, at

1. For a statement of this approach, see my "Art, Practice and Narrative," *The Monist* 71 (1986): 140–56.

2. Nelson Goodman, "When Is Art?" in his *Ways of Worldmaking* (Indianapolis: Hackett Publishing Co., 1978).

3. Kendall Walton, review of George Dickie's *Art and the Aesthetic, Philosophical Review* 86 (1977): 97–101.

4. Monroe Beardsley, *Aesthetics: Problems in the Theory of Criticism* (New York: Harcourt, Brace & World, 1958).

the same time, it is true that our energies might have been spent more fruitfully elsewhere.

However, even if it is granted that this has been *a* central question for philosophers, it has been noted less often that this question may be taken in a number of different ways—ways that diverge from the interpretation that contemporary philosophers are often predisposed to give it, and ways that do not connect in a neat package of interrelated answers. That is, the question "What is art?" may, at different times, signal a request for different kinds of information, and that information, furthermore, may not be linked logically in the manner most contemporary philosophers anticipate.[5]

Some of the primary issues that the question "What is art?" may serve to introduce include the following. First of all, how do we identify or recognize or establish something to be a work of art? That is, how do we establish that a given object or performance is an artwork? This request for information has, of course, become increasingly pressing for nearly a century, a period that we might label the "age of the avant-garde." For in its urge to subvert expectations, the art of the avant-garde, which would appear to have the most legitimate historical claim to be the high art of our times, has consistently and intentionally produced objects and performances that challenge settled conceptions about what one is likely to encounter on a visit to a gallery, a theater, or a concert hall. It can be no accident that the art theorists of the last century have become so obsessed with the question "What is art?" during the age of the avant-garde. For theory here would appear to be driven by practical concerns: that is to say, given the consistently anomalous productions of the avant-garde, how does one establish that these works are artworks? Indeed, recalling what Stanley Cavell has identified as the modern audience's fear that it might be the butt of a continuously floating confidence game, we surmise that the issue is one of how we are to go about establishing that the works in question *are* works of art in the face of worries, if not downright skeptical objections, to the contrary.[6] Again, it can be no accident that one of the most tempting theories of art to emerge in this period was George Dickie's institutional theory of art which, if nothing else, was perfectly suited to perform such a service for the works of Dada and its heritage.

5. The realization that the question "What is art?" may represent different requests for information has been noted by T. J. Diffey in his "The Republic of Art," *British Journal of Aesthetics* 9 (1969): 45–56. My thinking has been influenced by this article and by discussions with Dale Jamieson.

6. Stanley Cavell, "Music Discomposed," in his *Must We Mean What We Say?* (Cambridge: Cambridge University Press, 1969).

This, of course, is not said in order to claim that in previous times there never arose the question of how to identify something as a work of art. The explosion of romanticism certainly anticipates some of the quandaries of the age of the avant-garde. And there are other precedents. My point is simply that in the age of the avant-garde, the question of how one recognizes and establishes something to be a work of art is irresistible in a way that is reflected by the concerns of contemporary philosophy of art. Moreover, the question of how one establishes that something is a work of art gives rise to a deeper philosophical vexation: Are there indeed reliable methods for establishing or identifying something to be a work of art?

Another issue that might be introduced by asking "What is art?" may be the question of whether art has an essence. Here, following T. J. Diffey,[7] by essence I mean some general, shared feature or features of artworks which are useful to mark but which are not shared by artworks alone. When Plato and Aristotle agree that poetry and paintings are imitations, they point to what they take to be such an essence, though this feature, despite its significance for art as they knew it, was also shared, even in their own times, by childhood games of emulation. In this sense, an essence may be a necessary condition, and it is my suspicion that art theory before the age of the avant-garde was concerned primarily to isolate only such conditions, especially where identifying these shed illumination on artistic practices. To say that art is essentially communication or that it is essentially historical is to claim that art has an essence in this sense which is a matter of pointing to an informative general feature of art without maintaining that it is a feature which uniquely pertains to art. When, for example, George Dickie says that an artwork is of a kind designed for public presentation,[8] he marks an essential feature of art, though neither essential public presentability, nor historicity, nor communicativeness is a property of art alone. In asking "What is art?" we may be introducing the question of whether art has a noteworthy essence or necessary condition—a question that, if answered affirmatively, will be followed by a specification of what that general feature might be. Moreover, citation of that feature need not be proposed for the sake of saying something unique about art, but only as something that helps us understand art—that points us in the direction of something we have missed or helps us get out of some problem into which we have backed ourselves. Again, much previous art theory might be read profitably as presenting answers of this general sort.

7. T. J. Diffey, "Essentialism and the Definition of Art," *British Journal of Aesthetics* 13 (1973): 103–20.

8. George Dickie, *The Art Circle* (New York: Haven Publications, 1984), p. 80.

Thirdly, "What is art?" may also be taken as a request for a *real* definition in terms of necessary conditions that are jointly sufficient. This is the interpretation of the question that Morris Weitz attributed to the conversation of art theory that preceded his neo-Wittgensteinian de-Platonization of it. Whether Weitz's diagnosis of the tradition was an historically accurate conjecture is open to debate. However, the particular spin that Weitz put on the question—construing it as a request for a real definition—is the one that subsequent theorists, like George Dickie, have taken to be the most "natural" interpretation (though it pays to remark here that it may only seem natural in the context of a debate where Weitz and the other neo-Wittgensteinians had laid down the dialectical challenge that it cannot be done).

These three issues—Is there a reliable method for identifying art? Does art have an essence? and Does art have a real definition?—are the primary questions that may be introduced by asking "What is art?" However, there are two other questions worth mentioning, even though I will have little to say about them. They involve requests for information about the importance of art as a human activity, which some theorists, though not I, regard as inextricably linked with what I have identified as our three primary questions.[9] These questions—which I think of as secondary—are as follows. First: Why is art valuable as a human activity? Here we might be told that art is a cognitive instrument or a means of moral education. Moreover, this request can be made in an even more demanding manner. Specifically, we may be asked what makes art *uniquely* valuable—that is, What is the peculiar value of art in contradistinction to the values available in every other arena of human activity?

Now it seems to me that the reason all these questions—ranging from "How do we tell something is art?" to "What is the peculiar value of art?"—have been lumped together is that there is an underlying philosophical dream such that, ideally, all the relevant answers in this neighborhood should fit into a tidy theoretical package.

Consider the primary variants of our question: Is there a reliable method for identifying artworks? Does art have (some) essential feature(s)? Can art be defined? The philosophical dream to which I have alluded wants to answer each of these questions affirmatively, in such a way that each affirmation supplies the grounds for subsequent affirmations. That is, an affirmative answer to the question of whether art has any essential features may be registered in the expectation that these can be worked into a

9. The debate here would center on the issue of whether there is a purely classificatory, nonevaluative sense of "art." Here I agree with Dickie in thinking that there is.

real definition such that the relevant necessary conditions are jointly sufficient for identifying something as an artwork. Thus, the definition functions as the reliable standard for assessing whether or not something is a work of art.

Of course, there is an even more ambitious dream in these precincts, one that hopes not only to link up the answers to our primary questions but to link up our secondary answers as well. That is to say, there is the expectation that we shall be able to say why art is important, even uniquely important, in the course of defining art. Here there is the conviction that, among the necessary conditions listed in our definition, there will be some feature or features whose citation makes it evident that art has value or even a unique value. An example of this variation of the dream is Monroe Beardsley's aesthetic definition of art, in which affording aesthetic interest is related to the value of art as a human activity. That Beardsley supposes that some such account of the value of art should be part of the definition of art, moreover, is indicated by Beardsley's criticism of the institutional theory of art in terms of George Dickie's failure to say anything about the "pervasive human needs that it is the peculiar role of art to serve."[10]

Stated in its most ambitious form—that an identifying, real definition of art will yield an account of what is uniquely valuable about art—the dream seems exactly that. For, save embattled defenders of aesthetic theories of art, the remaining consensus is that art may serve a motley of purposes and, in consequence, that it possesses a motley assortment of values. But even the less ambitious dream—that artworks might be identified by means of a real definition which comprises sets of necessary conditions that are jointly sufficient—is dubious. For as the neo-Wittgensteinians—Weitz, Kennick, perhaps Ziff and others—maintain, it is at least possible to answer what I have called our three primary questions in ways that are independent of each other. That is, there may be no reason to suppose that the relevant answers dovetail—indeed, they may come apart.[11]

For example, it is possible to deny that a real definition of art is possible,

10. Monroe Beardsley, "Is Art Essentially Institutional," in *Culture and Art,* ed. Lars Aagaard-Mogensen (Atlantic Highlands, N.J.: Humanities Press, 1976), p. 106.

11. See Morris Weitz, "The Role of Theory in Aesthetics," *The Journal of Aesthetics and Art Criticism* 15 (1956): 27–35; Morris Weitz, "Wittgenstein's Aesthetics," in *Language and Aesthetics,* ed. Benjamin Tilghman (Lawrence: University Press of Kansas, 1973); William Kennick, "Does Traditional Aesthetics Rest on a Mistake?" *Mind* 67 (1958): 317–34; William Kennick, "Definition and Theory in Aesthetics," in *Art and Philosophy,* ed. William Kennick (New York: St. Martin's Press, 1964); and Paul Ziff, "The Task of Defining a Work of Art," *Philosophical Review* 62 (1953): 58–78.

as Weitz did,[12] and to deny that artworks share any general features or essences, as Kennick did,[13] and still argue that we do possess reliable methods for identifying or establishing that a given object or production is a work of art. That is, we may be able to identify candidates as art even if art lacks an essence. After all, we manage to identify a great many other things for which we lack a real definition. Of course, the leading candidate for a reliable method of art identification—the one that the neo-Wittgensteinians championed—was the notion of family resemblance. In fact, it may be the only well-known alternative to definition to be found in the literature so far, though, by way of preview, I should say that I plan to introduce narration as another alternative.

On one variation of the family resemblance approach, we begin with a set of cases of acknowledged or paradigmatic artworks. Given a new candidate for membership in the set, one identifies it or establishes it to be a work of art by determining whether it is sufficiently similar to our starting cases in a number of respects. This resemblance to our paradigm is called a family resemblance. Establishing that something bears a family resemblance to our paradigms, or to works whose resemblance to our paradigms has been previously recognized, is enough to establish a new candidate to be an artwork. However, whether the family resemblance approach is a reliable method is subject to a number of challenges.

The first objection takes note of the logic of resemblance. Starting with a handful of paradigms, we can identify a second generation of what Arthur Danto has called "affines"—things that share discernible similarities with our paradigms.[14] Yet these affines also have a great many properties that are not shared with our initial group insofar as things that are similar to each other in some respects also differ from each other in further respects. Consequently, a third generation of affines can be constructed that bears a large number of resemblances to the second generation but few to the first. Clearly, in the fourth and fifth generations of affines, we can get very far away from the package of properties possessed by the first generation. In fact, in short order, since it is also a feature of the logic of resemblance that everything resembles everything else in some respect, enough generations of affines of the sort that I have in mind can be arrayed so that anything can be said to bear a family resemblance to either an artistic paradigm or an affine thereof.

12. Weitz, "The Role of Theory in Aesthetics."

13. Kennick, "Does Traditional Aesthetics Rest on a Mistake?"

14. Arthur Danto, "Thoughts on the Institutional Theory of Art," a paper delivered at the San Francisco Art Institute, July 10, 1991.

Now this may not seem to be a particularly bothersome consequence in a world that has been shaken by Dada. However, the family resemblance method seems liable to identify anything as art for the wrong reason. A given snow shovel might be recognized to be art as it is in the case of Duchamp's *In Advance of a Broken Arm;* but I cannot claim that my snow shovel, which resembles Duchamp's in a hundred ways, is art on that basis. Perhaps my snow shovel could be made into a work of art—maybe as a deadpan counterexample to the family resemblance method. But it would require more than resemblance for that. In such a case, it would require what Danto calls a "background of theory."[15]

One may worry whether the preceding demolition of the family resemblance approach has not proceeded too hastily. For the family resemblance approach depends upon our starting with some paradigmatic exemplars, and one might suspect that the use of paradigms here could provide some constraints that would halt the headlong rush to the conclusion that everything is art. For example, the relevant resemblances, which this approach invokes, are said to be family resemblances. So perhaps that places suitable restraints upon what resemblances can count in the process of establishing that a candidate in question is art. That is, the collection of paradigms is a family, and any candidate that is to resemble them in a family way must share whatever property (or properties) makes the collection a family. But, of course, it has long been a criticism of the family resemblance approach that the notion of "family" that figures so prominently in its name really performs no work in the theory.[16] Nor is this an accidental oversight, given the other commitments of the most radical neo-Wittgensteinians. For if there were criteria of family resemblance or criteria for what sort of resemblances count as family resemblances, then the neo-Wittgensteinians would appear to be committed to the concession that there are at least necessary conditions for art. And that is *not* a concession they will make.

At this point, one attempted rejoinder might be to say that the neo-Wittgensteinians need not rely upon the notion of necessary conditions in order to cash in the idea of family resemblance, but instead need only claim that a family resemblance to our paradigmatic artworks is a resemblance by

15. Arthur Danto, *The Transfiguration of the Commonplace* (Cambridge: Harvard University Press, 1981). It is interesting to note that Danto's point—that art is something the eye cannot descry—counts against the family resemblance approach to identifying artworks as well as against certain well-known aesthetic theories of art (such as Clive Bell's).

16. See Maurice Mandelbaum, "Family Resemblances and Generalizations Concerning the Arts," *American Philosophical Quarterly* 2 (1965): 219–28; and Anthony Manser, "Games and Family Resemblances," *Philosophy* 42 (1967): 210–25.

virtue of correspondence to one or more members of a disjunctive set of the paradigmatic artmaking properties of our paradigmatic artworks—that is, those properties by virtue of which the artworks in question belong to our collection of paradigms. In other words, our collection of paradigmatic artworks yields a disjunctive set of paradigmatic artmaking properties; and, so, a family resemblance is a similarity to the paradigms in terms of one or more paradigmatic artmaking properties. Thus, not anything could become art, because in order to be art a candidate would have to possess one or more of a disjunctive set of paradigmatic artmaking properties.

However, this maneuver is not open to the neo-Wittgensteinian because such a theorist is committed to the view that one cannot fix a paradigmatic set of artmaking properties. And if such a set cannot be fixed, then we are back to sorting candidates in terms of resemblance rather than family resemblance. And that, combined with the principle that everything resembles everything else in some respect, will leave intact the *reductio ad absurdum* initiated four paragraphs earlier.

The preceding dilemma demonstrates the inadequacy of the family resemblance approach as a reliable method for identifying artworks. And this, along with the recognition that, *pace* Weitz, a definition of art, properly framed, need be no impediment to artistic creativity, encouraged a return to the dream of finding an identifying definition of art in terms of sets of necessary conditions that are jointly sufficient. This drama has been played out most explicitly with reference to Dickie's institutional theory of art.[17] Yet, to date, despite the voluminous exchanges on the topic, the prospects for securing a real definition of art along institutional lines seem slim.

George Dickie's most recent version of an institutional theory is advanced in his monograph *The Art Circle.* The core of the theory is a definition which proposes that "a work of art is of a kind created to be presented to an artworld public."[18] This definition, in turn, is elucidated by the following four definitions: "A public is a set of persons the members of which are prepared in some degree to understand an object which is presented to them"; "An artworld system is a framework for the presentation of a work of

17. It is instructive to note that even though George Dickie exploited the criticisms of people like Maurice Mandelbaum in terms of the latter's suggestion that the properties which the family resemblance theorists overlooked were nonmanifest relational ones, he did not also take Mandelbaum's suggestion that the relevant properties might be functional. Perhaps the reason for this is that the most obvious candidate for the pertinent functional properties in this area involved the putative capacity of artworks to engender aesthetic experiences. And, of course, Dickie was already opposed to the invocation of anything aesthetic.

18. Dickie, *The Art Circle,* p. 80.

art by an artist to an artworld public"; "An artist is a person who participates with understanding in the making of an artwork"; and "The artworld is the totality of all artworld systems."[19] The first thing to note about this set of definitions is that it is circular insofar as the concept of a work of art is material to the definition of the artist which, of course, is presupposed by the definition of an artworld system which, in turn, supplies the basis for identifying an artworld public upon which the very notion of a work of art depends. Of course, noting this circularity is no news. Dickie himself calls attention to it, arguing that the definition is circular because the concept of art, like other cultural concepts, is inflected. Perhaps, however, rather than saying that the concept of art requires a special sort of inflected definition, it might be more to the point to admit that this reformulation of the institutional theory of art has just given up the aim of producing a real definition of art where that is understood in terms of the challenge that the neo-Wittgensteinians advanced.

Moreover, it seems to me, there is a real question as to whether the new institutional theory is really a theory of *art*. For the inflected set of definitions, though mentioning "art" at crucial points, could be filled in just as easily with the names of other coordinated, communicative practices like philosophy or wisecracking. For example, we might say that "a work of philosophy is a discourse of a kind created to be presented to a philosophyworld public" or that "a wisecrack is a discourse of a kind created to be presented to a jokeworld public" while also adjusting the related, elucidating, inflected propositions so that the structure they picture is analogous in terms of functional positions to the artworld and its systems.

But then the question arises as to whether George Dickie has really said anything specific about art, as opposed to merely producing something like the necessary framework of coordinated, communicative practices of a certain level of complexity, where such practices cannot be identified in terms of their content. Art is an example of such a practice. But in illuminating certain necessary structural features of such practices, Dickie has not really told us anything about art *qua* art. Rather, he has implied that art belongs to the genus of complex, coordinated, communicative practices, and he has shown us by example some of the features that such practices presuppose by way of interrelated structural functions. Undoubtedly, such an analysis is not without interest. But it is not what disputants in the conversation of analytic philosophy expected in the name of a definition.

19. Ibid., pp. 80–82.

Another way of making this point might be to agree that Dickie's new version of the institutional theory does tell us something about the necessary conditions of art insofar as art is the product of a coordinated social practice. But the necessary conditions in question are features shared also by social practices other than art. This is not to say that the reformulation is uninformative. It points in the direction of a social framework for artmaking that many philosophers may have heretofore ignored. However, if at best George Dickie can claim only to have elucidated some necessary conditions for artmaking of the sort shared by comparable coordinated social practices, then he should give up talking about defining art. For he is no longer playing that game according to its original rules, and it only confuses matters to pretend that a real definition is still in the offing.[20]

Dickie's response to the failure of family resemblance as a reliable means for identifying artworks was to return—undoubtedly egged on by Weitz's challenge—to the project of framing a real, identifying definition of art. However, there may be another lesson to be derived from the neo-Wittgensteinian episode and another response to the failure of the family resemblance method. We may provisionally accept the neo-Wittgensteinian suggestion in one of its weaker forms—to wit: that a real definition of art is at least unnecessary—and agree that we nevertheless have reliable means at our disposal for establishing whether or not a given candidate is an artwork. Such a method will not be the family resemblance approach, of course, since the objections of George Dickie and others do seem pretty compelling. However, the refutation of that particular approach does not preclude that there may be other methods for establishing that something is art and that these other methods are not susceptible to the objections leveled at the family resemblance approach. The particular method I have in mind is historical narration of the sort that I will characterize in the next section of the present essay.[21]

But before turning to that analysis, let me summarize my argumentative strategy in light of the framework set forth in the preceding pages. I intend

20. Dickie's theory of the art circle is also criticized by Robert Stecker in his "The End of an Institutional Definition of Art," *British Journal of Aesthetics* 26 (1986): 124–32. Dickie has answered Stecker in his "Reply to Stecker," in *Aesthetics: A Critical Anthology,* 2nd. ed., ed. George Dickie, Richard Sclafani, and Ronald Roblin (New York: St. Martin's Press, 1989). See also Jerrold Levinson, review of Dickie's *The Art Circle, Philosophical Review* 96 (1987): 141–46.

21. Throughout this essay, when it is claimed that identifying narratives are distinct from real definitions, I mean that they are distinct from definitions in terms of necessary conditions which are jointly sufficient. I take this to be the relevant sense of "definition" for a discussion such as the present one because that is the kind of definition which has been at the center of our controversies since the 1950s.

to answer the question "What is art?" (where that question is taken to pertain to answering affirmatively whether we have a reliable method for identifying art) by specifying the nature of that method. My proposal is that we do have a reliable method for identifying a candidate to be an artwork and that that method is historical narration.[22]

Concerning the question of whether art may be characterized by means of a real definition, I remain agnostic: not only have George Dickie's attempts to provide one failed, but, as I shall try to show in a later section of this essay, recent attempts by Jerrold Levinson and Arthur Danto appear deeply problematic as well. Needless to say, such failures do not prove that there is no essential definition of art. But since I maintain that we do not really need such a definition, our agnosticism is not of the anxious variety. For the question of whether art can be defined is "academic" in the strong sense of the term, since artworks can be identified by other means.

Narration and Identification

As suggested above, a major impulse for a great deal of what we call art theory derives from the practical pressure of adjudicating momentous shifts within the practice of art. This is an historical conjecture. Perhaps some evidence for this conjecture is that the greatest variation in art theories corresponds to the period in Western art history that is marked by the fastest rates of innovation and change. That is, the most seismic shifts in art theory have occurred during what I referred to above as the age of the avant-garde. Again, this is not said with the intention of denying that in previous epochs major changes called for theoretical accommodation; I claim only that the seminal role of theory in negotiating spiraling historical transitions becomes particularly salient in the age of the avant-garde.

The dialectical conversation of the analytic philosophy of art has unfolded

22. This method identifies works as art where the works were art at the moment of their inception. Identifying narratives do not constitute works as art; thus, they are not susceptible to the kinds of objections that were leveled at Dickie's notion of the conferral of status. Identifying narratives are typically mobilized in contexts where questions about whether some work is an artwork are likely to arise. In such contexts, identifying narratives establish the credentials of something that is already art. Identifying narratives do not, so to say, turn nonartworks (or not-yet-artworks) into artworks.

Furthermore, this procedure is classificatory insofar as it in no way implies that the work in question is good. For even if an unproblematic application of the procedure implies that an artist succeeded in making art, that success is logically independent from the question of whether the art is good.

against the backdrop of avant-garde practice. Whether or not this has always been explicitly acknowledged by the major participants in that conversation, it should be clear that developments in the avant-garde have motivated what are identified as the crucial turning points in the dialogue. Implicit in the theories of Clive Bell[23] and R. G. Collingwood[24] are defenses of emerging avant-garde practices—neoimpressionism, on the one hand, and the modernist poetics of Joyce, Stein, and Eliot on the other. Indeed, these theories might be read as an attempt to realign the compass of art in general according to a grid extrapolated from the previously mentioned avant-garde movements. Susanne K. Langer's theory of dance, in turn, might be read as a gloss on the aesthetics of modern dance;[25] while, given the premium they place on innovation and originality, neo-Wittgensteinians would appear to have virtually incorporated the ideals of avant-gardism into their concept of art.

Likewise, George Dickie's initial version of the institutional theory of art requires something like the presupposition that Dada is a central form of artistic practice in order for its intuition pumps (like Walter de Maria's *High Energy Bar*) to work; while Arthur Danto wondered at the end of his "The Last Work of Art: Artworks and Real Things" whether his essay was not just another avant-garde artwork.[26] In any case, Danto has freely admitted that the historical conditions for initiating a philosophy of art, as he construes it, were secured by the avant-garde production of what he calls "indiscernibles," such as Warhol's famous Brillo boxes.[27]

Moreover, the linkage between art theory and avant-garde practice is evident outside the canonical progression of analytic philosophers of art. Russian formalism was intimately connected with Russian futurist poetry,[28] while the recent influential essays of Barthes and Foucault concerning the death of the author promote the explicit modernist ideals of cited authors, such as Mallarmé and Beckett, as the conditions of all writing.[29]

23. Clive Bell, *Art* (New York: Capricorn Press, 1958). For an analysis of Bell's theory in relation to the avant-garde art of his contemporaries, see Noël Carroll, "Clive Bell's Aesthetic Hypothesis," in *Aesthetics: A Critical Anthology*.

24. R. G. Collingwood, *Principles of Art* (Oxford: Clarendon Press, 1935).

25. Susanne K. Langer, *Feeling and Form* (New York: Scribner's, 1953).

26. Arthur Danto, "The Last Work of Art: Artworks and Real Things," *Theoria* 39 (1973): 1–17.

27. Arthur Danto, *The Philosophical Disenfranchisement of Art* (New York: Columbia University Press, 1986).

28. See *Russian Formalist Criticism: Four Essays,* ed. Lee T. Lemon and Marion J. Ries (Lincoln: University of Nebraska Press, 1965); and Victor Erhlich, *Russian Formalism* (New Haven: Yale University Press, 1981).

29. See Roland Barthes, "The Death of the Author," in his *Image-Music-Text* (New York: Hill & Wang, 1977); Michel Foucault, "What Is an Author," in *Twentieth-Century Literary Theory,* ed. Vassilis Lambropoulos and David Neal Miller (New York: State University of New York Press, 1987).

The recurring correspondence between developments in art theory and developments in the avant-garde supplies a clue to the aims of art theory. Though art theory may appear to be a purely abstract activity, it, like other forms of theory, has a point and a purpose within the tradition and practice from which it has emerged.[30] Stated bluntly, the task of art theory in the age of the avant-garde has been, in fact, to provide the means for explaining how the myriad modern subversions of traditional expectations about art—or at least some subset thereof—could count as art. The question "What is art?" as it is posed by the art theorist in the age of the avant-garde has generally, though perhaps in many cases only tacitly, been a question of fitting innovations into the continuum of our artistic practices. That is, on my interpretation of the history of art theory, the task of modern analytic aesthetics has really been one of providing the means for identifying the revolutionary productions of the avant-garde as artworks. Theory does not blossom in a vacuum; it is formulated in a context which shapes its agenda. And the context that motivates theoretical activity in the branch of art theory concerned with the question "What is Art?" is one in which change, transition, or revolution is a central problem.

As noted above, in many cases in the analytic tradition it is said that the answer to the problem is sought in terms of real definitions; however, the family resemblance method has also attracted a vocal minority. So far, neither of these strategies has proven to be entirely satisfactory. So perhaps another approach—the narrative approach—is worth considering.

On my view, the paradigmatic problem that is, in effect, addressed by contemporary art theory is one in which the public is confronted with an object or performance which is presented by an artist but which is at odds with the public's expectations about what counts as art. Some, often outraged, members of the public and their critic-representatives charge that the new work is not art; others claim that it is art. The question of whether or not the work is art is then joined, with the burden of proof placed on those who maintain that the new work is art.

How does one go about meeting this challenge? I think that the most common way in which this is accomplished is to tell a story that connects the disputed work x with preceding artmaking contexts in such a way that the production of x can be seen as an intelligible outcome of recognizable processes of thinking and making within the practice.

Typically the question of whether or not x is art arises in a context where

30. Benjamin R. Tilghman, "Reflections on Aesthetic Theory," in *Aesthetics: A Critical Anthology,* p. 161.

a skeptic fails to see how the object in dispute could have been produced in the network of practices with which she is already familiar—that is, if those practices are to remain the same practices with which she is already familiar. There is a perceived gap, so to speak, between the anomalous avant-garde production *x* and an already existing body of work with an antecedently acknowledged tradition of making and thinking. In order to defend the status of *x* as art, the proponent of *x* must fill in that gap. And the standard way of filling in that gap is to produce a certain type of historical narrative, one which supplies the sequence of activities of thinking and making required to, in a manner of speaking, fill in the distance between a Rembrandt and a ready-made.

In order to counter the suspicion that *x* is not a work of art, the defender of *x* has to show how *x* emerged intelligibly from acknowledged practices via the same sort of thinking, acting, decisionmaking, and so on that is already familiar in the practice. This involves telling a certain kind of story about the work in question: namely, a historical narrative of how *x* came to be produced as an intelligible response to an antecedent art-historical situation about which a consensus with respect to its art status already exists. With a contested work of art what we try to do is place it within a tradition where it becomes more and more intelligible.[31] And the standard way of doing this is to produce an historical narrative.

The paradigmatic situation I have asked you to recall in order to motivate my hypothesis is one in which a work is presented and challenged and in which the challenge is met by means of a narrative. However, equally typical is the situation in which the narrative is told proleptically—that is, told ahead of time in order to forestall an anticipated challenge. This proleptic story may be told or published by an artist, perhaps in the form of a manifesto or an interview, or, more likely, by a critic. Indeed, much of the task of the critic who champions the work in question is to place it in a framework that will render its connections with acknowledged portions of the tradition intelligible.[32]

For example, in order to allay misgivings about a painting by Morris

31. R. A. Sharpe, "A Transformation of a Structuralist Theme," *British Journal of Aesthetics* 18 (1978): 160.

32. This view of criticism may seem to be at odds with the influential view of Arnold Isenberg, who holds that what critics do, essentially, is to point at specific features of artworks in order to get audiences to see their properties. The view of criticism sketched above, however, does not preclude this sort of critical activity. Rather, it sees this sort of "pointing" as proceeding within a larger framework of contextualization. The critic contextualizes in order to orient and to give sense to her pointings. For Isenberg's view of criticism, see Arnold Isenberg, "Critical Communication," in his *Aesthetics and the Theory of Criticism* (Chicago: University of Chicago Press, 1973).

Lewis, Clement Greenberg provides a narrative that connects it to the program of analytical cubism. To a certain extent, the choice of the starting point of the narrative may be strategic. That is, the defender of the disputed work *x* begins the story with a body of artmaking techniques and purposes that she supposes the target audience acknowledges to be within the artistic tradition. However, in principle, such narratives are always open to being, so to say, pushed back further in time under the pressure of skeptical questioning. Thus, if analytical cubism is not a pragmatically effective starting point for defending the painting by Lewis, one may have to tell the narrative that gets us from impressionism or even realism to analytical cubism before one tells the narrative from analytical cubism to Lewis.

Nevertheless, though these narratives may be "strategic" in the sense in which I have just conceded, this does not entail that they are arbitrary or imposed in the way that historical constructivists maintain. For there is no reason to suspect that the historical connections which figure in our narratives are not literally truth-tracking.

Obviously, this method for identifying or establishing a proffered work *x* as an artwork presupposes some body of work and associated practices that are agreed to be artistic by the various parties involved in a given debate. That is true, but it is not a problem for the narrative approach to identifying artworks. For example, it makes no sense to charge the narrative approach with circularity on the basis of these assumptions. For circularity is a defect in real definitions, and the narrative approach to identifying art does not entail definitions. Narratives are not definitions.

Furthermore, presupposing that we approach our problem knowing some examples of artworks and their associated practices is an assumption made not only by the narrative approach but by its competitors as well. Clearly, the family resemblance approach makes such assumptions in presuming that we can designate a set of paradigmatic artworks. Likewise, George Dickie admits that knowledge of art as we know it is requisite for mobilizing his conception of the art circle; at the same time, definitionists in general must allow that we have some core knowledge of art and its practices in order to frame their theories and to weigh the force of counterexamples. Consequently, the presupposition which the narrative approach assumes—that there is already some knowledge about art and its practices—should be no obstacle to its potential as a means for identifying art.

Previously I claimed that the question "What is art?" serves as an umbrella under which a series of questions might be advanced, including these: Is there a reliable method for identifying artworks? Does art have any essential or general features? and Can art be defined? The narrative approach answers the question about whether there is a reliable method for identifying art affirmatively. That is, the narrative method is one reliable method. On the question of whether art can be defined, we are, as noted, agnostic; like many agnostics in the realm of religion, though, we are not tortured by our suspense in this matter. For if our earlier historical conjecture is correct, if what drives art theory is the quest for a reliable means of identifying artworks, then the narrative method satisfies our needs in a way that makes answering the question of art's definition academic. Whether art has a definition may remain a question of some marginal philosophical interest; but art theory can discharge its duties without answering it.

I have supplied answers to two of the three primary questions sketched earlier, but the issue remains as to where the narrative approach stands on the matter of whether art has any essential or general features. Here the version of the narrative approach that I wish to defend delivers an affirmative answer. Though I am convinced that art has more than one essential or general feature, for the purpose of advancing my narrative approach it is necessary only to argue that art has at least one necessary feature: historicity.

Art, as R. A. Sharpe nicely puts it, is an affair of ancestors, descendants, and postulants.[33] Each artist is trained in a tradition of techniques and purposes to which her own work, in one way or another, aims to be an addition.[34] The artist learns the tradition, or at least crucial parts of it, in the course of learning certain procedures of production, along with their attending folkways, self-understandings, rules of thumb, associated values, and even theories. In producing artworks, the artist remains in conversation with her teachers—sometimes repeating, sometimes improving upon, and sometimes disputing their achievements. But in every instance, the artist is always involved in extending the tradition; typically, even the artist who repudiates large portions of it does so in order to *return* it to what she perceives to be its proper direction.

Alongside the artist's traditions of production, there are also traditions of reception—that is, traditions of appreciating and understanding works of art on the part of audiences—which include paradigms for looking at, listening to, and interpreting works of art. However, such traditions are not entirely

33. Sharpe, "A Transformation of a Structuralist Theme," p. 170.

34. W. B. Gallie, "Art and Politics," in *The Aristotelian Society* 46 supp. (1972): 111. See also Gallie's "The Function of Philosophical Aesthetics," *Mind* 57 (1948): 302–21; his "Essentially Contested Concepts," *Proceedings of the Aristotelian Society* 56 (1956): 169–98; and his "Art as an Essentially Contested Concept," *The Philosophical Quarterly* 6 (1956): 97–114.

disjunct from those of production, if only because artists are audiences as well. That is, they attend to their own works and to those of others in the ways provided by our traditions of reception and, in consequence, these artists then produce works governed by the internalized norms and purposes that they, the artists, have derived from our practices of appreciation and understanding. Of course, to a lesser extent, especially in modern society, audiences are also introduced to the artist's side of the exchange, typically receiving some rudimentary training in some artmaking practice *along with* training in various practices of appreciation (e.g., interpreting stories for their morals).

The coordinated traditions of production and reception provide artists, audiences, audience/artists, and artist/audiences with the means for orienting their activities. Understanding a work of art, in large measure, is a matter of situating it, of placing it in a tradition. This may not be immediately apparent to some because the degree to which historical sensitivities, categories, and concepts are enmeshed in our art education blinds us to the influential, sometimes constitutive, role that they play in our appreciative responses. People deploy far more art-historical knowledge than they are often self-consciously aware of deploying. But even the simple identification of a drama as Shakespearean or a film as a silent comedy mobilizes historical knowledge which, in turn, shapes appreciation in terms of appropriate modes of response, including the postulation of relevant comparisons, expectations, and norms. Producing art, on the other hand, also, often unavoidably, involves awareness of the tradition—awareness of precedents and predecessors, of available techniques and purposes, of influences and the anxieties thereof,[35] of audience expectations, and of the historically rooted reactions that are apt to be engendered by subverting such expectations at a given moment.

Art has an inexpugnable historical dimension because it is a practice with a tradition. Moreover, this tradition is taught historically. Artists study their predecessors, their aims, and their breakthroughs in order to prepare themselves for their own contribution to the tradition. And the audience learns to appreciate and to interpret the productions of artists in terms of period concepts, in terms of generational strife and competition between artists, in terms of evolutionary solutions to preexisting problems as well as through historically grounded standards such as innovative/conservative, original/unoriginal, revolutionary/retrograde, not to mention the very idea of the avant-garde. Without art history, there is no practice of artmaking as

35. For one, perhaps not pellucid, account of these anxieties, see Harold Bloom, *The Anxiety of Influence* (New York: Oxford University Press, 1973).

we know it, nor is there the possibility of understanding that practice to any appreciable extent. In this sense, history is a necessary condition for art; and, thus, art has at least one essential feature.

Moreover, the assertion that art has this essential feature is connected to the strategy—historical narration—that I advocate as a reliable method for identifying art. If understanding a work of art involves placing it within a tradition, then challenging a particular claimant amounts to the charge that it cannot be placed in any intelligible way within the tradition. Meeting that challenge, then, is a matter of placing the claimant within the tradition. The challenge, if unwarranted, is a failure of historical understanding. Deflecting the challenge involves delivering historical understanding. And the most straightforward way of supplying historical understanding is historical narration.

Of course, I have said that a historical narrative will do the job if the challenge is unwarranted. This allows that a challenge may be warranted which, at the very least, effectively implies that there is no adequate historical narrative available to connect the work in question to the tradition.

The perplexity that the work of the avant-garde provokes in the skeptic is a function of the skeptic's inability to discern a plausible connection between the work in dispute and the rest of the tradition. The task of historical narration in this context is to make such a connection visible to the skeptic. Historical narration is an appropriate means for establishing whether or not the work under fire is art because it is a way of showing whether or not the work is part of a developing tradition.

So far, a great deal of weight has been placed on the role of historical narratives in identifying art. However, little has been said about the nature of these narratives. At this juncture, then, it will be useful to characterize the relevant features of the species of historical narrative that we deploy in order to identify and establish a claimant to be a work of art.

The first and perhaps most obvious thing to say about such narratives is that insofar as they are *historical* narratives, rather than fictional narratives, they are *committed* to reporting sequences of events and states of affairs accurately or truthfully. That is, in order to succeed fully in establishing the claim that a given work is a work of art by means of a historical narrative requires at the very least that the narrative be true. This means that the reports of events and states of affairs which constitute the narrative must be true and that the asserted connections between those events and states of affairs must obtain. If it is an ingredient in the narrative that x influenced y, then it must be true that x influenced y. If the narrative in question is at best plausible, given our state of knowledge, then it must be plausible that x influenced y.

The historical narratives that identify art are, among other things, *ideally* accurate reports of sequences of events and states of affairs. That they are accurate reports of sequences indicates that they respect a certain temporal order. A narrative is a time-ordered series of events and states of affairs. This does not mean that the order of exposition in the narrative must mirror the order of the chronology to which it refers, but only that the actual chronology of events be available from the narrative. This is consonant with the requirement that the narratives be truthful, since in order to be truthful the narrative should not rearrange the chronology of events. But this requirement does not follow from the demand for truthfulness, since the requirement for time ordering would be violated where it is impossible to discern the actual sequence of events and not only where the proposed time-ordering is false.

Thus far we have said that the relevant type of narrative aspires to be an accurate report of a time-ordered sequence of events. In other words, it must be at least what is often called a chronicle.[36] But more is required for the sort of narrative we need. The kind of narrative we are looking for has an explanatory role to play: it has to explain how an anomalous work in the present is part of the previously acknowledged practices of artmaking. Before undertaking a narrative of this sort, we already know where it must end in order to be successful. Specifically, it needs to end with a presentation of the work or works, or the performance or performances, whose status is contested. The task of the narrative is to show that this event is the result or outcome of a series of intelligible decisions, choices, and actions that originate in and emerge from earlier, already acknowledged practices of artmaking. That is, the narrative must represent the presentation of the contested work as part of a whole process which can be recognized to be artistic.[37] Moreover, though it may be controversial to claim that all historical narratives have unified subjects, the historical narratives discussed here

36. For a discussion of the distinction between chronicle and narrative, see Arthur Danto, *Narration and Knowledge* (New York: Columbia University Press, 1985), pp. 112–43.

37. This picture of historical narration differs from the one proposed by Danto in *Narration and Knowledge.* There Danto maintains that historical narration shows the significance of earlier events in the series by connecting them to their consequences. The point of historical narration, on his construal, is to elucidate the significance of the earlier events in the series. However, the kinds of historical narratives we are talking about—identifying narratives—aim at illuminating the final event in the series; therefore, identifying narratives represent a counterexample to Danto's general view of historical narration.

will have such a subject insofar as they are organized around the dominant purpose of explaining why some contested work is art.[38]

The endpoint of such a narrative—its moment of closure, if you will—is the presentation or production of the contested work. On the other hand, the *beginning* of the story sets the stage by establishing the art-historical context of the work—generally by describing a set of prevailing artmaking practices about which there is consensus that the works produced in that context are bona fide art. Pragmatic considerations may determine how far back into history the story must go in order to be convincing for given audiences. However, wherever the story begins, it must be connected to the subsequent events recounted in terms of real historical relations such as, for example, causation and influence. Pragmatically, the choice of where to begin such a narrative may be relative to an audience's consensus about what is indisputably art, but whether the states of affairs are part of the series of events recounted is not arbitrary. And, perhaps needless to say, I am presuming that there will always be some earlier point in time about which there is consensus about acknowledged artmaking practices.

By now, we have some sense of where the kinds of historical narratives in question begin and end. But what constitutes the middle of the story or, as I would prefer to call it, the complication?

The narrative begins by describing an acknowledged artmaking context. For simplicity's sake, let us imagine that there is consensus about the art status of the artistic practices that exist just prior to the appearance of the disputed work. In this case, the story begins with a sketch of the relevant artworld at the time the artist, whose work is contested, enters it. Thus, if our subject is the work of Isadora Duncan—of which Vaslav Nijinsky charged, "[H]er performance is spontaneous and cannot be taught. . . . [I]t is not art"[39]—then we are likely to begin our story with an account of the turn-of-the-century theatrical dance scene in the West which was dominated by academic ballet.

The complication in the story then emerges as we outline the artist's assessment of the artworld as she finds it. Of course, an artist may assess a given artworld to be unproblematic and simply go on to produce works in the same manner to which she has become accustomed.[40] But then the story is a very short one. However, in the case of innovative work of the sort that is likely to cause dispute, the artist is apt to assess the existing artworld as

38. For the view that historical narratives need not have unified subjects, see L. B. Cebik, *Concepts, Events and History* (Washington, D.C.: University Press of America, 1978).

39. Quoted by Bronislava Nijinska, *Early Memoirs* (New York: Holt, Rinehart & Winston, 1981), p. 224.

40. In my "Art, Practice and Narrative," I call this option "repetition."

requiring change or alteration either in the direction of solving some problem internal to existing artworld practices or in the direction of radically reorienting the project of the relevant artworld.[41]

Duncan, for example, assessed the ballet-dominated dance scene in late-nineteenth-century America to be tired, rigid, and stifling—features she associated with the Old World. In contrast, she searched for forms which were spontaneous and natural (by her lights) and which would serve to emblematize the Whitmanesque strains of her vision of the American spirit.[42]

The complication in our narratives commences as we introduce the artist's conception of the context in which she finds herself. The story gets rolling when we establish that the artist is resolved to change that context in one way or another. In noting the artist's conception of the situation and her resolve to change it, we elucidate the impetus of her assessment of the need or opportunity for change. Here the impetus may come from pressure within the artworld or from concerns derived from broader cultural contexts, or from a mixture of the two. In Duncan's case, for example, the aim of rejuvenating dance as well as the impulse to align it with romantic aesthetics might be thought of as imperatives internal to the artworld, while the desire to forge a style of dance with a distinctly American identity implemented a broader cultural politics, one heralded, for example, in Emerson's essay "The American Scholar."

Once we have established the artist's resolve to change artworld practices, and once we have shown how it is intelligible that someone in that context might come to have the resolve in question, then we go on to demonstrate how the artist's choice of the means to her end makes sense in the historical context under discussion. That is, we show how the means adopted would be deemed appropriate for securing the artist's purposes given the alternatives the situation afforded. Or, in other words, we must show that what the artist did in the existing context was a way of achieving her purposes. This involves sketching the situation in such a way that it becomes evident why certain artistic choices make sense given the values, associations, and consequences that are likely to attach to them in the pertinent historical context.[43]

41. These options are called, respectively, "amplification" and "repudiation" in my "Art, Practice and Narrative."

42. Information on Duncan's career is available in Deborah Jowitt, *Time and the Dancing Image* (New York: William Morrow & Co., 1988), chap. 2, and in Sally Banes, "Twentieth Century Dance," in *The Great Ideas Today: 1991* (Chicago: Encyclopaedia Britannica, 1991), pp. 65–68.

43. Narratives of this sort would seem to be the most straightforward way of representing the "heuristic pathways" that are so crucial in Gregory Currie's *An Ontology of Art* (New York: St. Martin's Press, 1989); see esp. chap. 3.

Thus, to return to the case of Isadora Duncan, we continue her story by noting the way in which her choice of the bare foot as her medium contravened the constrained pointwork of ballet in a way that within the presiding cultural framework would be associated with freedom, spontaneity, and naturalness. Similar observations might be made about her choice of loose-fitting tunics in opposition to tight ballet corsets.

In order to show that the disputed work of an artist is art, we must show in the course of our narrative that the artist's assessment of the initiating situation and the resolve she formulated in response to that assessment were intelligible. To do this we need to show that the artist had a reasonable interpretation of certain general understandings of the purposes of art which were abroad and alive in her culture. These general understandings include such purposes as the following: that art is expressive, or that it challenges complacent moral views, or that it is about itself. It is the artist's reasonable interpretation of these general purposes that ground her assessment and her resolve. In the case of Duncan, her claim to return to the natural expressivity of Greek art situated her revolution in recognizable artistic purposes.

Once it is established, by narrating the conditions which give rise to her assessments, that the artist's resolve is intelligible, we go on to show that the techniques, procedures, and strategies she enlists are effective ones for realizing her purposes, given the lay of the artworld—that is, given the alternative, available strategies and their associated values.[44] Finally, this elaboration of choices and rationales—including, possibly, a citation of the artist's experimentation with different alternatives—eventuates in the production of the contested work. My claim is that if through historical narration the disputed work can be shown to be the result of reasonable or appropriate choices and actions which are motivated by intelligible assessments that support a resolution to change the relevant artworld context for the sake of some recognizable aim of art, then, all things being equal, the disputed work is an artwork.[45]

44. For further discussion of the idea of associated values, see Noël Carroll, "Post-modern Dance and Expression," in *Philosophical Essays on Dance,* ed. Gordon Fancher and Gerald Myers (Brooklyn: Dance Horizons Press, 1981).

45. It has been asserted above that the assessments in question be intelligible. This allows that the assessments might be wrong, especially in the hindsight of historical research. For example, Isadora Duncan supposed that the art of the Greeks was natural. Her assessment might not stand up to the scrutiny of classical scholars today. Nevertheless, her view was intelligible for someone in her situation. That is, we can see how a reasonable person in her situation could, in a perfectly reasonable way, come to develop her view of Greek art even if, when all the research is in, it turns out that her view was

In theory, these stories sound immensely complicated; in practice they are not. For example, gathering together the fragments, recited so far, of the Isadora Duncan story, when someone denies that her barefoot prancing and posing in *Chopin Waltzes* is art, we could tell the following narrative:

> Turn-of-the-century theatrical dance in the West, excluding Russia, was dominated by forms of academic ballet that contemporary commentators, like Bernard Shaw, felt had become tired and clichéd. From Isadora Duncan's point of view, the problem was that ballet was an ossified discipline, mechanical and uninspired. As a child of the New World, she saw in it all the vices Americans attributed to Europe. It was artificial, lifeless, and formal. It was the epitome of the Old World. Duncan aspired to new dance forms that were spontaneous and natural. She found her sources in disparate places, including social dancing, physical culture, gymnastics, and the Delstarte deportment movement. From 1904 to 1914, Duncan was at the peak of her career. She replaced the toeshoe and the corset of ballet with the bare foot and the loose tunic. And her ebb-and-flow movement in pieces like *Chopin Waltzes* was designed to recall the natural rhythms of waves. At the same time, the use of running and walking in her choreography exchanged the measured and predetermined cadence of academic ballet for the more personally inflected gesture. Undoubtedly her conception of art as a means to individual expression derived as much from romantic poetry as it did from the tradition of American individualism. But Duncan did not see herself as creating something completely new. She conceived of herself as returning the dance to the founding values of naturalness which she identified with Greek art. Thus, with *Chopin Waltzes,* Duncan was able to solve the problem of the stagnation of theatrical dance by repudiating the central features of the dominant ballet and by reimagining an earlier ideal of dance.

---

incorrect. In terms of our historical narratives, we require that the artists make the assessments we claim they make, but those assessments need only be intelligible—reasonable conclusions reached in a reasonable way—and need not be art-historically correct according to retrospective historical research. This notion of intelligibility is analogous to the way in which Amelie Rorty thinks that the principle of charity should be employed in explaining certain emotions. See Amelie Oksenberg Rorty, "Explaining Emotions," *The Journal of Philosophy* 75 (1978): 139–61.

Narratives like this can be expanded in many directions. Further details may be included about the initial art-historical context: more background on the artist's influences, assessments, and decisions can be added, along with further descriptions of central and/or exemplary events, experiences, and experiments that contributed to the artist's resolutions and actions. Such narratives may appear seamless in the hands of an accomplished art critic, but they have a great deal of structure. So, to return from simple practice to abstract theory, let me try to capture that structure with a formula:

> *x* is an identifying narrative only if *x* is (1) an accurate and (2) time-ordered report of a sequence of events and states of affairs concerning (3) a unified subject (generally the production of a disputed work)[46] which (4) has a beginning, a complication, and an end, where (5) the end is explained as the outcome of the beginning and the complication, where (6) the beginning involves the description of an initiating, acknowledged art-historical context, and where (7) the complication involves tracing the adoption of a series of actions and alternatives as appropriate means to an end on the part of a person who has arrived at an intelligible assessment of the art-historical context in such a way that she is resolved to change (or reenact)[47] it in accordance with recognizable and live purposes of the practice.

Undoubtedly some clarificatory remarks about this formula are in order. My point has been that art theory has been driven by the question of how we identify innovative works as art, especially in contexts where such works are subject to dispute. I claim that the way in which this is done is by historical narratives of the sort we call "identifying narratives." An adequate identifying narrative establishes that a work in question emerged in recognizable ways from an acknowledged artworld context through an intelligible process of assessment, resolution, and action.

46. "Generally" has been added here to allow for the possibility that an identifying narrative might be told with reference to a work that is not disputed—for example, a "repetition," to use the language of my essay "Art, Practice and Narrative."

47. "Or reenact" has been added in order to allow for resolutions that do not involve changing the artworld. This adjustment is meant to accommodate the option of repetition (see note 46, above).

If we review the conditions I have advanced for an identifying narrative, it is probably pretty apparent that the explanatory force of this sort of narrative relies on the fact—most evident in my characterization of the complication—that underlying this narrative is the structure of practical reasoning.[48] The artist's assessment leads to a resolution, which leads to the choice from alternatives of means to that end, which choices then ensue in the action we want explained—the production of the disputed work. If in our reconstruction of this process we are able to show that the assessments, resolutions, and choices were intelligible in context, we are well on our way to showing that the work in question is an artwork.

It is not my contention that the explanatory power of *all* historical narratives rests on an underlying structure of practical reasoning, but only that the explanatory power of many historical narratives, including identifying narratives, does so. That many narratives are similarly based in the structure of practical reasoning should be noncontroversial. Think of the degree to which most popular narrative films, like *Terminator 2,* are founded almost exclusively on the problem/solution structure. That it should turn out that identifying narratives are also of this sort would seem to follow from a natural interpretation of the question which motivates them. That is to say, when confronted with an anomalous production which forces the question of whether it is art, a natural path to the answer is to hypothesize why someone would, in a given context, produce such an object for presentation to an artworld audience. And answering that question is a matter of reconstructing a process of intelligible assessment, resolution, choice, and action.

Though the example I have developed of the identifying narrative is relatively simple, it is easy to envisage more complex, expanded identifying narratives. Identifying narratives may include "embedded" narratives—for example, identifying narratives within identifying narratives dealing with cases where certain avant-garde experiments prove unsatisfactory (from the artist's point of view) until the final production of the disputed work. And identifying narratives can be "enchained"—that is, several identifying narratives may be arrayed "back to back," as in our example concerning the Morris Lewis painting.[49]

48. Compare my account of the complication with accounts of the logic of the situation in Alan Donagan, "The Popper-Hempel Theory Reconsidered," in *Philosophical Analysis and History,* ed. William Dray (New York: Harper & Row, 1966); and Michael Martin, "Situational Logic and Covering Law Explanations in History," *Inquiry* 11 (1968): 394.

49. For more information on embedding and enchainment, see Shlomith Rimmon-Kenan, *Narrative Fiction* (New York: Methuen, 1983); Claude Bremond, "La logique des possibles narratifs," *Communications* 8 (1966): 60–76; and Claude Bremond, *Logique du recit* (Paris: Seuil, 1973).

Furthermore, though the reliance on practical reasoning seems to restrict identifying narratives exclusively to the productions of individuals, there really is no reason why identifying narratives cannot be extended to movements. That is, not only may we mobilize identifying narratives to say why Richard Long's huddle of rocks called *Cornwall Circle* is art, but we may also employ such narratives to say why movements like Dada, given the Dadaists' assessments and resolutions, confronted the artworld with certain objects and antics. Ultimately, such narratives may have to be cashed in with reference to the activities of specific artists. But if that constraint is understood, there is no problem in depicting a movement in terms of its corporate assessments, resolutions, and choices when we explain why the movement in question produces the kind of objects it does.

One objection to the narrative approach might be that there are intelligible processes of assessment, resolution, and choice in artworld contexts that do not issue in artworks. Thus, identifying narratives of certain objects and performances might be told of productions that are not art. In the lore of film history, for example, the story is told that as a result of their heated and long-standing debate about the nature of film montage, Sergei Eisenstein named his dog "Pudovkin" in dishonor of his rival V. I. Pudovkin. In this, Eisenstein was not some sort of precursor of William Wegman. Eisenstein was not turning his dog into an artwork. He meant to insult his competitor Pudovkin. But surely a true story could be told about the way in which Eisenstein, in the context of an artistic debate, came to an assessment which resulted in the naming of his dog Pudovkin as a means of expressing his resolution that the "linkage" version of montage (Pudovkin's version) be discarded. Does this show that Eisenstein's dog was a work of art? How can the narrative approach keep dogs out of the artworld?

But, of course, we do not really want to keep dogs out of the artworld *simpliciter.* We only want to keep Eisenstein's dog out of the Soviet filmworld in particular and out of the pre–World War II Soviet artworld in general. In order to do so, it seems that we need to add to our account the constraint that the thinking and making which our identifying narratives reconstruct be localized to activities occurring within recognizable artworld systems of presentation: that is, artforms, media, and genres which are available to the artist in question. Thus, Eisenstein's naming of the dog Pudovkin, though a creative act by an artist, is not counted among the accomplishments of the golden age of Soviet art because the relevant thinking and acting was not transacted in the context of a recognizable artworld system of presentation. Surely the dog was not a film or a poem. Soviet Russia before World War II simply lacked a structure or convention of presentation in which Eisenstein's dog could—through an act of christening—become an artwork.

To say that the solution to this problem is that identifying narratives be restricted to thinking and making within recognizable artworld systems of presentation may appear simply to move the problem up a notch. But I would prefer to say that what it does is move the *solution* up a notch. The putative problem with relying on recognizable systems of artworld presentation is this: How are we to identify those systems? Here I feel we can say that, for the most part, there is an acknowledged consensus about a large body of available artworld systems of presentation in our culture, just as there is a large body of objects that we agree are art. In most cases, the question of whether the relevant thinking and making transpired in such a system can be settled straightforwardly. Of course, we can also point to cases where there are disputes about whether or not a putative system of presentation is an artworld system. The issue then becomes a matter of how one identifies a system of presentation as a recognizable artworld system which is available to the artist in question.

Not surprisingly, perhaps, my answer to the question of how we go about establishing that certain presentational systems are artworld systems is "by means of historical narration."

Novel artworld systems of presentation do not simply appear on the landscape by magic or by acts of nature. They are evolved from preexisting artistic practices by their proponents through self-conscious processes of thinking and making. Early filmmakers succeeded in turning a new technology into a recognizable artworld system of presentation by initially adapting it as an effective means for discharging the preexisting purposes of already acknowledged arts such as theater, painting, the short story, and the novel. Establishing that film was an artworld presentation system is a matter of explaining how the choices of early filmmakers flowed in a recognizable manner from the intelligible assessments and resolutions they made with respect to the artistic potential of the new technology.

Of course, there are other ways of introducing novel presentational systems. Film was introduced initially by mimicking existing, acknowledged forms of artmaking and their purposes. But novel presentational systems have been introduced in living memory by other strategies. For example, "happenings" seem to have developed as a reaction to existing artworld practices, notably practices in the precincts of painting and sculpture. Artists like Allan Kaprow, feeling the constraints of a high modernist aesthetic which bracketed the exploration of space and content from the canvas and which prized what was called "objecthood" (by the likes of Michael Fried) over participation, invented the happening as the arena in which those preexisting artistic concerns that had been repressed under the Greenbergian dispensation could return. Similar and indeed related stories can be told about the emergence of conceptual art and performance art. But in all these cases, the point remains the same. Contested presentation systems are established to be artworld systems when we can account for their emergence through narratives of thinking and making which connect them in recognizable ways with preexisting artworld systems and their purposes. Eisenstein's dog Pudovkin was not art because there was no artworld system available to Eisenstein through which he might have implemented an intention to make his dog art. That Eisenstein might have introduced such a system is irrelevant. For that is quite literally *another* story.[50]

Levinson and Danto

The narrative approach I have developed for identifying art emphasizes the importance of art history. However, it is not the only contemporary approach to look to art history for ways of answering the question "What is Art?" Powerful, alternative, historicist theories have been advanced by Jerrold Levinson and Arthur Danto. In this section, I would like to examine the viability of these rival theories.

One difference, of course, between the narrative approach and the theories of Levinson and Danto is that their approaches remain definitional. That is, they attempt to provide the means for identifying and establishing that something is art by means of real definitions.

50. By including the constraint that identifying narratives track activities localized in art-presentational systems, I think I can provide the kind of framework whose absence from my "Art, Practice and Narrative" Stephen Davies criticizes in his recent *Definitions of Art.* Also, Davies seems too quick to assimilate my notion of repetition with the family resemblance approach's notion of similarity. For, on my account, the similarities in question must be the result of *real* historical processes: that is to say, similarities which are not rooted in real historical relations are not enough. For a statement of Davies's criticisms of the narrative approach, see his *Definitions of Art* (Ithaca: Cornell University Press, 1991), pp. 167–69.

Levinson's method, which he explicitly calls *defining* art historically,[51] contends that

> X is an artwork at t = df. X is an object of which it is true at t that some person or persons, having the appropriate proprietary right over X, nonpassingly intends (or intended) X for regard-as-a-work-of-art—i.e., regard in any way (or ways) in which objects in the extension of 'artwork' prior to t are or were correctly (or standardly) regarded.[52]

This is a definition of art at a given time (t) in terms of what art has been in past times. To be art at t is to be intentionally related in the required way to something that is art prior to t. Furthermore, the intention has to be stable or, as Levinson puts it, "nonpassing." That is, in order to turn something into a work of art it is not enough just to have it flash momentarily through your mind that a certain object might be regarded as an artwork; Duchamp would not have turned a urinal into an artwork if he just momentarily thought that a urinal might become an artwork. The intention required has to be long-lived, firm, and stable; as Levinson puts it, nonpassing. And lastly, the artist in question has to have a proprietary right over the object. This stipulation appears to be intended by Levinson to block the possibility of artists scurrying willy-nilly through the world, christening as art everything in sight.

Levinson's theory contains two necessary conditions—the proprietary condition and the intention condition—which are jointly sufficient. Let us look at these proposals in turn.

The proprietary right condition seems irrelevant to the question of art status. Suppose a well-known artist stole her painting materials—stole the canvas, stole the paints—and painted the work during hours when she was contracted to be doing some other project. Nevertheless, she paints the work with the nonpassing intention that it be regarded in an art-historically, well-precedented mode of appreciation. Such a work might involve illegality, but surely, all things being equal, it would be a work of art.

Questions of legality are independent of art status. There may indeed be certain art forms, like urban graffiti, that require as a condition of class membership that they be illegal—that the graffiti be drawn on objects, like subway cars or tenement walls, over which the artist possesses no proprietary rights.

51. See Jerrold Levinson, "Defining Art Historically" and "Refining Art Historically," in his *Music, Art & Metaphysics* (Ithaca: Cornell University Press, 1990).

52. Ibid., p. 15.

The motivation behind this condition is Levinson's desire to block certain types of appropriationist or conceptual art. Levinson wants to deny that simply by pointing at something—or by writing out a specification of what an audience is supposed to look at (à la conceptual art)—the artist can turn Marilyn Monroe, the Empire State Building, or a slice of life of a family in Queens into a work of art.

But even if these things cannot be turned into works of art, the reason cannot be that the artist does not own them. For, presumably, if the artist did have a proprietary right—if Marilyn Monroe and the Queens family consented to being artistically transfigured, or if the artist bought the Empire State Building—then anyone who was inclined to be skeptical about the art status of the result would still be skeptical.

Levinson appears to presuppose that where an object is used to realize two conflicting intentions—where one of the intentions attaches to the owner and the other to an appropriator—the intention which determines its use is the owner's. So the appropriationist artist's intention that the object be used to support some art-historical regard will be trumped by the owner's intention wherever it conflicts with the artist's. But I do not see why the owner's intentions have so much ontological weight. Someone can certainly use my shotgun to shoot me despite my intentions that my shotgun not be so used. I might wish that my shotgun not have the status of a murder weapon. It might not be very nice to shoot me with my shotgun; but you can do it nonetheless. Similarly, I do not see how my ownership of the Empire State Building would be enough to stop someone else from turning it into a ready-made.

My recommendations about identifying art come closest to Levinson's with respect to his second condition.[53] However, even though he speaks of his method as a matter of defining art historically, Levinson's theory is really very ahistorical. For Levinson supposes that something might be art now just in case it supports *any* type of regard, treatment, or mode of apprecia-

53. In his "The Boundaries of Art," Robert Stecker suggests that my narrational approach may be open to the same objections to which Levinson's approach is open. This conjecture is undoubtedly owing to my remark, in "Art, Practice and Narrative," that in certain ways the narrative approach is compatible with Levinson's view. What I had in mind there, but did not fully explicate, was that my notions of repetition, amplification, and repudiation could serve as the basis of some of the art regards that might be relevant to Levinson's theory. That is, artists might create works with the intention that they be regarded as repetitions, amplifications, and repudiations. Still, I do not think the narrational approach falls with Levinson's in the face of the kinds of objections that Stecker advances, if only because the narrative approach *does not propose a definition of art.* See Stecker, "The Boundaries of Art," *British Journal of Aesthetics* 30 (1990).

tion that was appropriate to at least some works of art in the past. The problem here is that not every mode of appreciation that was lavished on artworks in the past is eternally available. Some modes may have become historically obsolete. Making artworks in the present to support such obsolete, historically outmoded, and historically unavailable modes of appreciation should not, on the face of it, result in things that we now count as artworks. Levinson's theory is ahistorical at least in the respect that it does not allow for the historical obsolescence of art regards. He treats his art regards as ahistorically eternal—as always available modes of appreciation. But modes of appreciation may pass away. This is something that any theory claiming to be historically sensitive should acknowledge. But Levinson's does not.

This may sound like a somewhat abstract objection. Let me introduce a counterexample in order to give it some purchase.

It seems fair to suppose that sometime in the past artworks were thought to perform such services as propitiating the gods. That is, artworks—such as those performed at religious festivals—were offerings to the gods (offerings predicated on either exciting their favor or, at least, mitigating their disfavor). Since this was once a function of what we call artworks, presumably one way of appreciating such artworks was in terms of how suitable or how effective such works were in propitiating the gods. Perusing some works in this light, we might think that they were very powerful examples of propitiation; other works might be assessed as less powerful. We might appreciate such works with respect to propitiation in the way that we appreciate thoroughbreds with respect to their racing potential.

Now if what I have said so far is plausible, then assessing, appreciating, or regarding some historically acknowledged artworks as vehicles of propitiating the gods was an appropriate way of regarding artworks. On Levinson's view, it must count as an integral form of artistic regard. It is, in other words, a form of regard which a contemporary artist might seek to facilitate with respect to a contemporary candidate for the status of artwork.

But consider this case. Jones is a person who knows something of the history of art. He knows that artworks were sometimes used to propitiate certain gods. Let us even suppose that Jones believes in these gods and thinks that they ought to be propitiated. Jones also owns a chicken farm and an automatic assault rifle. He has a proprietary right over both the relevant chickens and the rifle. By dint of these property rights and a certain intention, Jones sets out to make an artwork. Specifically, he shoots a mass of chickens in record time in order to propitiate the gods. Moreover, he presents the massacre as an artwork: onlookers are invited to appreciate it, to assess it, or to regard it in terms of its effectiveness as a means of propitiating the gods. This was a correct way of regarding some artworks in the past; and Jones intends to facilitate this way of regarding his massacre of the chickens as a means of producing a contemporary artwork.

Here it is important not to confuse Jones's activity with the activities of other proponents of the art of slaughtering chickens. Jones is not a conceptual artist who seeks to make some kind of statement about art or life by means of slaughtering chickens; nor does Jones hope to turn chicken-slaughtering into art by creating something that is full of dramatic excitement and color. His intention is simply to make something that is to be regarded and assessed as an effective vehicle for propitiating the gods, where propitiating the gods *was once* an acknowledged purpose of art and where regarding the work's viability in discharging this function is one correct way to treat artworks.

So Jones makes a work at *t*—September 25, 1992—with the nonpassing intention that it, the chicken massacre, be an object for regard as an artwork. In particular, it is to be regarded in terms of its efficacy for propitiating the gods—which, of course, was a way of correctly regarding artworks in the past (prior to September 25, 1992).

It is hard to see how Levinson's theory can avoid admitting Jones's chicken massacre to the roster of art. But surely Jones's chicken massacre is *not* a work of art, even if an indiscernible chicken massacre by the modern artist Herman Nietze is. There must be something wrong with Levinson's theory if it entails that Jones's chicken massacre is art.

Moreover, I do not think that this counterexample is idiosyncratic. Rather, it points to a systematic flaw in Levinson's theory—namely, that it is ahistorical (despite its claims to being historical) in the sense that it fails to take account of the fact that some regards-as-a-work-of-art may pass away. Indeed, it is very easy to multiply counterexamples of this sort when one recalls that a great deal of art in the past was produced for religious purposes and was properly regarded as the focus of devotion. But when I was a first-grade student in Catholic school and I put two Popsicle sticks together in the shape of a cross with the intention that it be a devotional object, the result was not a work of art, even though it was correct to regard some artworks in the past as devotional objects. Obviously, the religious functions of art and their attending regards can produce, in fairly predictable ways, a substantial number of problem cases for Levinson's theory.

Arthur Danto's theory of art is another rival to my narrative approach, for in it, too, art history performs an important role in identifying works of art. But Danto's theory, like Levinson's, differs from the narrative approach insofar as it proposes a definition as the reliable means for identifying art.

Danto never states his definition of art outright. But he does seem to believe that something is a work of art just in case it (1) is about something (2) about which it projects some attitude or point of view (this is what Danto means by the work's possession of a style) (3) by means of metaphorical ellipses which (4) depend on some enthymematic material from the historico-theoretical artworld context (this material is generally what Danto thinks of as art theories), and which (5) engage the audience in interpreting the metaphors elliptically posed by the work in question.[54]

This is an immensely complicated theory of art, and full justice cannot be given to it in a page or two. But, *prima facie,* it does seem to be far too exclusive to serve as an adequate definition of art. Surely some tap dancing, such as the work of Honey Coles, counts as art. But that work need not be about anything; it need not propose a metaphor about anything; it does not engage or require an interpretation about its (probably nonexistent) metaphorical import by audiences; and its reception does not depend upon art history, where that is construed narrowly in terms of art theory.

Admittedly, it will require some art-historical background to establish that such dancing is art, if it is challenged; but it need not be background of the order of art theories. Rather, that background can be woven into suitable art-identifying narratives without recourse to theories of dance. For there is probably nothing that we would count as a theory of dance in the actual historical background of Honey Coles's tap dancing. That is, where Danto proposes to identify artworks in terms of their connection to historically existing art theories, I think it is enough to tell stories about their connection to preexisting art contexts which may or may not possess anything like art theories.

Of course, Danto might modify his view, as he sometimes seems to do, by dropping the emphasis on the background of art theory. But even with this modification, his definition seems too strict. Surely some artworks are not about anything. Do not certain works of pure pattern count as art? And even

54. I have derived this interpretation of Danto's theory from his book *The Transfiguration of the Commonplace.* I have also presented a less restrictive interpretation of Danto's theory in my review of his recent art theory in the journal *History and Theory.* The less restrictive definition was produced in order to avoid certain of the difficulties with Danto's view that I rehearse above. Nevertheless, though a more charitable version of Danto's theory can be produced, I think that the version of Danto's theory which I attack above is his official theory. See my review in *History and Theory* 29 (1990): 113.

of those remaining works which are about something–those which have a semantic component–many need neither be construed as metaphors nor interpreted that way. There are plain-speaking works of art. Hogarth's "Cruelty in Perfection," from his *The Four Stages of Cruelty,* is not a metaphor (not even a visual metaphor), and it does not elicit or require metaphorical interpretations from viewers. Indeed, it is not clear that the work requires any sort of interpretation, metaphorical or otherwise, if one agrees with Annette Barnes's argument that interpretation is an activity we engage in only when the point of what we are attending to is not obvious.[55]

Perhaps Danto thinks that all works of art are about something because they "comment" on their tradition. But surely this is a figurative use of the notion of commenting. Many works of art bear relations to their tradition upon which we comment. It is strained, however, to relocate what are *our* comments in the work of art. Moreover, there is no reason to suppose that those works of art which do comment on other works of art always do so in a metaphorical mode. Daumier's 1856 lithograph *Photographie: Nouveau Procede* comments disparagingly on the art of photography, but without metaphor.

Danto's emphasis on the importance of the art-historical context, especially where the latter is not associated strictly with existing art theories, is a valuable insight. In fact, it is an insight that led me to my own thoughts about the role of historical narration in identifying art. However, many of the other conditions that Danto adds to the condition of historical relevance seem to render his theory far too exclusive.

The theories of Danto and Levinson seem the closest competitors to the sort of historical approach I advocate. Their accounts, of course, are both definitional. The problems I have sketched in regard to their theories reveal that there are continued difficulties with definitional approaches, even when putatively informed by historical considerations. In a dialectical sense, the failure of these theories at least recommends attention to the narrative approach.

In the present essay I have maintained that in asking the question "What is art?" we may be requesting different types of information. We may be asking whether there are reliable methods for identifying and establishing that something is art; whether art has any general or essential features; whether there is a real or essential definition of art. Moreover, as a historical conjecture or diagnosis, I have claimed that the actual project of philosophical art

55. See Annette Barnes, *On Interpretation* (New York: Basil Blackwell, 1988).

theory in the age of the avant-garde is, in fact, the issue of how to identify and establish whether the often unexpected productions of the avant-garde are art. In this context, I have proposed that identifying narratives provide us with a reliable method for establishing the artistic status of the works in question. Such narratives ideally explain the way in which a disputed production is an artwork by showing how it emerged through intelligible processes of assessment, resolution, choice, and action from acknowledged artworld practices within a context of recognizable presentational systems. Securing such narratives for contested artworks represents a sufficient condition for establishing that such candidates are art. Moreover, my invocation of acknowledged artworld practices and systems should raise no worries about circularity, since we are talking about identifying art, not defining it.

One criticism of my emphasis on identifying narratives rather than on art definitions might be that this is not really philosophy. But isolating the reliable methods of reasoning and argument that we use in our practices certainly has a *prima facie* claim to the status of philosophy. Another worry about the narrative approach might be that it makes it seem easy to establish that something is art. This does not strike me as a problem. Establishing that something is art is generally not a very daunting task.

The narrative approach offers a way of answering the question "What is art?" that is different from the one George Dickie proposed. It employs narration rather than definition, and it makes much more explicit reference to art history than Dickie's more explicitly sociological approach does. However, the move to art history that I advocate might be thought of as a matter of seizing an opportunity opened by Dickie's seminal emphasis on the indispensability of context for art theory.

Jeffrey Wieand

Perceptually Indistinguishable Objects

In *The Art Circle,* George Dickie endorses the argument that "if there are two visually indistinguishable objects and one is a work of art and the other is not, then there must be some context or framework in which the work of art is embedded which accounts for the different statuses of the two objects."[1] The same argument figured prominently in Dickie's earlier book, *Art and the Aesthetic.*[2] I will call an argument of this kind, for want of a more elegant characterization, a perceptually indistinguishable objects argument (PIOA).

PIOA is one of the cornerstones of Dickie's approach to the philosophy of art and was thought by him to entail an institutional, or at least a contextual,

1. George Dickie, *The Art Circle* (New York: Haven Publications, 1984), p. 11. Dickie also characterizes the argument as "Danto's 'indistinguishable-pairs' argument" (p. 82). For Arthur Danto's formulations, see, for example, his *The Transfiguration of the Commonplace* (Cambridge: Harvard University Press, 1981); "The Artworld," *The Journal of Philosophy* 61 (1964): 571–84; and "Artworks and Real Things," *Theoria* 39 (1973): 1–17.

2. George Dickie, *Art and the Aesthetic* (Ithaca: Cornell University Press, 1974).

theory of art. The most aggressive version of this theory is that there is an institution (such as a convention, practice, or social group) which confers or otherwise establishes the art-ness of the artwork. An examination of PIOA, therefore, is not only interesting in its own right; it also illuminates the underpinnings of Dickie's work and the institutional theory of art with which he is identified.

In this essay I will not attempt to establish how PIOA or some version of it is formulated by Dickie, Danto, or anyone else; nor will I attempt to identify what specific conclusions anyone has drawn from the argument. My purpose will be to inquire whether Dickie was right to accept PIOA and what, in general, can be learned from it. This requires, in turn, that PIOA be formulated in the most plausible way possible.

Perceptual Indistinguishability

In the passage quoted above, Dickie refers to "visually indistinguishable objects" as being the subject of PIOA. Artworks that are meant to be looked at have indeed been the focus of PIOA, but if a more general conclusion is to be drawn about works of art, the argument must go beyond visual properties. I take PIOA in its broadest form to be about perceptual properties in general. To state the argument baldly, if two objects are "perceptually indistinguishable," but the first is a work of art and the second is not, then the first could not be a work of art because it possesses any perceivable property or combination of such properties, since the second object has all of the same perceivable properties. Imagine, for example, a can of tomato soup which, though it looks like (i.e., merely like) an ordinary can of tomato soup, is considered to be a work of art.

PIOA depends upon the idea that some objects are perceptually indistinguishable from one another. What does it mean for two objects to be "perceptually indistinguishable"? There could be several answers to this question. Leibniz advanced a principle known as the "identity of indiscernibles," which finds its way into modern logic as Leibniz's Law. Leibniz thought that if two objects, *A* and *B*, have all the same properties, then they must be one and the same object. It apparently follows that you will not be able to find two indiscernible objects. Leibniz tells the story of one "ingenious gentleman" who ran all over Princess Sophia's garden in search of two leaves perfectly alike.[3] Naturally he failed to find them. But if the ingenious gentleman had claimed to be successful, he would not have refuted Leibniz. For the "identity of indiscernibles" is a principle with a misleading name. There is no reason that *A* and *B* cannot have individuating properties which are not discernible, or which so far have not been discerned, by human perception. Indeed, after poking fun at the "ingenious gentleman," Leibniz observes that "two drops of water, or milk, viewed with a microscope, will appear indistinguishable from each other."[4] One can only guess as to the result if no microscope is available; perhaps the drops will be indistinguishable. If, even with the aid of a microscope, the drops appear identical, this must still be mere appearance. A better microscope, a more skilled observer, another form of sensory perception (touch, hearing) should point out the differences; and if not, well, such are the disappointments of perception in the face of logic. The "identity of indiscernibles," then, is better denominated the "identity of identicals," for it has to do with what is, not with what we do or can discern.

Not so with PIOA. PIOA does not demand that *A* and *B* have all the same properties; at best, it demands only that *A* and *B* have all the same *perceptual properties*. (For this reason, the advocate of PIOA need not reject Leibniz's Law.[5] This is not to say that the idea of a "perceptual property" is clear as a bell. Perceptual properties certainly do not include spatial or temporal location, as some form of individuation of *A* and *B* is essential. If we define a perceptual property as a monadic property which can be discerned by perceptual examination, we will need, in turn, to define "perceptual examination." This concept may prove as difficult to understand as the concept of a perceptual property. Is taking an X-ray or performing a chemical analysis, for example, a way of conducting a perceptual examination? How close should I stand? How good does my hearing have to be? And why should we suppose that perceptual properties, whatever they are, are intrinsic? Do these properties require the existence of perceiving beings and exist only in relation to their perceptual faculties? Clearly the analysis of "perceptual property" cannot lead to a relational property masquerading as a monadic one.

The advocate of PIOA may become impatient with the foregoing considerations. PIOA is interested only in the sort of properties which can

3. *Leibniz-Clarke Correspondence,* ed. H. G. Alexander (Manchester: Manchester University Press, 1956), p. 36.

4. Ibid.

5. See R. A. Goodrich, "Danto on Artistic Indiscernibility, Interpretation and Relations," *British Journal of Aesthetics* 31 (1991): 358.

reasonably be expected to figure in the evaluation of something as a work of art. Consequently, perceptual properties (for purposes of PIOA) are those properties which can be detected by someone who has what Hume called "delicacy of taste." If experts on photography cannot discern any difference between photograph *A* and photograph *B* (using only unaided eyesight), then it is irrelevant, from the point of view of PIOA, that differences between *A* and *B* emerge when they are magnified by a hundred power. No photographer could have intended such a feature to be aesthetically relevant—unless, of course, he makes some unorthodox arrangements, such as displaying the photograph in an installation under a microscope. In that case, microscopically detectable differences might (who could say for sure?) be relevant in assessing the photograph's perceptual indistinguishability from another photograph.

Let us, then, distinguish three forms of indistinguishability. First, there is the kind which interested Liebniz—the identity of all properties as between *A* and *B*—which is not, strictly speaking, "perceptual indistinguishability" at all. Then there is what we might call the strong theory, according to which *A* and *B* are perceptually indistinguishable just in case no one can tell them apart. Had Leibniz's ingenious gentleman found his two identical leaves, he would have produced a useful illustration of the strong theory. The weak theory, by contrast, holds that *A* and *B* can be perceptually indistinguishable with respect to a given property. The weak theory thus concedes that *A* and *B* may appear manifestly different, but it claims that these differences—or indeed any perceptual examination—will show which has the property in question. Two apples, for example, will be perceptually indistinguishable with respect to the property "grown in the west orchard" (which applies to only one of them) if there is no way to tell by examining the apples which one was indeed grown there, despite the fact that the apples appear quite different.

The examples provided by Danto and Dickie in support of PIOA often suggest, I think, that PIOA is committed to the strong theory. The phrase "perceptually indistinguishable" itself suggests this. But if "indiscernibility" was not strong enough for Leibniz's logical principle, "perceptual indistinguishability" is too strong for PIOA. This is easily demonstrated by one of Danto's examples: artist One has his assistant paint a 10 × 10 blank canvas vermilion as a ground for a future painting; artist Two brings his new painting, a 10 × 10 canvas painted vermilion, to artist One's studio. Soon the artists become hopelessly confused as to which is which, and artist Two leaves with the wrong canvas. This case does not depend on there being no perceptual differences between the two canvases. The point is rather that whatever differences exist are not supposed to be able to show One or Two (unless they give One or Two insight into the production process of a given canvas) which canvas is the work of art.

I offer, then, the following characterization of perceptual indistinguishability: two objects, *A* and *B*, are perceptually indistinguishable with respect to the property "is a work of art" just in case one (but not both) is a work of art, but it cannot be determined by examination of the perceptual properties of *A* and *B* which one this is.[6] A monadic perceptual property of a work of art is, again, a property which can be discerned by persons with delicacy of taste using their unaided senses (or using such aids as would be envisioned and welcomed by artists: e.g., eyeglasses). I do not think the terms of PIOA can be made much clearer than this.

What Does PIOA Show?

PIOA in its weakest form could be taken to claim that

(1) It is not the case that all objects which are artworks are such because of any perceptual properties they possess.

But it does not follow that

(2) No object is a work of art solely because of the perceptual properties it possesses.

To show (1), PIOA needs at least one example of an artwork which is perceptually indistinguishable from a nonartwork. To show (2), which is the view embraced by Dickie, we need to make a logical point about the relation between "work of art" and "perceptual property." Lacking this, we could at least build support for (2) by citing (from various fields of art) many cases of the kind used to argue for (1), and then lay down the challenge to produce a counterexample. Alternatively, we could seek to establish (2) by demonstrating the following thesis:

6. I realize that saying two objects are "perceptually indistinguishable with respect to a property" seems confused. It should be clear, however, what is meant by this. An alternative approach would be to replace "perceptually indistinguishable" with "aesthetically indistinguishable," but I am unconvinced that any advantage is to be gained by doing so.

(3) No examination of the perceptual properties of an object will tell me that it is (or is not) an artwork.

Now it is not as easy for PIOA to establish (1) as might be supposed at first glance. The most obvious sort of thing which is likely to be perceptually indistinguishable from a work of art is a copy or forgery. Unfortunately, there is no reason not to regard copies and forgeries as works of art in their own right. In *Art and the Aesthetic,* Dickie argued that fakes are not works of art because the authentic work used up the originality that is requisite to being an artwork.[7] The trouble with this argument is that it assumes that to be an artwork the fake must be the same work as the original. The fake, however, is a completely different work, and its art-ness (as well as its artistry) consists in something entirely different from the original. It is extraordinarily unlikely, of course, that a copy will be anywhere near as good as the original. Perhaps what good copies teach us is that the quality of a work of art need not rest entirely on its perceptual properties. Although a brilliant copy of Courbet's *The Stone Breakers* might be perceptually indistinguishable from the original with respect to the property "painted by Courbet," and although it is important to recognize such a copy as a work of art in its own right, no one would suggest that the copy is as good as the original; or, anyway, no one would say that it is good in the same way.

PIOA needs, therefore, to find a counterpart to an artwork which is not a copy. What about the can of tomato soup? Here, surely, is an illustration of a work of art that is perceptually indistinguishable from legions of nonartworks. Yet the case is not so simple. First, the status of the soup can as an artwork is open to question in a way that *The Stone Breakers'* status as an artwork is not. It was Dickie who initially drew attention to the act of putting an object forward as a work of art.[8] One question that arises in this connection is, What exactly is the work being put forward? Thus, the significance of the soup can might be that, in putting it forward, the artist made (or intended to make) *all* such cans of tomato soup works of art. The "original" soup can is merely, as it were, an exemplar of millions of similar artworks in every pantry and grocery in America, none of which could serve as an indistinguishable counterpart. Alternatively, the soup can may simply be the token of a type,

7. Dickie, *Art and the Aesthetic,* p. 47.

8. George Dickie, "Defining Art," *American Philosophical Quarterly* 5 (1969): 253ff; Dickie, *Art and the Aesthetic,* p. 34.

as my copy of *Lord Jim* is a token of a type. In this case, the soup can would enjoy a privileged status, as the manuscript of *Lord Jim* enjoys a privileged status, though neither is itself the work of art. Finally, the art of the soup can could reside in the *gesture* of putting it forward, as Ted Cohen has suggested in his critique of Dickie's institutional theory.[9] Similar reasonings can apply to any work of art which is perceptually indistinguishable from common or mass-produced objects.

PIOA, then, is faced with the following problem: when dealing with traditional artworks, we imagine a perceptually indistinguishable counterpart as a copy; that is, as something which ought itself to be called a work of art. On the other hand, when dealing with Dadaist or pop works like the soup can, we can say either that every other soup can is also a work of art or that the soup can itself is not an artwork at all, but that the real work is a type or a gesture. To make a convincing case for (1), therefore, PIOA needs a counterpart to a work of art that is not produced by copying *and* is not a mass-produced object. An ideal case would be an accidental duplicate.

One kind of accidental duplicate suggested by Danto was presented earlier: the two 10 × 10 blank vermilion canvases. The proper response here, it seems to me, is: Does it matter? Who cares? If the artists cannot tell the difference, there is nothing special about artist Two's canvas for us to care about or study. (Once again the art seems to consist in putting the canvas forward or displaying it.)

The truth about such cases is that it is not really necessary to perceive the work of art at all. The canvases are really generic objects which, once they are described, need not be perceived. We could just as easily look at the "wrong" vermilion canvas as at the "right" one (or at this soup can or that soup can) or, apparently, not look at either of them but just entertain the idea of the thing. The "right" canvas is perceptually undistinguishable from the "wrong" canvas because, in the end, perception is irrelevant. Notwithstanding Dickie's reference to *Fountain*'s "gleaming white surface,"[10] the whole point about *Fountain* has nothing to do with "perceptual properties," whether or not you think *Fountain*'s art consists in a gesture or a urinal. Similar observations can be made about a host of imaginary works involving (unlike the soup can) some degree of work or fashioning (e.g., ties with paint dribbled on them or mounds of clay run over by automobiles), though not

9. Ted Cohen, "The Possibility of Art: Remarks on a Proposal By Dickie," *Philosophical Review* 82 (1973): 69–82.

10. George Dickie, "A Response to Cohen: The Actuality of Art," in *Aesthetics, A Critical Anthology*, ed. George Dickie and Richard Sclafani (New York: St. Martin's Press, 1977), p. 199.

the sort of work or fashioning required by something like *The Polish Rider.*

Is it possible to imagine accidental duplicates of works where perception is crucial? Surely this is not an easy thing to imagine. Why, for example, would anyone produce something which, by accident, looks exactly (but exactly) like a target by Jasper Johns? What would such a thing be for? (Do not say: a target.) How would a duplicate of Rembrandt's *Polish Rider* be produced accidentally? Arthur Danto imagines that a centrifuge is filled with paint, the centrifuge is spun over a canvas, and voilà (by, Danto says, "a kind of statistical miracle")[11] we have a canvas which is indiscernible from *The Polish Rider.* But cases like this are bound to be unsatisfactory. Danto's idea is reminiscent of Nietzsche's eternal return: if we just wait long enough (given that we have an eternity to wait), the required accidental copy will turn up. Of course, if we have an eternity to wait, I suppose we might end up waiting an eternity, but the "statistical miracle" conveniently solves that problem. Unfortunately, works of art do not have a monopoly on statistical miracles. The centrifuge is enormously fecund; there is no end to what it can produce. I am aware of no logical reason why there cannot be, by a statistical miracle, a pear tree which, apart from spatial location, no person could ever distinguish from the pear tree in my yard. I leave it to the reader to decide whether this means that pear trees are not what they are by virtue of properties they possess which can be perceived.

What PIOA is really searching for is a work of art that is intended to be unique but accidentally fails to be. The best I can do is the following: hiking in the Brooks Range, I come upon a configuration of rocks perceptually indistinguishable from a Smithson rock sculpture. Because Smithson could hardly anticipate the existence of such a configuration, we could not say that he also intended to make *it* a work of art; nor could we say that he intended his own sculpture as a token of a type. Others may be better at producing cases like this than I am. But the foregoing discussion reveals that PIOA is hardly the deft instrument its proponents have taken it to be. PIOA is portrayed as something which arises easily and naturally from modern art, but if PIOA succeeds in establishing (1), it is only after much arduous labor.

In the end, (1) is not a terribly interesting thesis. The true goal of PIOA is to establish (2). The problem, as I have already suggested, is that it is hard to imagine how perceptually indistinguishable counterparts to most works of art would come about except through design, and it is hard to imagine, in

11. Danto, *The Transfiguration of the Commonplace,* p. 31.

turn, how such design could fail to make a work of art. I do not think there are any circumstances under which something perceptually indistinguishable from Wright's *Robie House,* Diaghilev's original production of Stravinsky's *Firebird,* or the ceiling of the Sistine Chapel would not be a work of art.

But let us suppose that we can imagine perceptually indistinguishable counterparts (in the weak sense) to these works. Proposition (2) is still dubious. To borrow a point from Nelson Goodman, we cannot be sure, when presented with an object perceptually indistinguishable from some work of art, that we will not in the future be able to detect perceptual differences that today we are unable to detect. To this sort of point Danto has replied that in the case of artworks like the soup can or painted ties by Jim Dine and John Duff, the refined peering that would turn up perceptual differences is inappropriate. The gross perceptual properties are all that count.[12] As an argument in favor of (1), Danto's point is well taken, but as an argument in favor of (2) it is self-defeating. For in the case of something like *The Polish Rider,* the perceptual differences we may eventually notice may be of *aesthetic* significance. Goodman has noted that "extremely subtle changes can alter the whole design, feeling, or expression of a painting. Indeed, the slightest perceptual differences sometimes matter the most aesthetically."[13] The proponent of (2) might reply that such differences could not be the reason that *The Polish Rider* is a *work of art,* but the problem is that this is precisely what PIOA is supposed to *show.* That is, as an argument for (2) and (3), PIOA begs the question. In order for PIOA to show that you cannot tell that an object is a work of art by examination of its perceptual properties, PIOA has to show that the object can be perceptually indistinguishable from a nonartwork with respect to the property "is a work of art." In the case of works like *The Polish Rider,* however, *any* perceptual differences between it and the proposed counterpart could be of aesthetic importance. There is no reason why these differences could not show which is the work of art. PIOA, then, can establish (2) and (3) only if it can also establish that we can imagine for any work of art a perceptually indistinguishable counterpart in the *strong* sense; that is, a counterpart which no expert *could* distinguish from the work of art. This is something, I take it, that no argument could ever establish. The impulse to imagine this lies behind the "statistical miracle" caused by the centrifuge, for this case *stipulates* that the objects are identical.

12. Ibid., pp. 43–44; Danto, "Artworks and Real Things," p. 8.

13. Nelson Goodman, *Languages of Art* (Indianapolis: Bobbs-Merrill, 1976). See also Robertson Davies, *What's Bred in the Bone* (New York: Penguin, 1986).

Given the sort of works of art that provide fodder for PIOA, the foregoing result is not surprising. It is entirely plausible that only a majority of works of art are such by virtue of perceptual properties they possess. We could say (if inclined to say this kind of thing) that perceptual properties of a certain sort are a sufficient but not necessary condition of something being a work of art.

The Role of Intention

The fact that PIOA does not establish (2) and (3) does not, of course, show that (2) and (3) are false. Whatever plausibility these propositions have rests not so much on PIOA as on the feeling that in order for something to be a work of art it must be meant to be such. When we try to imagine a perceptually indistinguishable counterpart to a work of art, we are trying to imagine something which was not intended as art or, better, which was not intended at all (but is the product of the winds and rains, or of a short circuit in a centrifuge). Things are works of art because they are produced by creative acts. We can infer such acts by "perceptual examination" of artworks, but of course the acts themselves are not (ordinarily) perceptual properties of the works. Consequently, we can never tell "for certain" by examining something that it is a work of art simply because such examination cannot tell us "for certain" what the artist's intentions are (no more than your words can tell me "for certain" what you intended by them). The reason that PIOA is comfortable with particular kinds of modern art (e.g., soup cans) and much less comfortable with traditional works (e.g., *The Polish Rider*) is that it is hard to imagine how something perceptually indistinguishable from a traditional work could come about except by intentions that would make it art.

This point about intentions shows two things. First, the fact that an object is a work of art because of a relation it bears to something else (intentions) can be brought out by comparing the object to ordinary objects like staplers and pinecones. No reference to "perceptually indistinguishable" objects is necessary. Second, as Danto recognizes, PIOA does not entail an institutional theory of art. George Dickie moved from the idea that being a work of art does not consist in the possession of perceptual properties to the idea that being a work of art must consist in the possession of an institutional status.[14] But even if we think that perceptual properties do not

14. Dickie, *Art and the Aesthetic*, p. 34.

make something a work of art, we can explain this by reference to artistic intentions.

It should not be supposed, however, that "intention" is a concept foreign to or incompatible with the institutional theory. On the contrary, intention has been an unsung hero of Dickie's work from the beginning. In maintaining that works of art must be artifacts,[15] and that an artifact becomes a work of art by having the status of candidate for appreciation conferred on it, the intentions of artists have played a crucial role in Dickie's thinking. This is clear in *The Art Circle,* where Dickie defines "art" by reference, in part, to a definition of "artist" as "a person who participates with understanding in the making of a work of art."[16] Dickie goes on to explain: "This definition of 'artist' . . . makes it clear that art-making is an intentional activity; although elements of a work of art may have their origin in accidental occurrences which happen during the making of a work, a work as a whole is not accidental. Participating with understanding implies that an artist is aware of what he is doing."[17]

PIOA, then, shows at best that you cannot always tell something is a work of art by examining it. (This is something I suppose we knew all along.) But it cannot show that you can never do this. Its importance lies in pointing to the fact that works of art, like utterances in language, are *meant* and, therefore, that they are what they are as a result of the intentions of the people who make them.

15. Ibid.
16. Dickie, *The Art Circle,* p. 80.
17. Ibid.

Susan Feagin

Valuing the Artworld

Emma was "incapable of understanding what she didn't experience, or of recognizing anything that wasn't expressed in conventional terms."

—Gustave Flaubert, *Madame Bovary*

George Dickie initially established his reputation as a debunker of certain myths: namely, the myths of aesthetic experience and the aesthetic attitude. He also argued for what has come to be known as an institutional theory of art, according to which some object, entity, or event is an artwork according to whether it occupies a certain kind of position in relation to an institutional framework or context.[1] Though Dickie's *objectives* in defending these positions were hardly political, his philosophical achievement in showing the limitations of certain traditional aspects of the concepts of art and the aesthetic provides independent grounds (i.e., independent of political views) for growing suspicion about both their utility within a theory of art and the way they reinforce certain cultural values. He was thus a precursor of those

1. This is Dickie's more encompassing characterization of an institutional definition. See his paper "Aesthetics," in *Proceedings of the Eighth International Wittgenstein Symposium,* pt. 1, ed. Rudolf Haller (Vienna: Holder-Pichler-Tensky, 1984), p. 47; reprinted as "The New Institutional Theory of Art," in *Aesthetics: A Critical Anthology,* 2nd ed., ed. George Dickie, Richard Sclafani, and Ronald Roblin (New York: St. Martin's Press, 1989), pp. 196–205.

who today are challenging the very notions of art and the aesthetic, who see them as an historically bound residue of eighteenth-century thought, which arose out of a certain cultural climate and served (and continue to serve) to reinforce its attendant social and cultural values.

Yet, Dickie's exhortations in his early works to pay attention to the work and its properties instead of to characteristics of the perceiver's attitude or experience are themselves illustrative of tendencies which he and the philosophical community at large have transcended. For example, Dickie argued that the unity and coherence which Monroe Beardsley attributed to "aesthetic experiences" were in fact features of the *work* rather than features of our *experiences* of the work.[2] It is fair to assume that it is currently agreed on practically all sides that appreciating a work of art requires active contributions on the part of perceivers, not merely attention to what is "really there," the sets of properties the work "really has." Dickie's later writings on the nature of aesthetic value judgments and on the nature of taste display his concern with the age-old philosophical debates over the relationships between properties of the object and the contributions of appreciators.

Artworks move us in profound, amusing, frightening, sometimes appalling ways. We sympathize with the characters and share their pains, pleasures, joys, and despair. Artworks can change our moods, shift attitudes and points of view, create vague feelings and strong emotion. These experiences are certainly important aspects of an appreciation of artworks, and they constitute, in some sense, at least *part* of what is valuable about works of art. But these experiences do not come from *simply* attending to the qualities of "the work itself." One's own attitudes, values, mental sets, and past experiences affect how one sees and hears, and *a fortiori* how one affectively responds: as philosophers have been pointing out ad nauseam over the years, there is, psychologically, no such thing as an innocent eye or unmarked mental tablet which receives "pure," "uninterpreted" impressions from the world.

Dickie's debunkings have thus left us in a troubling position. The lack of any univocal analysis of the kind of experience we are supposed to have in response to art in general casts doubt on whether there is any specifically *aesthetic* value to artworks or to our experiences of them. And once we have eliminated any appeal to a special kind of attitude which prescribes what we are to *do* with a work of art, it is difficult to establish what kinds of mental sets and active involvements are appropriate (i.e., "*aesthetically* relevant").

2. See Dickie, "Beardsley's Phantom Aesthetic Experience," *The Journal of Philosophy* 62 (1965): 129–36, and "The Myth of the Aesthetic Attitude," *American Philosophical Quarterly* 1 (1964): 56–64.

While not denying that there may be value in the character of appreciative experiences themselves, I will instead discuss a) the importance of having a capacity to engage in the activities which culminate or result in those experiences and b) the roles such activities play in an appreciation of an artwork. These activities are of at least two kinds. First, there are psychological shifts and adjustments which culminate or result in our having *affective* feelings or emotional responses to works of art in general. Second, there are imaginings, wonderings, and hypothesizings which one engages in to understand the roles one's affective responses play in one's appreciative experience. However, it should be recognized that making judgments about the relevance, appropriateness, or justifiedness of the former activities requires reflection, and hence it requires hypothesizing and whatever else one might do to figure out how to assess them. Both these kinds of activities can loosely be called exercises of imagination, and my focus will be on what I deem to be an important function of the artworld, which is to develop these capacities of our imagination. The values of engaging in these exercises of imagination, which are manifested in the various emotional and affective responses we have, as well as the reflections we make on their appropriateness and relevance, are linked with the values of developing imagination as an end in itself: for example, expanding the flexibility of the human mind so that it can move beyond the mere apprehension of a stimulus object, or what is "really there." In saying that it is valuable to develop imaginative flexibility as an end in itself, I am rejecting the assumption that the importance of imagination depends *solely* on its mental or behavioral effects—for example, on the contributions it makes to our store of knowledge or the morality of our behavior.

After some brief preliminary and, for many, largely familiar distinctions among the kinds of things which can have functions, and after some comments on the nature of functions, I will describe the sorts of imaginative capacity—what I call mental flexibility—which it is at least one of the functions of the artworld to develop. I think it likely to be less controversial that it *could* be a function of the artworld to develop this capacity than that it is *desirable* to promote the artworld as having this function, and some of my remarks will address that concern. Finally, I will return to the distinction between functions of the artworld and functions of individual works of art to explain how, when we recognize many different kinds of things as being valuable or important, these values may conflict with one another.

My views on these matters are, in some major respects, decidedly old-fashioned. In contrast with recent trends, they are in accord both with recognizing the concept of *art* as an important and useful concept and with an account of something which can plausibly be called *aesthetic* value. Indeed, I think it is important to recognize a category of phenomena called "art" precisely because I think it is important to recognize that stretching and exercising human imagination is an important thing to do. But I argue this without positing the existence of some mythical aesthetic attitude or aesthetic experience, and without claiming that art and the aesthetic are cultural universals. My argument is rather that something important can be preserved by recognizing these categories, something which may well be lost if we do not do so.

The artworld has many functions; I have tried to delineate one which is appropriately thought of as aesthetic. But I do not claim that every individual work of art has or ought to have this agency—the development and exercise of imagination—as at least one of its functions. Nor do I claim that all good works fulfill this particular function. I am not even sure I would want to claim that *most,* or even *a high percentage,* have or fulfill this function. It is not the functions of individual works of art that interest me here, but *a* function of the artworld.

The Artworld, Member Institutions, and Artworks

The artworld of late-twentieth-century Western Europe and America comprises a multiplicity of institutions, in the broad sense of people, organizations and significant patterns of activity, such as museums, dealers, collectors, auction houses, magazines, criticism, schools, departments, and governmental and private sources of monetary support earmarked specifically for the above. Our concept of art conceptually underwrites these institutions by defining a particular subset of existing museums as *art* museums, and by identifying a class of dealers as *art* dealers, and so on for collectors of art (or artworks of specific kinds), art magazines, art criticism, art schools, departments of art and art history, endowments for the arts, and the rest.

This artworld has a multitude of effects on individuals and on society at large, both good and bad. But there is a difference between something's function in this sense—the way something does in fact function; that is, what its actual effect is—and something's function in the sense of what it is supposed to be doing, which it may or may not accomplish. Astute and informed observation lets you find out what the functions of a set of institutions in the former sense in fact are.

Unfortunately, the basis for drawing conclusions about something's function in the latter sense, what something is *supposed* to be doing, is not at all that clear. Indeed, the deciding factors or criteria for identifying functions in this latter sense may vary, depending on whether one is talking about the function or functions of an individual object, or of an institution whose function is to produce such objects, or of the set or collection of institutions whose function is to maintain and enhance the member institutions of the set. However, one thing should be clear: it is too strong to require that either an individual object, institution, or set of institutions be *uniquely* suited to fulfill or perform a function in order to conclude that it does have, or that it is desirable for it to have, that function. On the other hand, if the artworld *can* plausibly be shown to be well suited to fulfill or perform some *desirable* function or role in society, then this provides a reasonable basis for saying there is a special *value,* which could perhaps even be called "aesthetic value," in having a society which recognizes the existence of something we call "art" and which supports institutions that compose an "artworld."

The primary function or purpose of member institutions of the artworld—what they are individually apparently *supposed* to be doing within the society—is to play various specific roles from among the general categories of guiding the production, study, understanding, appreciation, and distribution of individual works of art. In saying merely that the institutions of art ought (i.e., their function is to) guide the production and so on of individual works of art, a lot is being left unsaid. Guidance to what end? In ways that reinforce existing social values or moral codes, or in ways that challenge them? In ways which ensure, as much as possible, that they contain some "truth"? In ways which encourage virtuosity rather than sentiment, discipline rather than experimentation, the traditional over the innovative? It is clear that various policies, explicit or implicit, can tilt the balance in different directions. Minimum kinds and degrees of skill might be considered a requirement for completing one's education as an artist or for obtaining a favorable critical assessment. Museums might adopt purchase policies (and galleries might adopt policies for shows) which favor some kinds of works over others. And so on.

The actual effects of member institutions can be both more and less extensive than what it is their function to do. When evaluating the benefits and disadvantages of an institution, one must consider not only what it is supposed to be doing, whether it is doing it, and whether that is worth doing, but also what *else* it is doing: that is, what other effects the existence of the institution has. It is often difficult to distinguish, moreover, the effects of the institution per se from the effects of the institution in its present form, since some deleterious effects might occur from mismanagement or peculiarities of organization, but not necessarily if the institution were reorganized.

Conclusions about what any single museum, gallery, critic, school, magazine, and so on *ought* to be doing are complicated by the sheer numbers. The variety and balance among member institutions and the relationships various member institutions have to one another, rather than the characteristics of any given institution considered in isolation, can be the source of the artworld's social effects. It is a fallacy of composition to assume that the functions of the individual member institutions merely dictate additively the functions of the artworld as a collection of institutions. Similarly, to conclude that the functions of the artworld are the functions of its individual member institutions is to commit a fallacy of division. Moreover, whether it *is* desirable to have certain sorts of institutions in one's society with certain functions depends on the structure of other aspects of that society.

There is one worthwhile function, in the second sense mentioned above, which it seems to me the artworld should be recognized as having but which in my view is not sufficiently recognized or emphasized in the popular mind. That function is to develop certain capacities of mind—in particular, both its cognitive flexibility and its affective flexibility; that is, flexibility with respect to one's emotional and affective sensitivities. In this essay, I will concentrate primarily on explaining affective flexibility. I will describe this mental capacity and how it relates both to mental abilities and to emotional sensitivities. I will also address briefly the issue of why it is desirable to recognize such a function as a function of the artworld.

Capacities to Develop the Ability to Feel

It is important first to distinguish between capacities and abilities.[3] Abilities are the powers to do things, while capacities are the states or conditions which enable one to acquire those powers. Certain degrees of strength and

3. An anonymous reviewer of the present essay suggested that this distinction might be irremediably fluid. I think that may well be so; however, it does not follow that the distinction is nowhere useful. I hope my discussion here shows the utility of the distinction for understanding the *capacities* which I take it as a function of the artworld to develop, rather than for understanding either certain abilities or the results achieved through the exercise of those abilities.

flexibility are capacities; that is to say, they are conditions of an organism which are necessary for acquiring and developing certain (physical) abilities, as are endurance, coordination, and quick reflexes. The powers we have to *control* and *direct* the movements and successive states of our bodies and minds are commonly called "abilities," especially when those powers have been enhanced or developed with practice or experience and when they can be put to the service of some chosen end. This control may be conscious or intentional, or it may simply be a mode of action adopted "automatically" in a given sort of situation. We speak of the ability to control *ourselves* as well as the ability to *do* things and to do things *to,* or make changes *in,* the world.

It is something of a terminological decision whether capacities, like abilities, can be enhanced by *learning.* You can learn techniques, like mind control, to enhance your endurance; and capacities can be enhanced by *training,* as strength and endurance can be enhanced by the right kinds of exercise. This is true even of what we might call "mental abilities," such as abilities to make fine perceptual discriminations, the ability to see things from different points of view, and imaginative abilities. As with physical abilities, it is often difficult to draw a line between where a capacity ends and an ability begins—whether, for example, repeated exposure to early Renaissance paintings, and feedback on who did what, enhances one's perceptual *capacities* for discrimination or whether it enhances one's *abilities* to discriminate; that is, whether we already have the capacity but learn how to control and direct it. (The case of perception also illustrates the automaticity which often, and often essentially, attends the exercise of abilities.)

I am especially interested in our *capacities* for emotional and affective response, as distinguished from our *abilities* to respond appropriately and justifiedly to given sorts of situations. It is the development of a certain capacity—affective *flexibility*—which I will argue is an important function of the *artworld.* Affective flexibility is the capacity to respond to a variety of different kinds of perceptual phenomena and ideas in a variety of ways. It is also the capacity to respond to the same kind of phenomena in a variety of ways. Unfortunately, it sounds natural to describe flexibility—both physical and mental—as an ability as well, but such descriptions are at best elliptical. Flexibility is not an ability; an ability would be a particular controlled and directed utilization or exercise of a capacity. I have the ability to touch my toes, but being sufficiently flexible to do that is a condition of my body, or a bodily capacity, rather than an ability.

Affective flexibility requires that one have, and be able to come to have, a great variety of sensitivities. A sensitivity is the psychological state or condition which makes it the case that one affectively responds in a given way to a given sort of phenomenon. There are things we can do, sometimes directly and sometimes only indirectly, to expand and alter our sensitivities, to get into a condition such that we respond in a given way to a particular kind of phenomenon. On the other hand, sometimes our sensitivities change whether or not we *do* anything, or whether we want them to or not. In the latter case, it is unclear whether the alteration of our sensitivities is something which simply happens to us or whether it is something which we *allow* to happen. This is not an issue which we need to adjudicate here, but it is important to recognize tendencies to respond emotionally and affectively as what they are: susceptibilities which can to a substantial degree be changed, which can increase or decrease with experience and practice, and which we can come to control and manipulate. It is my position that one of the functions the artworld should be recognized as having is that of developing and exercising a capacity to have a wide variety of sensitivities (and perhaps also *in*sensitivities, when those are considered to be "acts of omission"); that is, a capacity to be moved emotionally or affectively in an extraordinary variety of ways to an extraordinary number and variety of things.

It is not the function of the artworld as a whole to encourage or facilitate the use of any *particular* sensitivity or ability to feel. If this were the case, one would have to explain not only what that experience is (aesthetic experience?) but also what the benefit (i.e., value) is of having that *particular* sensitivity. Explaining this benefit, of course, is not always difficult. Certain sensitivities may manifest themselves in quite pleasurable experiences, or may even enable us to "know what it's like" to be in a certain kind of situation. They could thus have hedonic or epistemic value. There might also be extrinsic value in these experiences: for example, insofar as they lead us to reflect on the sources of our emotions and feelings and thereby to acquire knowledge of ourselves.[4]

4. Alternatively, one might say, we learn how the fictional character feels. Many would argue that doing this *enables* us to learn important things about the world; thus, its value is instrumental, not intrinsic. The defensibility of such a claim rests on the extent to which responses to fiction can be effectively used in this way. It is far beyond the scope of this essay to discuss such issues, but for a defense of useful knowledge see David Novitz, *Knowledge, Fiction and Imagination* (Philadelphia: Temple University Press, 1987), chap. 6, "Fiction and the Growth of Knowledge." On the other hand, Martha Nussbaum argues that emotions are themselves "pieces of recognition" (p. 390), rather than that they provoke us to examine things so that we come to know. See Nussbaum, *The Fragility of Goodness* (New York: Cambridge University Press, 1986), "Interlude 2: Luck and the Tragic Emotions."

Be that as it may, what is crucial to my purposes is that it is desirable to have a capacity for a wide variety of emotions and feeling responses to art (i.e., emotional and affective flexibility). This places a value on the extent and variety of one's sensitivities, rather than on the character of individual ones. There may be value in the former—indeed, I think there is—even if there is no value (e.g., pleasure or knowledge) in having each and every one of its components. Nor does this mean that it would be just as well to leave out those components which do not themselves have intrinsic or extrinsic value, for this would show that one's mental flexibility was decreased.[5]

Thus, it may be the function of an *individual work of art* to exercise a particular sensitivity, or to produce a particular sort of experience, which it is not either intrinsically or extrinsically desirable or valuable to have. This may seem paradoxical: it is an object's function to do something, according to which it is to be judged good or bad, which it is not at all worthwhile to do.[6] Yet, I would go even further: it may be an object's function to do something it is downright harmful to do. This follows from the purely *logical* distinctions between the functions of a collection of institutions (e.g., the artworld), the functions of each individual organization or the practice of a member institution of that collection (e.g., museums or schools), and the functions of the individual objects which it is the function of the organizations and practices to develop, distribute, and so on (i.e., individual works of art). And though to argue that the artworld is a valuable part of our society and that it should be retained in some form or other requires specifying the respects in which it has a valuable function (and also, perhaps, requires specifying how overriding detrimental effects can be avoided), it does not require showing that every *object* which the component organizations produce and even applaud has a *valuable* function.

An analogy may prove to be illustrative at this point. The analogy involves a very simplistic characterization of the human mind as having a function. Let us suppose that it is the function of the human mind to obtain true beliefs about oneself and the world. Nothing hangs on whether this supposition is true: it is advanced simply to illustrate the logical distinctions between functions of a collection, functions of the entities which compose

5. Such experiences will certainly be valuable insofar as they are *manifestations* of a capacity which it is valuable to have. But they will not necessarily be valuable because of their inherent phenomenological character (as pleasurable) or because they constitute "knowing what it's like" (a nonhedonic intrinsic value) or because of their effects (extrinsic value).

6. Monroe Beardsley denies this in *Aesthetics: Problems in the Philosophy of Criticism* (New York: Harcourt, Brace & World, 1958), p. 526.

the collection, and functions of what is produced by the entities which compose the collection. Let us also suppose that this mind is a collection of hierarchically arranged processes (each of which has a function or functions) and that each process is supposed to interact with the others so that one does end up with true beliefs. Now let us suppose, not too implausibly, that a person rarely if ever has conclusive evidence for the truth of any given thought, so that if one's mind is constructed in such a way that it will not generate thoughts unless it has conclusive proof for their truth, it will rarely do what it is supposed to be doing (i.e., have true beliefs). One way of designing a mind which gets around this problem would be to have some subsystem or "faculty" whose function it is to generate thoughts irrespective of the extent to which any belief in their truth is justified. This would allow us to speculate about the unseen, to hypothesize for purposes of testing, and even to accomplish a "paradigm shift," where what was formerly thought to support one belief or set of beliefs could be found to support a belief or set of beliefs inconsistent with it.[7] For convenience, let us call this faculty "imagination."

Clearly, even though the function of the mind (as we are supposing) is to generate true beliefs, it does not follow that this "faculty" should be condemned because it generates thoughts of things which, as it turns out, have no chance of being true (and which we have no reason to believe would stand such a chance). Furthermore, the thoughts themselves are not to be evaluated according to whether they are true or likely to be true, since it is not the function of the particular subsystem which generates them to produce *true* thoughts, and it is not the function of those *thoughts* to be true. Of course, the higher-order systems are always assessing the products of the subsystems (if the mind is working properly) with respect to whether one should believe these things. Nevertheless, the *most* imaginative thoughts may do no earthly good, either intrinsically or extrinsically. A *given* thought may not be true (and hence not have "intrinsic value"), or it may not play any role in helping one find the truth (and hence not have "extrinsic value"). Such thoughts may nevertheless be precisely the kinds of things the subsystem is supposed to be generating, for they indicate the subsystem is working the way it is supposed to be working: namely, to generate ideas *irrespective* of whether one has reasons to believe them. To condemn the thoughts ("It's stupid to think such things, and you shouldn't do it") will muck up the higher-order system, whose proper functioning *depends on* having a subsys-

7. There must be limitations to this, of course. We do not want this faculty to keep generating ideas at the expense of the operation of other faculties, such as considering whether there are any good reasons for believing any of them. But such niceties of mind design need not concern us here.

tem which operates *independently* of anything one has reason to believe is true.[8] If the subsystem internalizes the objectives of the higher-order system so that it acts as a censor on imagination's production of thoughts, the imagination will cease to fulfill its function.

Psychological Exercise

It does not seem implausible to me that, analogously, it is at least one of the functions of individual works of art to do things which in themselves are no earthly good—for example, to provide experiences which are not morally elevating or pleasurable or which do not constitute knowing what some kind of situation is like (to mention the most commonly discussed candidates). A work of art may be a good work of art when it produces certain kinds of experiences, even when they lack both intrinsic and extrinsic value. Affective responses to artworks *may* themselves be pleasurable, and they may also enhance one's cognitive or moral understanding of the world. Yet, artworks need not be defended as good or valuable only insofar as they afford experiences which are, for example, hedonically, epistemically, or morally valuable.[9] But what is left?

Let us return to the idea floated above that one of the functions of having an artworld (one of the things it *should* be doing) is to develop our capacities for emotion and feeling. It will do this by provoking and facilitating the exercise and development of a wide variety of sensitivities. It is this capacity for a wide range and variety of responses which I have been calling "mental flexibility." Essential to this capacity is having the potential for making various kinds of psychological shifts and adjustments that are necessary for having affective responses to works of art. Making these psychological shifts is what we *do* which eventuates in our having an emotional or affective response. These can include shifts in attitude,

8. One may attempt a "rule utilitarian" justification of the individual thoughts, though it appears to me that this will collapse into a functional justification (i.e., they are "good" because they are the kinds of things the subsystem is supposed to be producing), which I am arguing is the right basis for their assessment.

9. If so, of course, the question remains open as to what makes one experience, rather than another, appropriate to have in response to a given work. Are these the experiences which *are* morally or epistemically valuable? Highly implausible. So we need criteria of relevance. What will ground these criteria—the kinds of things which will make it most likely that one has a morally or epistemically rewarding experience in response to the work? A sketch of my own alternative follows.

point of view, or frame of mind or a shift in cognitive or affective orientation. In this section I will give a more detailed explanation of the nature of such shifts.

There is one kind of situation, a perceptual situation, where (most) people can, quite intentionally, effect a "mental shift" which results in their having different kinds of experiences. "Double-aspect" figures, such as the duck-rabbit and the Necker cube, provide the perceiver with a clear opportunity to change how sensory data become *perceptually* organized to produce a perceptual experience. Looking at a drawing of a Necker cube, one can see the lower square *as* representing the front face of a cube or *as* representing its back face. With a little practice, it is possible to bring this "flipping" under one's control, so that it is possible to tell oneself, "This is the front face of the cube" and have the rest of the lines fall into their perceptual places. I *do not* have to tell myself, "These lines are supposed to be receding" and "That square represents the back face"; that is, I do not have to know what role each aspect of the figure will play in my perceptual experience in order to make the shift. My mind simply operates in such a way (no doubt having something to do with the lure of closure) to ensure that as many segments of the drawing as possible are "interpreted" accordingly, without my having to think through the representational significance of every portion of the image.

When someone effects a change in perception, in point of view, in what one sees something "as," or in affective or emotive orientation, psychological adjustments are made, many of which occur more or less automatically, lower down in the hierarchy of "programs" that process memories, beliefs, ideas, desires, and perceptual stimuli.[10] Though we can describe the effects of these adjustments—e.g., perceptions, beliefs, thoughts, or emotions and other affective responses—and though we may have some techniques for producing them intentionally, we do not really know just what it is at the preconscious level which constitutes the implementation of our executive order to make this psychological shift. Moreover, a shift in perspective is not always initiated intentionally or deliberately. It can just happen, and sometimes one would rather it did not. My old shoes looked perfectly fine until I saw them next to a new pair, at which point they looked worn and battered. A contrasting perceptual environment can serve to highlight different proper-

10. "Programs" is a useful *metaphor* for capturing the differences among psychological processes. But it is only a metaphor. Strictly speaking, programs are *sets of rules* governing behavior. I do *not* mean to imply that the mental or psychological processes I am discussing are rule-governed (though they may be describable by rules).

ties of an object, both the straightforwardly perceptual and their affective or valuational accompaniments, and can trigger a new visual organization of what is sensed.

Often in the process of becoming acquainted with an artwork, one should psychologically readjust oneself, or at least *become* psychologically readjusted: one should shift into, or slip into, a different mental gear. And the relevance or appropriateness of the shifts may not depend at all on the accumulation of evidence or reasons for believing that the psychological shifting will reveal some kind of truth. Nor does it depend on the nature of one's values and desires. The point may well be to see and experience things from a point of view which does *not* value what one does and which embodies a very different belief system.

The independence of one's capacity for psychological shifting from one's reasons for believing (what one ends up thinking of or perceiving something *as* being like) is perhaps most clear in a shift of *mood.* One's mood need not lift because all of a sudden one has recognized *that* the world is not so terrible as one thought, but can occur because something "triggered" a change in perspective. The "trigger" *can* take the form of a belief, or an intention or decision of one's own, or it can be something someone else says or does. But the trigger does not *have* to be anything like *evidence* or a *reason* for seeing things differently. Nevertheless, once the shift has occurred, the world may look very different, and one may find oneself in a position to *acquire* reasons or evidence to support a claim about the truth or veracity of how one now sees things. A shift in perspective can give access to new information or ideas, without being itself produced for a reason or because one has reasons or evidence for the claim that such is the *correct* way to view things.

Being in third gear is a state of an automobile, but it is a state which ensures that certain sorts of events go on as the car moves. Shifting into third gear, that action or event which culminates in being in third gear, has a major effect on how the car runs and on what it will do. What is psychologically analogous to being in third gear is to be in a given frame of mind or to take a certain kind of mental perspective on things, to have a given sensitivity. One's frame of mind or perspective will affect how one interprets or analyzes what one sees or reads, what it does to oneself, and what significance it has. Psychologically, slipping into a "new gear" gets one into a condition which results in activity that would not take place if one were not in that "gear." Psychological shifts do not *make* things happen in the sense of ensuring that an experience will occur, because whether or not one has the experience depends on (at least) what the conditions are under which one is operating: what the "environment" is like, what sorts of perceptual stimuli one is exposed to.

The fact that our psyches *can* become emotionally or affectively sensitive to various kinds of things is crucially important for having emotional and affective responses to works of art. We are psychologically malleable (affectively and conatively), and one of the things we are *supposed to do* in order to appreciate individual works of art is to make use of this malleability. This is, so to speak, the converse of an Aristotelian position in virtue ethics, where the emphasis is on our deeply rooted, permanent character traits. On the contrary, certain aspects of a work are supposed to change us, and we are supposed to change ourselves, in such a way that we do affectively respond in a given way to something in the work. The point is that we are supposed to *alter* our sensitivities, not simply respond by using the ones we already have.

One often must change, psychologically, during the process of confronting an artwork in order to appreciate it. One "uses" progressively encountered aspects of the work to effect a change in one's sensitivities, so that one *becomes* sensitive to something one perceives later on. Not surprisingly, the parts of a work of art are supposed to work *together,* to coordinate with one another, to accomplish their functions. Making the work "work" requires using the various parts to do what they are supposed to be doing. *Some* parts should be functioning to alter our psychological condition, very often at a preconscious level, in a way which does not necessarily issue in a conscious experience—either a thought or an affect. This change in our psychological condition is a change from not being sensitive to being sensitive to a certain sort of thing—or the converse—or perhaps, at an even more subtle level, becoming more susceptible to the influence of something which will effect this change. *Other* parts of a work should be producing emotional or affective responses: we should already have become, or have made ourselves, sensitive to the aesthetically or artistically significant properties of the work.[11]

11. Gabriele Taylor has provided an illuminating example, taken from James Joyce's short story "The Dead" (see Taylor, *Pride, Shame, and Guilt: Emotions of Self-assessment* [Oxford: Clarendon Press, 1985], chap. 1). She argues that in order to explain or understand why a person (in the story, Gabriel) had a given response to a particular kind of situation, it is necessary to understand why he focused on the particular set of properties of the situation that he did. In other words, to experience an event as he did, we must perform certain "mental actions" which result in our being or becoming sensitive to certain kinds of things in the same way Gabriel was. The story assists us in performing these actions by providing a context for understanding Gabriel's emotional response in terms of his previous

Punching Bags for the Mind

About the functions of individual works of art, I have said virtually nothing which could serve to generate criteria for an assessment of such works as good or bad, as opposed to one's assessment of the institution of the artworld as a whole.[12] Naturally, the functions of individual works that I am interested in are their roles in developing one's various mental capacities and abilities—in particular, a) one's sensitivities and capacities for becoming sensitive to various sorts of phenomena and b) one's ability to adopt a given attitude, perspective, or point of view. Another function may be to get the reader to have an experience of a given kind; but clearly this is not to have the function of developing a given capacity or ability, unless having the experience is seen as instrumental to the development of something else. An example would be that having a given experience is instrumental to gaining some sort of knowledge or understanding of oneself. As I indicated above, I believe this achievement is less likely to be part of the *function* of a work and more likely to be part of the benefit of being able to *appreciate* a work.[13] The knowledge and mental capacities one might acquire *as a result of appreciating* artworks may indeed be among the benefits of developing the capacity to appreciate them, but it is not necessarily itself part of the *function* of the artwork or part of what might be called its *aesthetic* value.

The boundaries between functions and benefits are of course fluid, though this fact does not alter the significance of the conceptual distinction between them. Moreover, one's *realization* that bases for an assessment of a given work—reasons for judging it to be beneficial to have such things around and to appreciate them—may be different from what it is the *function* of that work to do can lead to a psychological tug-of-war which I like to call "axiological schizophrenia." Axiological schizophrenia occurs because recognition of the benefits of a practice tends to infiltrate one's thinking about

experiences, a series of failures which have served gradually to erode his sense of self-worth. Those experiences made him sensitive to his wife's remarks in a way that a more well-adjusted person would not have been.

12. This is at the core of Beardsley's instrumentalist theory (see *Aesthetics*, chap. 9, sec. 28). Also see Paul Ziff, "Reasons in Art Criticism," in *Philosophical Turnings: Essays in Conceptual Appreciation* (Ithaca: Cornell University Press, 1966).

13. And the benefits need not always come from appreciating the work: one could use the work to learn something about oneself in a way which is quite divorced from any reasonable understanding of what is actually going on in the work itself.

why to do something. Hence, those benefits come to provide reasons for doing it which conflict with specifications of the work's function. This seems to be exactly what has happened with much theoretical writing about the arts, which sees the arts in terms of their epistemic (or their social, moral, or political) roles and functions, rather than in terms of anything which might be describable as their "aesthetic value." The insinuation of these other concerns into the functions of art is especially tempting if the *importance* of such things as knowledge, morality, and social impact are seen to outweigh or override any value which the development and exercise of various mental capacities might have in and of themselves. These latter may be seen as insufficiently significant to stand on their own if they conflict with other concerns, and hence to pale in comparison with them. However, recent debates about the plausibility of the "overridingness principle" should give us pause when it comes to assessing phenomena which conflict with what we recognize to be *morally* required.[14] The importance of the development and exercise of one's mental flexibility may well outweigh at least some consequences it might have in the form of inclining us to have false or unjustified beliefs, or to feel or emotionally respond in what one judges to be morally questionable ways. One way of *avoiding* possibly deleterious consequences is to make sure one is aware of the differences between engaging in acts of imagination, making use of the flexibility of the human mind, and actually endorsing or committing oneself to believing in the truth or goodness of what one thinks or feels.

A function or value of the art*world* is to promote and perpetuate the member institutions, which in turn guide the production, study, understanding, appreciation, and distribution of art*works*. Art*works* are the equipment used for a certain kind of mental fitness: using them properly—at least, many of the good ones—increases and maintains the affective flexibility of the human mind. If the capacity is already there, artworks utilize it; if it is not there, they give us an opportunity to expand and develop it. Whether increasing one's capacities and using these abilities is pleasurable is another matter: some people enjoy a physical workout and some do not, and one may enjoy it sometimes and not at others. Whether these increased capacities and abilities, and the exercise of

14. See Bernard Williams, *Moral Luck: Philosophical Papers, 1973–1980* (New York: Cambridge University Press, 1981) for a germinal discussion of the overridingness of the moral.

them, actually give us *knowledge* or make us morally better people is likewise another matter, analogous to whether increased athletic abilities are useful in any *other* avenue of our lives.

Nelson Goodman wittily parodied a view much like the one I have advanced above by characterizing it as holding that artworks are dumbbells and punching bags for the mind.[15] The "dumbbell" view need not say, as Goodman characterizes it, that the ultimate objective or function of art is for "survival, conquest, and gain." One can set fitness goals for oneself as ends in themselves: to press one's own weight, or to run five miles in fifty minutes. Art, at least good art, can strengthen or at least "tone" our "mental muscles," but not necessarily for "survival, conquest, and gain." It is highly unlikely that an Olympic gymnast's flexibility and specific physical skills are not likely to equip him or her better for the vicissitudes of everyday life. Indeed, the high polish of those skills fades very quickly with a diminution of training and practice. But we admire them nevertheless, and so we should admire the flexibilities of connoisseurs, many of whom have great mental endurance and agility, which are manifest in their capacities for appreciation.

However, it is not just the Olympic athlete who we think should partake in physical exercise. It needs to be borne in mind that the value or goodness to the amateur might be very different from that accorded to the expert. This difference is not just that different standards of competence are used for beginners and experts: the *value* of reaching a moderate level of competence might be different from the *value* of reaching a higher level, and hence the function of general physical fitness programs may be different from the function of Olympic training programs.[16] Unfortunately, it does not seem to me that our educational institutions have kept this in mind: what the introductory literature student should be getting out of a literary work may well not be the same as what the professor, having devoted many years to the study of it and its history and influence, gets.

Goodman, though roundly rejecting the idea that symbolizing in the arts has the *purpose* of serving other practical ends, nevertheless argues that symbolizing serves cognition as an end in itself: "the drive is curiosity, and the aim enlightenment. . . . [W]hat compels is the urge to know,

15. Nelson Goodman, *Languages of Art* (Indianapolis: Bobbs-Merrill, 1968), p. 256.
16. See James Wallace, *Virtues and Vices* (Ithaca: Cornell University Press, 1978), p. 48.

what delights is discovery."[17] With this I heartily agree. However, curiosity can be exemplified by a desire to *do,* not just a desire to *know.* One can desire to *exercise* one's mental capacities and abilities without desiring to have some kind of knowledge, just as one can desire to exercise one's *physical* capacities and abilities without wanting either to know *how,* to know what it's *like,* or to achieve some other end or goal. It is possible to desire to *use* one's mind in all sorts of ways, to develop one's facility and flexibility in such respects, as ends in themselves.

Flaubert's Emma, as indicated by the epigraph at the beginning of this essay, has no such curiosity. Similarly, I would argue that those who value individual works of art only insofar as they can give us knowledge or "right-thinking morality" are displaying ignorance of the role which art can play in expanding our imaginations, something which it is important to do in part because it increases our mental powers and capacities, and not necessarily or exclusively because each power or capacity it exercises or develops has some epistemic or moral benefit. The *artworld,* as I have been arguing, has the function of developing our general affective flexibility, so that we can make various psychological shifts and alter our sensitivities. It is important to have art*works* around which explore and expand new regions of the human imagination—even at the risk of epistemic and moral concerns.

I have sketched a way of understanding the notion of the aesthetic—as concerned with the development and exercise of various powers of imagination, a theme which is important in aesthetic theory from the eighteenth century. I have separated it conceptually from the moral and the epistemic, though admitting the axiological schizophrenia we can experience when evaluations from different realms conflict. This schizophrenia is healthy, however, in that it reveals the many values which we recognize as human beings as well as the fact that one sometimes cannot serve one without treading on another. It is a mistake, though, to try to analyze the aesthetic out of existence by making it, and the powers of imagination which fuel it, subservient to the moral or the epistemic. The artworld, it seems to me, is especially well suited to resist this moral and epistemic axiological tyranny (though, given the politics and economics which have

17. Goodman, *Languages of Art,* p. 258. Given Goodman's nominalism, his view and the one I defend here are closer than they might initially seem. Being more philosophically realistic about the nature of knowledge, I hesitate to use such words as "understanding" and "knowledge," much less "enlightenment," to describe the character of the effect of our encounter with works of art. However, bright people can learn from just about anything—that is part of what makes them bright—including their encounters with works of art.

driven the evolution of many of its member institutions, it may not fulfill this function in actual practice as well as it might). This is a *valuable* function of the artworld: to conserve and expand our sensitivities and affective flexibility, many exercises of which not only may not serve, but may even be impeded by the infusion of other concerns into an account of why it is important to have such a thing as an artworld.

2

RECONSIDERING THE EVALUATION OF ART

Bohdan Dziemidok

On the Need to Distinguish Between Aesthetic and Artistic Evaluations of Art

The aim of this essay is to justify the thesis that an aesthetic evaluation of art is not the only appropriate kind of evaluation; that is to say, it is not the only one that treats art as an autonomous correlate of man's cultural activity (rather than as a means to other ends, which tends to be the focus of the political, religious, or moral judgments).[1] Another kind of art evaluation also treats art as an end in itself: namely, an artistic evaluation of art. I would like to distinguish and organize various arguments offered in support of this view. Such an effort will be helpful for the following reasons.

First, the distinction between aesthetic and artistic evaluation is important for theorizing about art, especially in the context of the avant-garde and experimental movements, and for the consideration of purely theoretical problems the contemporary philosophy of art has to cope with. Second,

Translated by Wojciech Chojna with Stefan Sencerz.

1. A similar thesis can be found in an interesting essay by Noël Carroll, "Art and Interaction," *The Journal of Aesthetics and Art Criticism* 45 (1986): 57–68.

several contemporary aestheticians deny the legitimacy of the distinction itself. Third, even the advocates of the thesis which I will defend in this paper sometimes do not defend their views consistently, and sometimes they do not consider all of the important arguments that can be formulated in its defense.

These arguments are drawn from the praxis of evaluating art by critics and recipients, from the artistic praxis of the contemporary avant-garde and of earlier artistic movements, and from methodological and metatheoretical activities. This third kind of argument is motivated by the needs and difficulties of the theory of art. My distinction will help clarify the language of the philosophy of art; it will help solve some theoretical difficulties; and it will help avoid some pointless disputes. Before presenting the above-mentioned arguments, I will suggest working definitions for the concept of an "artistic value" and the concept of an "aesthetic value," as well as definitions of the correlative methods of evaluation.

An artistic value will be understood as constitutive and, to a considerable degree, characteristic of works of art. Owing to artistic values, art can be viewed as a relatively autonomous form of cultural praxis. Owing to them, people in all known types of cultures and epochs have regarded art as valuable, unique, and irreplaceable. Thus, a certain degree of artistic value seems to be a necessary condition for a cultural object to be considered as a work of art.

Artistic evaluation evaluates art *as art.* Its aim is to determine in what way and to what extent a given work of art realizes the values that are taken to be characteristic of the artistic form and genre to which it belongs. Artistic evaluation is applied only to artistic phenomena: works of art, methods of presentation and execution, and the experiments and situations in art. It pertains not only to the perceptual qualities of a given work but also to its place in the history of art, its role in breaking with the canons and traditional means of artistic expression. Artistic evaluation also focuses on the properties dependent on the cultural and historical context of creation, such as realism, stylistic qualities, adherence to a certain convention, craftsmanship, originality of form, artistic vision, as well as expressive and cognitive qualities. The above qualities can sometimes be discerned in a purely cognitive attitude (i.e., without aesthetic experience) not only by professional critics but also by some well-schooled and experienced perceiver.

An aesthetic value, on the other hand, is most frequently construed as a quality of natural and cultural objects which has the capability to evoke an aesthetic experience in an adequately prepared and aesthetically attuned perceiver. Thus, aesthetic evaluation and aesthetic values seem to be very tightly connected with an aesthetic experience, the latter being not only the basis but also a necessary condition and the most important criterion of aesthetic evaluation. Aesthetic evaluation pertains not only to art but to any objects, as well as to any natural and cultural states, capable of evoking positive or negative aesthetic experiences. The immediately perceived as well as imagined aspects of an object (its perceptual qualities and structural properties) are being evaluated in an aesthetic way.[2]

There are many different types of artistic and aesthetic values, depending on the variety of forms of art in different cultures and epochs, as well as on the multitude of artistic genres and kinds coexisting at the same time in a given culture. In the same way that a notion of art is a species to which literature, painting, and music belong, the notion of an artistic value is a species for the whole array of notions such as literary artistic values, musical artistic values, artistic values of painting, and so on.

Some of the most significant kinds of artistic value are the mimetic, formal, expressive, functional, constructive, and decorative values of a work. Some of the values that were once acknowledged as very important (e.g., resemblance, craftsmanship) or that are now regarded as significant for art (e.g., originality, innovation) are not uniquely artistic qualities, for they are also characteristic of other cultural objects, such as science, technology, and philosophy.

For a long time, beauty had been regarded as the only or, at least, the main value of art. Its varieties included prettiness, loveliness, charm, neatness, and the sublime. Subsequently, a few other aesthetic qualities were derived from individual genres, kinds, and categories of arts and were applied to art in general. These included vividness, picturesqueness, the lyric, the elegiac, the dramatic, the tragic, the comic, the melodramatic, the grotesque, and so on.

From the second half of the eighteenth century until our times, aesthetic qualities have been commonly taken as the characteristic and constitutive qualities of art. The advocates of this view identified the aesthetic value of a work of art with its artistic value. Nowadays, too, an aesthetic value

2. Cf. Ingarden's well-known distinction between aesthetic and artistic values in Roman Ingarden, "Artistic and Aesthetic Values," *British Journal of Aesthetics* 4 (1964): 198–213. Since Ingarden's distinction is based on different criteria, I do not discuss it in this essay. For a discussion of Ingarden's thesis, see my "Ingarden's Theory of Value and the Evaluation of the Work of Art," in *On the Aesthetics of Roman Ingarden*, ed. Bohdan Dziemidok and Peter McCormick (Dordrecht: Kluwer Academic Publishers, 1989).

is often regarded as decisive of an artistic value of a work of art.[3] The above claims, to which I will subsequently refer as the "thesis of aesthetic nature of art," have frequently been called into question by recent anti-aesthetic trends in the artistic avant-garde, not only in the praxis of art (i.e., through artworks) but also in art theory (e.g., manifestos, credos, art criticism, etc.). Generally, however, although few aestheticians dispute the possibility of making a distinction between the artistic and the aesthetic, there seems to be no consensus among them as to the exact nature of the relation between these two distinct values and evaluations.

Arguments justifying the possibility and necessity of the distinction between the artistic and the aesthetic might be found in the practice of art evaluation. Theoreticians who wrote on some complex aspects of art criticism and evaluation and who called for such a distinction include John Fisher, Piotr Graff, and Richard Rudner (in their articles from the end of the 1960s and the beginning of the seventies). Only Rudner, however, explicitly justified the need for such a distinction. Fisher and Graff, on the other hand, leaned toward the above position by questioning the necessity of the correlation between an aesthetic experience and an aesthetic evaluation.

Fisher acknowledges that a certain degree of aesthetic enjoyment almost always accompanies aesthetic evaluation.[4] He thinks, however, that it is possible to evaluate a work of art without a prior experience of aesthetic enjoyment. Sometimes the lack of enjoyment is compensated for by a perceiver's sensitivity to a work's formal aspects and by his knowledge of the current artistic norms. In actual practice, we often encounter statements of the following sort: "I don't like this object, but I have to acknowledge it is aesthetically valuable." If aesthetic enjoyment were to be a necessary condition of an aesthetic evaluation, then such a statement would not be possible. According to Fisher, the conviction that enjoying a work is a condition of its aesthetic valuing derives from the fallacy of confusing cause with effect. Fisher concludes that aesthetic enjoyment is neither a formal condition of aesthetic valuing nor a material condition of evaluation.

Like Fisher, Graff thinks that "the lack of a link between an aesthetic experience and evaluation is conspicuous in many contexts." Besides the context mentioned by Fisher ("I don't like it but I know it is aesthetically valuable"), Graff correctly identifies the possibility of the reverse situation: "I

3. See Bohdan Dziemidok, "Controversy About the Aesthetic Nature of Art," *British Journal of Aesthetics* 28 (1988): 1–17.

4. John Fisher, "Evaluation Without Enjoyment," *The Journal of Aesthetics and Art Criticism* 27 (1968): 135–39.

like it but I know it is kitsch."[5] Graff does not question the possibility of a positive experience accompanying the process of recognition of value, but he thinks it is not necessary; for the recognition of value can be accomplished without reference to any emotions.

Fisher and Graff call into question the claim that an aesthetic experience is either necessary or sufficient for aesthetic evaluation, but they do not generally deny that there is a correlation between the two. They think there are two equally legitimate types of aesthetic evaluation, one which is a necessary correlate of an aesthetic experience and is based on such experience and one which can be accomplished independently from any aesthetic experience. The two kinds of aesthetic evaluation may lead to evaluations which are significantly different, and which may even be opposed to each other.

Two types of art evaluation that can actually be distinguished in the existing praxis testify to the truth of the conclusions of Fisher and Graff. However, if these two types of evaluation can be distinguished with regard to their respective methodologies and structures, as well as with regard to their resulting judgments, then why should they be referred to by the common term "aesthetic"? In other words, should any evaluation which takes into account the uniqueness and relative autonomy of a work of art be called "aesthetic"?

Unlike Fisher and Graff, Rudner follows up in a more radical way on the conclusions of his investigations. Rudner describes the rejection of a short story by the editor of a literary journal who not only regards the piece as well written but actually experiences intense aesthetic emotions while reading it. The editor motivates his seemingly strange decision by saying that the rejected story thematically, stylistically, and emotionally clearly borrows from Borges. In this case, says Rudner, the distinction between the artistic and the aesthetic evaluation allows us to see that there is really nothing strange about the editor's decision.[6]

Theoreticians who looked for the justification of the distinction between artistic and aesthetic evaluations in the actual artistic praxis often found it in those avant-garde movements—say, minimal or conceptual art—which exhibit clear anti-aesthetic tendencies. These movements produced objects which were clearly works of art but at the same time were deprived of any

5. Piotr Graff, "O rodzjach braku zwiazku miedzy przezyciem estetycznym a ocena estetyczna" [On the Kinds of Lack of Connection Between Aesthetic Experience and Aesthetic Evaluation], *Studia Estetyczne* 7 (1970): 45–46.

6. Richard Rudner, "On Seeing What We Shall See," in *Logic and Art: Essays in Honor of Nelson Goodman,* ed. Richard Rudner and Israel Scheffler (Indianapolis: Bobbs-Merrill, 1972), p. 171.

aesthetic qualities. As examples of such works one can point to Duchamp's ready-mades (*Bottle Rack* or *Fountain*), Joseph Kosuth's *One and Three Chairs,* or Ken Friedman's *The Distance from This Sentence to Your Eyes Is My Sculpture.*[7]

Although the art of the past does not reveal such a conspicuous chasm between aesthetic and artistic values, these two types of values were sometimes perceived as separate. Arnold Hauser, for example, notices a certain incompatibility between two kinds of values one can ascribe to a work of art: an aesthetic merit of a work, on the one hand, and its historical significance, on the other. Hauser thinks that these two types of values might not have anything in common; they could even become incommensurate. A work of art might be significant because it was innovative and seminal, having initiated some artistic trend which produced many masterpieces, even though the work itself might not have been of the highest order aesthetically. "Second- or third-class works often play a decisive role in the history of art and literature; on the other hand, there have been very great masters—Bach and Raphael are examples who were not revolutionary artists and who, historically speaking, do not hold such a key position as many of their inferiors."[8]

The discrepancy between artistic and aesthetic values might go so far that "the course of art history would not be essentially different were it to ignore altogether many of the greatest artists; for example without Rembrandt the history of Dutch painting would remain essentially the same. It would of course be immeasurably poorer—it would have lost its peak—but it would not have lost its direction leading to that peak."[9]

In American aesthetics, Richard Rudner was the first to postulate the necessity of making the distinction between artistic and aesthetic values and evaluations. Motivated by Nelson Goodman's remarks on Hans van Meegeren's forgeries, and by his own analysis of the similar case of Guenther Dietz's copy of the abstract piece by Otto Bachman, Rudner wonders whether originality and authenticity are constitutive elements of an aesthetic value. If there were no perceptual differences between Bachman's original and Dietz's copy of it, then the aesthetic value of those two pieces would have to be the same, although the artistic value and the market value of the original would be much higher than the value of the forgery. Rudner's conclusion was that such cases would not yield an easy solution if we did not accept the

7. Cf. Göran Hermerén, *Aspects of Aesthetics* (Lund: Gleerups, 1983).
8. Arnold Hauser, *The Philosophy of Art History* (New York: Knopf, 1959), p. 165.
9. Ibid.

legitimacy of the distinction between the two different types of values, artistic and aesthetic, and between two different judgments—namely, a judgment of artistic value and a judgment of aesthetic value, respectively. The latter is sufficiently determined by our aesthetic experience—our response to its aesthetic qualities. An artistic value of a work, on the other hand, is not determined by our aesthetic experience of a work of art.[10] Having accepted this distinction, Rudner unexpectedly and unconvincingly concludes that an artistic value belongs to the domain of ethics. For, as he maintains, artistic evaluations are based on the conclusions of sociology and psychology of art as well as on our hierarchy of aesthetic preferences.

Tomasz Kulka picks up where Hauser and Rudner left off, although in Kulka's articles there are no references to either of them.[11] Kulka distinguishes between the aesthetic value and the artistic (or, rather, historico-artistic) value of a painting. Aesthetic value pertains to the perceptual qualities of a painting and is arrived at on the basis of an aesthetic perception. No other consideration, such as the knowledge of a painting's place in the historico-cultural context, or information about its origin, plays any significant role in the work's aesthetic evaluation. Such factors as authenticity, originality, or innovation also seem to lie outside the realm of an aesthetic value. On the other hand, all the above factors become significant when it comes to historico-artistic evaluation. Thus, an artistic value of a painting cannot be arrived at without taking into consideration the questions of its origin, its place in the history of painting, the originality of its style, its relation to the canon, the specific innovative artistic techniques it might employ, and so forth. It also matters whether a painting is an authentic piece or a forgery, an original work or an imitation.

Aesthetic and artistic values might not be compatible. Excellent copies, "masterpiece-forgeries," or successful imitations might have as high an aesthetic value as the authentic and original pieces, yet nevertheless be artistically worthless.[12] The opposite cases can also be found in the history of art. The whole of conceptual art has been ascribed little or no aesthetic value, yet it may be groundbreaking from an artistic point of view. Even Picasso's *Les Demoiselles d'Avignon,* painted in 1907, as groundbreaking

10. Rudner, "On Seeing," p. 169.

11. Tomasz Kulka, "The Artistic and Aesthetic Value of Art," *British Journal of Aesthetics* 21 (1981): 336–50.

12. Along these lines, see an interesting and convincing argument against the belief that the value of the work of art is exhausted by its aesthetic value: Robert J. Yanal, "Aesthetic Value and Genius," in *The Reasons of Art,* ed. Peter McCormick (Ottawa: University of Ottawa Press, 1985).

as that work was from an artistic point of view, was initially ascribed minimal or no aesthetic value by Picasso's contemporaries Braque and Apollinaire as well as by some critics contemporary with him. Picasso, in effect agreeing with such opinions, hid his painting for more than twenty years. It was first displayed in 1937.[13] Nineteenth-century academic painting generally focused on the development of aesthetic qualities, ignoring artistic innovation and originality, which became the primary focus of avant-garde art, which was programmatically anti-aesthetic. Kulka thinks, however, that the greatest works of art (Mondrian's works, for instance) successfully combine the highest aesthetic values with the highest artistic ones. He maintains that some minimal presence of aesthetic together with artistic qualities is necessary for treating something as a work of art.

A Finnish aesthetician, Ilka Oramo, also sees a need for making the distinction between aesthetic and artistic evaluation, but he objects to Kulka's synonymous use of "artistic" and "historico-artistic." Instead, Oramo suggests that an artistic value consists of aesthetic value *and* historico-artistic value, since the lack of either of these aspects amounts to a deficiency on the part of a work of art.[14] To illustrate his thesis, Oramo analyzes Bartók's 1908 *Bagatellas* which, though lacking notable aesthetic qualities, became valued for their artistic originality, "leading to completely new ways of musical thinking."[15] Were this little composition written in a conventional way, it would be worthless from an historico-artistic point of view. Yet, according to Oramo, an artistic value cannot be reduced to technical innovations. It consists also of specific cognitive values. It involves a "specific kind of knowledge," which is different from scientific knowledge or from knowledge characterizing those kinds of art which document objective reality. A "truth of art" is not truth in the usual sense of the word. More appropriately, one should use such terms as "verisimilitude" or "likeness to truth," says Oramo. Thus, the constitution of aesthetic, artistic, and historico-artistic values presents different methodological problems. Oramo suggests that we either construe an artistic value as a sum of aesthetic and historico-artistic values or regard an historico-artistic value as dependent on an aesthetic value and an artistic value.

Aesthetic and artistic are radically different with respect to the methods (the first being predominantly perceptual, the latter intellectual), the aspects

13. Kulka, "Artistic and Aesthetic Value," pp. 336–37.
14. Ilka Oramo, "Artistic and Aesthetic Value," *Acta Philosophica Fennica* 43 (1988): 217–227.
15. Ibid., p. 222.

that are being referred to, as well as to the respective exclusion and inclusion of any extraneous biographical and historico-cultural knowledge. Therefore, these two ways of valuing and their respective correlates (i.e., aesthetic and artistic values) should be distinguished theoretically as well as terminologically.

As early as 1928, Stanislaw Ossowski made a distinction between two types of evaluation of aesthetic objects and came up with two different concepts of an aesthetic value: "The objects of aesthetics are evaluated in some cases with respect to the experiences one had while perceiving them, and in some other cases with respect to the creative effort which was needed to bear them."[16] This view was later developed and argued for in his magnum opus *U podstaw estetyki.*[17] "I had no doubts," writes Ossowski in the preface to the third Polish edition, "that the concepts of an aesthetic and artistic value are not compatible, and that the general theses of aesthetic theories are incompatible with the domain of the phenomena to which these theses refer." Thus, a work of art can be evaluated with respect to its cause (the creative act) and with respect to the effect it has on a perceiver (aesthetic experience). "These two methods of evaluation in aesthetics might be called, briefly, *valuation with respect to beauty* and *valuation with respect to artistry.*"[18] Nonetheless, these two conceptions of value are not usually distinguished, either in current appraisals or even in general aesthetic considerations.

As a result, "in contemporary European cultural milieu, aesthetic value is *a collage of concepts.*"[19] The confusion comes about all the more easily since important correlations exist between aesthetic and artistic values. An aesthetic experience of a perceiver often constitutes the criterion of evaluation of creative effort; conversely, the awareness of high degree of artistry might intensify and enrich an aesthetic experience. Thus, Ossowski's conclusion seems to be that the domain of value is not univocal. Despite the practical difficulties and a methodological confusion, it is possible and necessary to distinguish two concepts of valuation: an aesthetic valuation and an artistic valuation. The latter pertains to art only and is done with respect to facts which can be established objectively, in such terms as

16. Stanislaw Ossowski, "O przeciwienstwie przyrody i sztuki w estetyce" [On the Opposition Between Nature and Art in Aesthetics], in Stanislaw Ossowski, *Dziela* [Works], (Warsaw, 1966–1970), 4 vols.

17. Stanislaw Ossowski, *U podstaw estetyki* (Warsaw, 1966); trans. by Janina and Witold Rodzinski as *The Foundations of Aesthetics* (Dordrecht: D. Reidel, 1978).

18. Ibid., p. 303.

19. Ibid., p. 304.

originality of conception, the overcoming of technical difficulties, perfection of execution, and so forth. It is an evaluation which does not have to be based on an aesthetic experience, but it requires competence and knowledge, which an ordinary perceiver might lack. That is why Ossowski calls artistic values "aristocratic." Aesthetic values, on the other hand, are "democratic," for they are based on an aesthetic experience only. Hence they are not objective but subjective-objective (relational). They cannot be reduced either to the properties of an object or to a spectator's sensations. Rather, they refer to the relation between the two.

A similar distinction can be found in the writings of Zdzislaw Najder. He also thinks that one can ascribe to art two kinds of values, but he names them "artistic" and "experiential."[20] The former pertain to an inherent structure of a work, as well as to its relations with other works of art of the past, present, and future. Artistic values are ascribed independently of any perceivers and aesthetic experiences. We talk about an artistic value in terms of "technique," "craftsmanship," "expressiveness," "relation to artistic tradition," "novelty," "originality," "plagiarism," "style," "artistic convention," "poetics of genre," and so on.

Experiential values, on the other hand, pertain to the relationship between a work and its perceivers. Hence, an aesthetic experience constitutes the necessary basis for such an evaluation. We take into account its richness, intensity, the quality of each of its sensual and emotional elements, the active role of our imagination and reflection. Like Ossowski, Najder realizes that "both kinds of values are closely related. We apply the criteria of artistic value that we do because we assume that the results of the qualities so chosen will be experimentally satisfactory; we evaluate works of art experientially using artistic categories of style, convention, trend, or motif."[21]

It is perhaps neither necessary nor even possible in practice to keep these two kinds of evaluations apart. Similarly, it would be very difficult to try to separate aesthetic evaluation of art from all the non-aesthetic evaluations in practice. It seems important, however, to be able to make a distinction between these two kinds of evaluations theoretically, not only to make aesthetic terminology more precise, so as not to contribute to already numerous misunderstandings caused by various equivocations of different meanings of the same term, but also to be able to meet, in a somewhat better way than traditional aesthetics could (advocating the thesis of the purely

20. Zdzislaw Najder, *Values and Evaluations* (Oxford: Clarendon Press, 1975), p. 142.
21. Ibid., p. 143.

aesthetic nature of art), the challenges brought against traditional aesthetics by the latest artistic avant-garde.

I think these were the reasons Carolyn Korsmeyer criticized George Dickie's denial of the possibility of the aesthetic attitude. One of her reasons is the inability of Dickie's theory to account for phenomena that are obviously aesthetic in nature. The "thesis of aesthetic nature of art," on the other hand, seems to be more effective in contrasting the aesthetic with other types of phenomena, values, and attitudes (e.g., the practical, moral, or theoretical). It seems, however, to limit the scope of the theory of art to one sphere only, without doing justice to all the values, broad "scope, and importance of art."[22] As a result, some advocates of the thesis of aesthetic nature of art rejected *The Brothers Karamazov* as a work of art, claiming that it cannot be read in a purely aesthetic attitude. In order to preclude the possibility of such undesirable consequences, some aestheticians broadened the term "aesthetic" to cover all the artistic categories as well. The price that has to be paid for such a maneuver is frequently dear: loss of precision or even of meaning. Korsmeyer thus opts for preserving the precise meaning of "the aesthetic," but she refuses to treat it as in any way superior to "the artistic." "Some artistic qualities and some types of artistic value extend beyond the narrowly aesthetic."[23] That is why one has to say that the notions of artistic value and aesthetic value overlap. Aesthetic qualities comprise, according to Korsmeyer, perceptual qualities, formal qualities, and so on. She does not specify, however, what kind of qualities are deprived of an aesthetic character. Perhaps, like Dickie, she would like to exclude the cognitive and moral values from the realm of the aesthetic.

Similarly, Peter Kivy distinguishes narrowly construed aesthetic evaluation from broader artistic evaluation. The former pertains to "sensual and structural properties" of a work of art; the latter "concern any relevant properties other than the aesthetic."[24]

Suppose then that, adopting the proposed distinction, we will also accept a) that artistic values are irreducible to aesthetic values; b) that an aesthetic experience is not the only legitimate reaction to an artwork; and c) that an aesthetic evaluation is not the only appropriate way of evaluating artworks. It seems that this will help solve two difficult, significant, and interrelated problems encountered by the contemporary theory of art. The first problem

22. Carolyn Korsmeyer, "On Distinguishing 'Aesthetic' from 'Artistic,'" *The Journal of Aesthetic Education* 4 (1977): 53.

23. Ibid., p. 55.

24. Peter Kivy, *The Corded Shell* (Princeton: Princeton University Press, 1980), p. 116.

is about the artistic status of the cognitive values of art. In other words, are cognitive values constitutive for all art or only for some kinds of art? The second problem has to do with the possibility of finding one universal value of art and one uniquely valid approach (way of reacting) to art. Is there such a unique value and approach characteristic for all the multifarious kinds of art?

The only theory of art which might successfully compete with the still popular thesis of aesthetic nature of art seems to be the "cognitive theory," which claims that the only essential function and value of art is its cognitive value. Originating in ancient Greece, the cognitive theory is the oldest in European culture. It found many advocates, especially among art realists, only to gradually lose popularity as the influence of the realist and representational approach to art waned. The questions raised by disputes over the nature of truth in fiction, relations between a fictional world and the real one, as well as the nature of statements in literature contributed to the initial rejection of the simplest, mimetic version of the cognitive theory. Nelson Goodman's *Languages of Art* as well as Arthur Danto's *The Transfiguration of the Commonplace* once again put the cognitive theory into the center of the dispute.

Goodman's views are more radical than Danto's: Goodman thought that the primary value of art is cognitive, since its basic purpose is cognition for the sake of cognition. An aesthetic experience is also a cognitive experience. I find such a thesis no easier to accept than the thesis of aesthetic nature of art discussed above.

George Dickie's views seem much less problematic to me. Dickie acknowledges the importance of the cognitive aspects of art: "It cannot be just an accident of no evaluative significance that such an enormous percentage of our art is referential in character."[25] All advocates of the aesthetic/artistic distinction who, unlike Kulka and Ossowski, construe the notion of an artistic value in a broader way, seem to think that, like the aesthetic, moral, political, or religious, the cognitive values of art are also constitutive of an artistic value. It is enough here to name a few representatives of many diverse trends who subscribe to such a view: M. S. Kagan,[26] N. Wolterstorff,[27] G. Hermerén,[28] I. Oramo, and recently George Dickie in *Evaluating Art.*

25. George Dickie, *Evaluating Art* (Philadelphia: Temple University Press, 1988), p. 126.

26. Kagan is a Marxist aesthetician who characterizes an artistic value as the function of all the other values, such as the aesthetic itself, the political, the religious, the moral, and the cognitive. The relations between the aesthetic and nonaesthetic aspects of artistic value are functions of the type of culture, historical epoch, kind, and even genre of art. See M. S. Kagan, "Esteticheskaya i khudozestvennaya cennost w mire cennostey" (Aesthetic and Artistic Value in the World of Values), in *Trudy WNIITE* (Moscow, 1981): 25–34.

27. See Nicholas Wolterstorff, *Art in Action* (Grand Rapids: Eerdmans, 1980), esp. pp. 157–60.

28. See Hermerén, *Aspects of Aesthetics,* pp. 66–68.

Dickie's recent views, as well as their evolution, are especially interesting. As is well known, he had rejected the thesis of aesthetic nature of art a long time ago, arguing, I think rightly, that the moral and cognitive values of a work of art cannot be ignored, for they might contribute significantly to its artistic value. Yet, still under the influence of Monroe Beardsley, he was not ready to reject the term "aesthetic" altogether. Instead, he broadened its meaning. In *The Art Circle,* for example, arguing with Robert McGregor and Carolyn Korsmeyer, Dickie distinguished two senses of "the aesthetic": one pertaining to aesthetic qualities as certain kinds of perceptual qualities, the second pertaining to the "aesthetic objects of a work of art." In this second, broader sense, an aesthetic value of a work was the function of all the appreciated qualities of a work of art, including aesthetic, expressive, moral, and cognitive qualities.[29] Thus, it seems that the aesthetic in the second sense is for Dickie part of an artistic value of a work of art. The next step was made in the article "Evaluating Art," where Dickie refuses to speak of a proper experience of art in terms of an "aesthetic experience" and suggests a more neutral expression: an "experience of art."[30]

Finally, in *Evaluating Art,* Dickie concludes that not all the significant values in art should be called aesthetic, and he suggests that the notion of an aesthetic value should be construed in a narrow way, as opposed to the broader notion of an artistic value comprising three kinds of cognitive qualities of a work of art. One of the components of the third kind of a cognitive value are, according to Dickie, moral qualities of art.

In conclusion, let me say a few words about the second problem aesthetics might be facing today: namely, the already mentioned difficulties with specifying the aesthetic universal (i.e., one uniform value which could be ascribed to all arts) in the context of an amazing variety of kinds and forms of art entailing considerable differences between the ways one values and reacts to each of the many types of art (literature, music, fine arts, etc.). In my opinion, one should either follow Wladyslaw Tatarkiewicz and acknowledge that there is no uniform class of aesthetic values characteristic of all arts or decide that aesthetic values are not the only significant values, constitutive of all arts.

The same holds true with respect to experiences of all these different kinds of art. The differences between an experience of a literary work of art and an experience of a painting or a piece of music are so significant that it

29. George Dickie, *The Art Circle* (New York: Haven Publications, 1984), p. 105.
30. George Dickie, "Evaluating Art," *British Journal of Aesthetics* 25 (1985): 3–16.

is doubtful whether they can all be classified in the same category of an aesthetic experience. An experience of a literary work of art, a film, or a theatrical performance is much richer and more complex than an experience of any other kind of art, for it contains cognitive and intellectual elements. Therefore, the view that an aesthetic experience is a uniquely appropriate means of perceiving or reacting to artworks seems to be no longer plausible.

Peggy Zeglin Brand

Evaluating Art: A Feminist Case for Dickie's Matrix System

George Dickie's *Evaluating Art* is an important contribution to the current body of literature that deals either directly or indirectly with the way society values artistic creation.[1] Though he denies any necessary connection between this project of evaluating and his prior work of defining, one is tempted to read this work as part two—a sort of completion of the classificatory theory of part one.[2] For some, it has arrived on the scene none too soon, as we approach the end of a century in which anything at all can become art on the revised institutional theory. Recurring controversy attests to the discomfort involved with ascribing value to certain objects or events that have come

My thanks to George Dickie, Carolyn Korsmeyer, Mary Devereaux, Flo Leibowitz, Hilde Hein, and participants in the October 1990 meeting of the American Society for Aesthetics for comments on an earlier draft of this essay.

1. George Dickie, *Evaluating Art* (Philadelphia: Temple University Press, 1988).

2. Earlier works that focus on the classificatory sense include *The Art Circle* (New York: Haven Publications, 1984) and *Art and the Aesthetic: An Institutional Analysis* (Ithaca: Cornell University Press, 1974).

to be classified as art. Having come full circle in classifying the unconventional as "art"—from Marcel Duchamp's *Fountain* to Andre Serrano's *Piss Christ* to Karen Finley's *The Constant State of Desire*—we have come to realize the interest and importance of what Dickie calls the "additional question" of the value of such works.

Dickie's project of an evaluative matrix system to assess artistic value provides an initial, though incomplete, framework for analyzing judgments that arise from works of art. According to Dickie, works of art are instrumental in bringing about experiences that are intrinsically valued in and of themselves or for the value derived in experiencing a representation of some valued thing. On this view, artistic value is a function both of a work's aesthetic values *and* its cognitive values. Dickie's matrix system provides a schema for tracking a work's particular aesthetic and cognitive values. (It does not—nor was it ever intended to—provide a matrix for assessing *overall* artistic value for artworks.)

Dickie's project is a good beginning toward isolating the elements that constitute the range of judgments made about a work. It guides us in the right direction in its emphasis—in contrast to previous theories of the aesthetic—on *cognitive* value (the way a work of art is tied to the world). It serves as a model for analyzing the reasons why some forms of art have enjoyed a more favored status than others; for example, why only certain artworks are considered "masterpieces" or why high art is more valuable than craft. This essay will utilize Dickie's matrix system to investigate the kind of claims that serve to undervalue a work by a woman artist of the seventeenth century in comparison to the work of her peers.

Dickie's approach, however, is not complete as it stands. It is incomplete in its failure to take "cognitive value" far enough in capturing the way art criticism and evaluation function in the everyday workings of the artworld. That is, it abstains from taking on issues like gender, race, class, and sexual orientation which inevitably bear on both how we conceive of the notion of cognitive value and how cognitive value is actually assessed. Such failure is twofold: first of all, there is no discussion as to when or how such factors affect the philosophical approach to an analysis of cognitive and artistic value; second, the discussion mentions so few artworks that talk of the evaluation of noncanonical works is basically moot.[3] Since works by women, minorities, and other underrepresented artists have clearly been shown

3. Twain's *The Adventures of Huckleberry Finn* and *The Adventures of Tom Sawyer* are analyzed in depth. Tolstoy's *War and Peace* is discussed at several points in the text, and the examples Hume provides of French theater, *Polyeucte* and *Athalie,* are mentioned only briefly.

to be *consistently* ignored and devalued by art historians, critics, and aestheticians, their devaluing is crucial to a discussion of artistic value; their omission reflects the incompleteness of a theory that purports to capture an operable notion of artistic value.[4]

In the first section below, Dickie's approach is applied to two divergent commentaries made by current scholars about the Baroque paintings of Artemisia Gentileschi and Michelangelo da Caravaggio. "Imitative cognitive value"—one of the three criteria for cognitive value—is clarified and expanded in order to introduce the topic of section two: the way that various sorts of critical remarks elucidate a work's "nonimitative or propositional cognitive value." In order to make the schema more complete and workable, feminist strategies for (re)claiming the value of women's artworks are discussed. These strategies open the matrix system up to new possibilities in assessing various aspects of a work's cognitive value. Concluding remarks offer to philosophers and feminist theorists alike the benefits of the proposed expanded approach.

Applying Dickie's Matrix System: A Case Study

In *Evaluating Art,* Dickie proposes a system of artistic evaluation of works of art which he unofficially calls the "amplified, compromise view."[5] The compromise is between those theories which hold aesthetic features to be the sole determinant of a work's evaluative status and those theories which hold cognitive features to be of sole importance. Dickie sees his own view as a progression beyond the two entrenched polarities of evaluation—one which involves attending both to aesthetic and cognitive properties, not just attending to one type exclusively. He offers us guidelines for assessing specific, individual works of art, guidelines which he claims most evaluative theories have failed to provide.

4. One might object that Dickie's approach naturally does encompass such concerns—that he need not address them directly. I believe it does not (most feminist concerns cannot be accommodated by the "add women and stir" approach). Thus, I offer not so much a criticism of his view as a healthy extension of it in ways he may have failed to anticipate.

5. Dickie prefers the broader term "artistic value," rather than, for example, Beardsley's "aesthetic value," since he believes aesthetic value to be only one type of many that art can have. See *Evaluating Art,* p. 157. Also, when Dickie speaks of a work's value, he intends his matrix system to result in weak evaluative statements like "This work of art has value," and not strong statements like "This work of art is good."

Guided by previous instrumentalist theories—such as those of Ziff, Beardsley, Sibley, Goodman, Wolterstorff, Hume, Vermazen and Urmson—Dickie summarizes his version as follows: "Works of art are valuable because they can be the instrumental source of a valuable experience that in turn is valuable because the experience or an element of it is intrinsically valued by some person or persons and/or because the experience or an element of it is of a representational feature of art that refers to a valued thing."[6] The first part is intended to capture the tendency to evaluate according to aesthetic properties, while the second is intended to capture the more recent trend to evaluate according to referential, cognitive properties.

From the outset, Dickie assumes, without question, the traditional dichotomy of aesthetic/cognitive. Aesthetic properties are such properties as a work's unity, complexity, beauty, gracefulness, garishness, elegance, and sentimentality. Cognitive properties are ones "that relate art to the world"; they are referential, thereby establishing a relationship between the artwork and "the rest of life."[7] They are a general category of which representational properties constitute one type. In the particular case of imitative art, the representational element ties the image to the real (or imaginary) object or event depicted.[8] Dickie advocates evaluation by means of situating a work in its historical context and attending to its nonaesthetic/cognitive properties as well as to its aesthetic properties. According to Dickie, it is easier to assign values to aesthetic properties than to cognitive properties. A test case demonstrates why.

Consider a specific comparison of two works on a very popular theme: two Italian Baroque versions of an Old Testament heroine, Judith, beheading the Assyrian general Holofernes. One is the well-known version by Caravaggio, painted in 1598–99 (144 cm. × 195 cm., Palazzo Barberini, Rome), and the other is by Artemesia Gentileschi, painted circa 1620 (47″ × 37″, Uffizi, Florence).[9] The story of Judith is one of bravery and devotion to her people; her plot to seduce and kill an enemy general on the eve of his attack

6. Ibid., p. 155.

7. Ibid., p. 15.

8. A work of art, of course, can refer to a fictional object (e.g., a painting of the goddess Venus) as well as to an actual object. The test of whether a work of art is "true-to-actuality" in the case of a fictional object depends on whether the work is "true to some *prior* and *independently established* fictional object in some respect." Ibid., p. 125.

9. There is evidence to believe that the Caravaggio painting may now be part of a private collection. An earlier treatment of this same theme by Gentileschi, dated 1612–13, is located in the Museo di Capodimonte, Naples. She completed two other depictions of Judith, *Judith and Her Maidservant* (c. 1613–14, Palazzo Pitti, Florence) and *Judith and Her Maidservant with the Head of Holofernes* (c. 1625, Detroit Institute of Arts), neither of which shows the actual beheading.

proved successful in averting battle. Thus she saved her people, albeit by unconventional means:

> Her sandal ravished his eye,
> Her beauty made captive his soul,
> The sword passed through his neck.[10]

Caravaggio's version of the act, *Judith Beheading Holofernes,* depicts a young, attractive woman at arm's length from the head she grasps, exhibiting little competency in performing the act (see Figure 1). This version, or at least the name of Caravaggio, is familiar to many viewers. He is the subject of many monographs, has been the focus of a recent showing at the Metropolitan Museum of Art, and is touted as "genius" and "Master of the Gesture" in recent reviews.[11] He is considered the expert of a brand of realism that bears his name—the Caravaggesque style—depicting figures in their most human and dramatic moments. The drama of this moment is focused in the general's face (not Judith's). Some believe that the image of Holofernes may even be a self-portrait of the artist, as in the case of Caravaggio's depiction of David, the Old Testament hero.

Mary Garrard, author of a recent monograph on Gentileschi, focuses on the way Caravaggio depicts Judith, describing her as "a beautiful but vacuous mannequin . . . a creature of masculine fantasy."[12] She is less than human: a stereotype of beauty in contrast to the more humanly realized screaming general. In addition, the other female in the scene, the maidservant at Judith's side, is depicted as terribly old, haggard, and ugly: a personification of "the evil and negative aspects of Judith's character."[13]

In contrast, Garrard heaps generous praise upon Artemisia's version, *Judith Slaying Holofernes* (see Figure 2), which she claims presents a "fully-sexed, mature woman, who is physical without being beautiful." Her strong forearms overpower the struggling general while a young maidservant aids in holding down the body. Both escape the "stereotypes of maiden, virago, and crone."[14] Garrard claims that the Caravaggesque style of por-

10. Book of Judith 16:9.

11. See John Ashberry, "Genius of the Low Life," *Newsweek,* February 18, 1985, pp. 86–87; and Robert Hughes, "Master of the Gesture: At the Metropolitan, Caravaggio's Turbulent Genius," *Time,* March 11, 1985, pp. 74–75.

12. Mary D. Garrard, *Artemisia Gentileschi: The Image of the Female Hero in Italian Baroque Art* (Princeton: Princeton University Press, 1989), p. 290ff.

13. Ibid., p. 298.

14. Ibid., p. 323.

Figure 1. Michelangelo da Caravaggio, *Judith Beheading Holofernes,* 1598–99, Galleria Nazionale d'Arte Antica, Rome (Alinari/Art Resource, New York)

traying intense, realistic human drama is much more exemplified in Artemisia's female figures than in Caravaggio's, and that it is no coincidence that Artemisia's treatment of the theme was influenced by the fact that she was raped by a coworker in her father's studio.[15] Artemisia's figures focus attention and concentration on their task, working to sever the head, even as the dying Holofernes ironically grips the drapery around the maidservant's neck. Gentileschi—though well known in her day, having pursued her career in Florence, Venice, Naples, and Rome—is not the subject of extensive monographs; Garrard's, in fact, is the first. Only recently has she had a show devoted solely to her work, and she has not even appeared, until the last decade, in major art history texts.[16]

15. Some residual doubt remains, though most are convinced that the episode took place in either 1611 or 1612 (at age fifteen or sixteen). The case was brought to trial, Artemisia was subjected to questioning under torture, and the artist was released. The transcript of the trial is included in Garrard's text.

16. The show did not travel to the United States. Now that Gentileschi is included in such texts, she is described as a follower of Caravaggio who "helped to propagate Caravaggio's manner throughout the

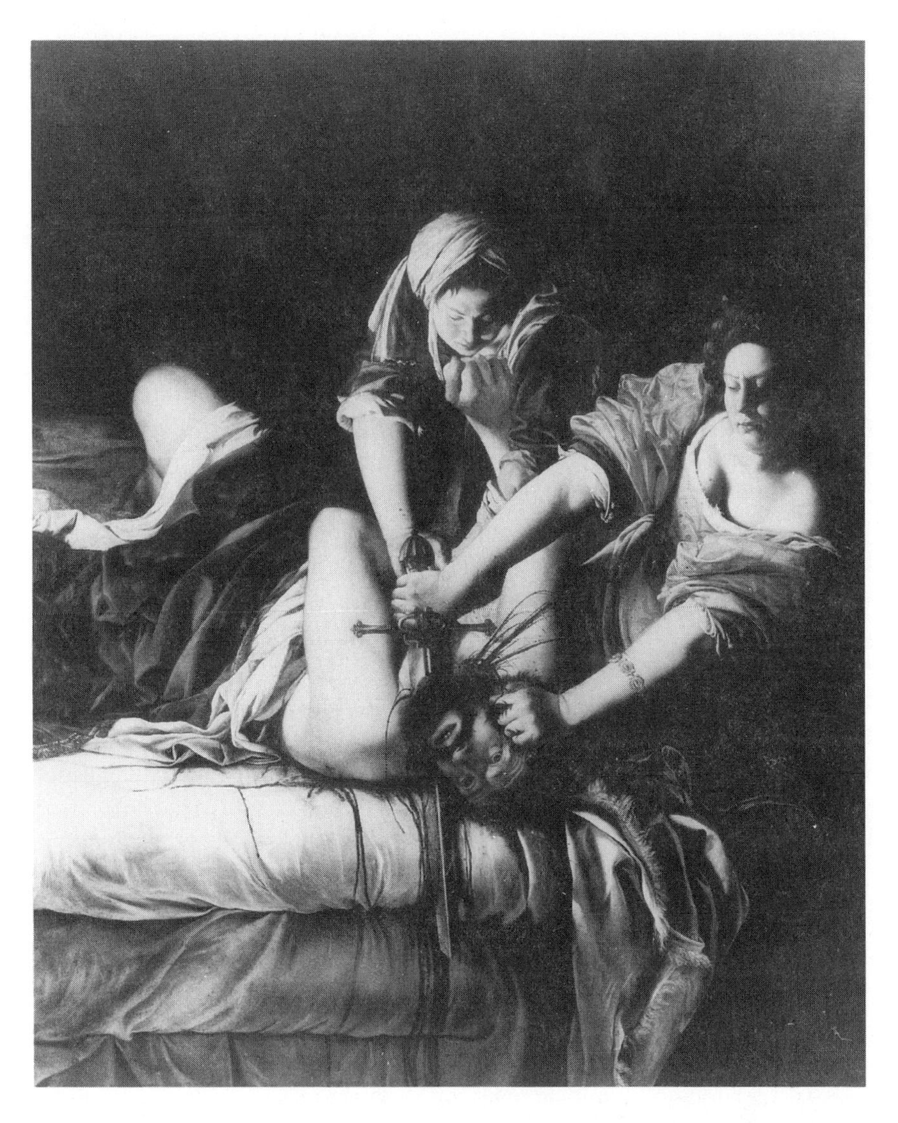

Figure 2. Artemisia Gentileschi, *Judith Slaying Holofernes,* c. 1620, Uffizi, Florence (Alinari/Art Resource, New York)

In 1989, Francis Haskell, a critic writing for the *New York Review of Books,* claimed that such respectable and valued artistic features as originality, complexity, and the capacity for expressing personal suffering—that is, features indicative of works "(almost) of genius"—were, "despite her great talent," "beyond the reach—or perhaps beyond the ambitions—of Gentileschi."[17] This devaluing of Artemisia's work was written in direct response to Mary Garrard's monograph. Here we are faced with a clear case of opposing viewpoints. As Garrard attempts to attribute (or reattribute) value to works previously neglected by art historians, she is thwarted by a critic who disagrees. And it is no simple disagreement. Some of the more extreme critics of revisionist art criticism and art history (e.g., Hilton Kramer) believe that works by women and feminist readings of those works are causally linked to the erosion of existing critical standards in art.[18]

How do we solve such a disagreement? Can Dickie's matrix system provide us with guidelines that serve to help us out of this dilemma? Consider a comparison between the two works that represents Garrard's and Haskell's evaluations according to Dickie's matrix system.

Once it is decided which particular aesthetic or cognitive properties are to be assessed (e.g., the aesthetic properties of complexity, unity, and balance), Dickie proposes assigning numerical values to those properties in order to rank them.[19] Using a scale of 1–3 (where 1 is the lowest) for the range of values of the aesthetic properties of complexity, unity, and balance, let values (3,2,1) represent Garrard's view that Artemisia's version of the beheading is very complex, rather unified, and somewhat balanced. Haskell might envision Caravaggio's work to be superior to Artemisia's, thereby assigning the values (3,2,1) to Caravaggio and the lowest values of (1,1,1) to Artemisia. A simplified version of Dickie's matrix yields the following:

---

peninsula." See Helen Gardner's *Art Through the Ages,* 8th ed. (Orlando: Harcourt Brace Jovanovich, 1986), p. 729. Interestingly enough, no major art history text mentions either version of the beheading; rather, other works by Gentileschi, particularly versions of Judith *after* the beheading, are discussed. See also H. W. Janson's *History of Art* (New York: Harry N. Abrams, 1986).

17. Francis Haskell, "Artemisia's Revenge?" *New York Review of Books,* July 20, 1989, pp. 36–38. Haskell actually compares Artemisia's work to the work of her contemporary Pietro Testa, a lesser-known artist than Caravaggio. I have taken the liberty of extending Haskell's comparison to a contrast of her work with Caravaggio's, since both artists actually completed works depicting the beheading of Holofernes.

18. Hilton Kramer, "Does Feminism Conflict with Artistic Standards?" *New York Times,* January 27, 1980.

19. The scale is arbitrary: it can range from 1 to 3, 1 to 5, or 1 to 10 and can even include the value 0. I assume these values represent ordinal and not cardinal numbers, and that 0 plays no special role in the system other than representing the lowest value of rank in the sequence. I thank Bruce Vermazen

		Aesthetic Values				
		Complexity	-	Unity	-	Balance
Garrard:	Artemisia	3	-	2	-	1
	Caravaggio	1	-	1	-	1
Haskell:	Artemisia	1	-	1	-	1
	Caravaggio	3	-	2	-	1[20]

This sample comparison of values simply reverses the ranking of the two works, based on the critics' assignment of values for three specific aesthetic properties. Where Garrard rates Artemisia high, Haskell rates her low, and vice versa. But is this the whole story? Does such a comparison of matrices capture what is implicit in Haskell's devaluation of Artemisia's work? Is he really devaluing her version because of aesthetic properties like complexity, unity, and balance, especially when he claims that her works fail in originality and expressivity? (In fact, some viewers have pointed out that, at least in terms of aesthetic properties, Artemisia's design is tighter, more unified, and more balanced than Caravaggio's.)

An opponent to Haskell's value judgment might insist that this is not the whole story—that what is missing is consideration of the work's cognitive properties: properties which tie the work to the world. Some opponents would insist that cognitive properties must be considered: that no evaluator has the luxury of ignoring them. Let me explain why.

The feminist task of restoring value to forgotten past artists and overlooked contemporary artists is not a simple chore of determining value of the aesthetic properties of works of art. If it were, feminist critics would be engaged in the task of "proving" that works by women possess unity or complexity or beauty: criteria traditionally utilized for determining *master*pieces of "genius." Rather, their task is to undermine and, in some cases, entirely discard the traditional apparatus of evaluation.[21] Skeptical of

for remarks on this topic, from an unpublished commentary on *Evaluating Art* read at the Pacific Division Meetings of the American Philosophical Association in March 1990.

20. The matrix system precludes comparisons of *overall* value of works (i.e., the interaction of all properties that would yield one overall value).

21. I hesitate to generalize "the feminist stance" in this way, since feminists hold differing views on the problem of evaluation; still, for most intents and purposes, feminists agree in their general skepticism of traditional methods of artistic evaluation, given the obvious consequences of producing white, male, European canons. Among the many spokespersons are the following: those who seek to eliminate evaluative criteria altogether (like Deborah Cherry, "Feminist Interventions: Feminist Imperatives," *Art History* 5 [1982]: 501–8, and Roszicka Parker and Griselda Pollock, *Old Mistresses: Women, Art and Ideology* [New York: Pantheon, 1981]); those who seek to work *within* existing "male" criteria to make them more inclusive (like Norma Broude and Mary D. Garrard, "Feminist Art History

such distinctions as high art versus low, fine art versus craft, and aesthetic versus cognitive, feminists view the entire history of the visual and literary arts as having been oppressively dominated by white, male authorities utilizing nonobjective criteria which masquerade as universal and objective. In their task of debunking the myth of "genius" and deconstructing the traditional standards of greatness for inclusion in the canon, they hold, "The personal is the political." For them, there is no separating political concerns from aesthetic ones. Translated into Dickie's terms, feminists' interest in political value is an interest in his notion of one type of cognitive value: what he calls "moral value." In fact (though this is a controversial claim) I offer the suggestion that they are nearly exclusively interested in moral value to the exclusion of an interest in aesthetic value.

In other words, in spite of their uneasiness with the given categories, one could say that feminists prefer to rank the cognitive properties over the aesthetic properties in importance. This naturally precludes ranking aesthetic properties as equal to or more important than cognitive properties. Thus, a feminist approach differs drastically from traditional philosophical approaches like Monroe Beardsley's, which favors aesthetic properties exclusively. It also differs from Dickie's approach, in which cognitive and aesthetic properties appear to be weighted equally, in that feminists build in an implicit hierarchy in which moral (or political) value always outweighs aesthetic value. Given this strategy, let us return, then, to Dickie's characterization of the aesthetic/cognitive distinction and his explanation of cognitive value.

According to Dickie, there are three types of cognitive value or disvalue that art can possess:

1. *Imitative cognitive value or disvalue,* which derives from the satisfaction or dissatisfaction of noticing [a] that the world of a work of art is true or false to actuality in some respect or [b] that a proposition asserted by means of a work of art is true or false;
2. *Supportive cognitive value or disvalue,* which derives from referen-

and the Academy: Where Are We Now?" *Women's Studies Quarterly* 15 [1987]: 10–16, and Myra Jehlen, "Archimedes and the Paradox of Feminist Criticism," *Signs* 6 [1981]: 575–601; and those who propose criteria alternative to the tradition (Annette Kolodny, "Dancing Through the Minefield," in Elaine Showalter, *The New Feminist Criticism* [New York: Pantheon, 1985], Toril Moi, *Sexual/Textual Politics: Feminist Literary Theory* [New York: Routledge, 1985], and the French feminists: Hélène Cixous, Julia Kristeva, Luce Irigaray). For an introductory though somewhat dated sampling of feminist viewpoints on visual art, see Thalia Gouma-Peterson and Patricia Mathews, "The Feminist Critique of Art History," *The Art Bulletin* 69 (1987).

tial features of a work of art being responsible for that work's having certain valuable or disvaluable aesthetic properties; and

3. *Referent-centered cognitive value or disvalue,* which derives from the value or disvalue of the object, event, or state of affairs that aspects of a work of art represent.[22]

If a feminist were to grant the feasibility of Dickie's three types of cognitive value, she would probably be most interested in imitative cognitive value and referent-centered cognitive value.[23] With the latter, a work gets rated highly because its referent—in the real world—gets rated highly. Dickie, following Hume, sometimes calls this a work's "moral" value in that the work is assessed in terms of the moral viewpoint taken toward the thing or event to which the work refers; hence the name "referent-centered."[24] There is overwhelming evidence to argue for the plausibility of this view. One need only consider the popularity of certain trends in the history of Western art to realize the value that referents (whether real or imaginary) held for viewers of religious and mythological art, landscape and genre painting, and portraiture. Additional evidence might be the number of works which persons fail to value highly because of their subject matter: for instance, images in which women are raped, seduced, vilified, or victimized.

On these grounds, it would follow that if one values the act of Judith slaying Holofernes, for example, one will naturally value the depiction of that act. If one does not value that act, then one will not value its depiction. As Garrard explains, one's reaction to Judith's act can be easily complicated, however, since men have traditionally shown an ambivalent attitude toward

22. *Evaluating Art,* p. 128.

23. Cognitive value type 2—or supportive cognitive value—includes cases in which aesthetic features of a work of art depend upon or are supported by cognitive features of a work of art. The example provided by Dickie focuses on the aesthetic property of unity: the central event of Huck and Jim floating down the Mississippi River, from the free state of Illinois into the slave state of Missouri, adds to the novel's "overall coherence." The coherence, or unity, of the novel is an aesthetic property enhanced by "references to these geographical and political realities." Ibid., p. 121. According to Dickie, cases of supportive cognitive value are not indicated on the matrix system because they are not *independently valued* properties. For this reason, I leave them out of the discussion of feminist concerns.

24. Hume's example, in his essay "Of the Standard of Taste," is the case of a French play intended by the playwright to reinforce viewers' feelings of religious sentiment. Since Hume deplores the actuality of religious sentiment (calling it "bigotry"), he judges the work to have low referent-centered cognitive value because it affirms such a deplorable state of affairs. See *Evaluating Art,* p. 117.

her "heroism." She is undoubtedly a religious savior of her people. Nonetheless, she achieves good by means of evil: deception, seduction, aggression, and treachery.[25] It would be easy to attribute Haskell's devaluing of Artemisia's version to a simple aversion for the subject matter, but it would also be naive and unfair to do so. Since many artists, throughout the centuries, have depicted this same subject matter, it is clear that artists and viewers value the incident enough to see it pictured repeatedly and in a variety of ways. What is crucial for our discussion is that some depictions are consistently valued more highly than others. Haskell and other critics who favor Caravaggio's version over Artemisia's are likely to do so because of the particular stylistic treatment of that subject matter which thereby affects the value they hold for the image and the referent. As Dickie claims, referent-centered value is affected by the conception one holds of the imagined event, the biblical beheading.

Let us look more closely at the way each artist presents the figures of Judith, maidservant, and Holofernes. One might claim that if Judith is portrayed as a strong, goal-driven woman and a male viewer feels threatened by the actuality of such a woman, he would naturally fail to value such a depiction.[26] This, in short, could explain the difference between male critics who devalue Artemisia's version of a decapitation, where an overpowering Judith is brutally sawing off the head of Holofernes, and the same male critics who value Caravaggio's version, where the deed is inflicted on a less-than-deserving male (after all, *she* seduced *him!*) by an artificially and prettily posed Judith. In these cases, the male viewer identifies with the male victim (as did Caravaggio, we assume), not with the perpetrator of the heroic deed. On the other hand, a viewer who identifies with the strength and will of Judith (or at least with the helpfulness of the maidservant, if one cannot picture oneself as Judith) would rate Artemisia's version highly for presenting a motivated and justified woman who acts to save her people, and would feel little empathy with the deserving victim of Caravaggio's version.

25. Garrard, *Artemisia Gentileschi,* p. 291ff, relates the story of the Florentine debate of 1504 over replacing Donatello's *Judith* with Michelangelo's *David* in the Palazzo Vecchio; proponents for the replacement argued that "the Judith is an omen of evil, and no fit object where it stands. . . . [It] is not proper that the woman should kill the male."

26. This is based on recent feminist theorizing of how a viewer responds to images: for example, images of women in Hollywood films, based on gender ("the male gaze"). For one strain of this lively discussion, sparked by Laura Mulvey, see her *Visual and Other Pleasures* (Bloomington: Indiana University Press, 1989) as well as the essays of Mary Devereaux, "Oppressive Texts, Resisting Readers and the Gendered Spectator: The 'New' Aesthetics," and Noël Carroll, "The Image of Women in Film: A Defense of a Paradigm," both of which appear in *The Journal of Aesthetics and Art Criticism* 48 (1990): 337–360.

This divergence of response points out the difficulty in assigning referent-centered value, since it is possible that rating the work will divide along the lines of gendered figure-identification: males more likely identifying with Holofernes, females more likely identifying with Judith or the maidservant. According to referent-centered value, viewers end up assigning high or low values based on how they would feel about an actual Judith performing the deed. Giving Haskell the benefit of the doubt, let us assume that both critics highly value the actual beheading of Holofernes by Judith (i.e., both see it as heroic), but that the difference in evaluation between the two rests on how each values the original event insofar as it has been depicted by the artists. Their valuing of referents in different ways, low or high (1 or 3), is reflected in the addition of cognitive, referent-centered value (RCV, for short) to the matrix:

		Aesthetic and Cognitive Values			
		Complexity -	Unity -	Balance -	RCV
Garrard:	Artemisia	3 -	2 -	1 -	3
	Caravaggio	1 -	1 -	1 -	1
Haskell:	Artemisia	1 -	1 -	1 -	1
	Caravaggio	3 -	2 -	1 -	3

According to this matrix, Garrard values Artemisia's depiction over Caravaggio's for the way in which the scene represents the imagined event, while Haskell rates Caravaggio's version over Artemisia's.

Leaving aside referent-centered value, another approach to evaluating these two works is by means of Dickie's related notion of imitative cognitive value. Dickie claims that imitative cognitive value consists of (a) a work's truth-to-actuality merit or (b) the truth of the propositions asserted by means of a work of art. He has since changed his mind on the characterization of disjunct (b), but let us first look at how (a) would work.

To determine the value assigned by means of the truth-to-actuality criterion, a question arises as to how one gauges the imitative value of a woman decapitating a man. Is she to be judged by her effectiveness or by her beauty? Judith was deceitful and seductive, but she also "smote twice upon his neck with all her might." Garrard, in arguing for the value of Artemisia's version, believes that Caravaggio's "vacuous mannequin" fails to portray realistically a successful beheading or even a capable heroine. Thus Garrard might assign a value of 3 to Artemisia for the criterion of truth-to-actuality but a value of only 1 to Caravaggio. Haskell, on the contrary, might assign a value of 3 to Caravaggio, maintaining that his Judith looks capable of seducing an Assyrian general and subsequently beheading him *because* she is beautiful. He would naturally, then, assign a low value of 1 to Artemisia for depicting Judith as too strong and physically unattractive. In each case, the identical value of 3 is assigned for the (ICVa)—the imitative cognitive value, as represented in clause (a)—but for very different reasons.[27]

		Aesthetic and Cognitive Values				
		Complexity	Unity	Balance	RCV	ICVa
Garrard:	Artemisia	3	2	1	3	3
	Caravaggio	1	1	1	1	1
Haskell:	Artemisia	1	1	1	1	1
	Caravaggio	3	2	1	3	3

Consider, finally, the assignment of value which is based on whether the proposition "This work of art expresses personal suffering" is held to be true or false with regard to each work of art. Let us call this (ICVb): imitative cognitive value, based on (b) the truth of the proposition asserted by a work. Haskell would definitely rate Caravaggio high (a value of 3) for this property, while rating Artemisia low.

		Aesthetic and Cognitive Values					
		Complexity	Unity	Balance	RCV	ICVa	ICVb
Garrard:	Artemisia	3	2	1	3	3	3
	Caravaggio	1	1	1	1	1	1
Haskell:	Artemisia	1	1	1	1	1	1
	Caravaggio	3	2	1	3	3	3

One could take issue with this judgment by arguing that Artemisia's work is surely more expressive than Caravaggio's because it represents *both* Judith and Holofernes in dramatic human moments, rather than simply Holofernes alone. Or one could argue that Artemisia's version is more expressive since—at least on Haskell's criterion of expressivity of human suffering; that is, based on the artist's personal experience of suffering—her

27. I assume this problem would arise in determining the truth-to-actuality value in many other sorts of cases: for example, the case of a realistic landscape versus an impressionistic landscape. One critic might argue that a realistic style is truer to the overall visual experience of the actual landscape, while another might argue that an impressionistic mode more realistically captures the intensity and interplay of lights and darks.

version depicts a Judith enraged at Holofernes' sexual advances much like she herself must have felt enraged at her rapist's advances. Surely she expresses her own rage better than Caravaggio could ever express the feelings of being decapitated based on personal experience!

Haskell's judgment, in addition to being unenlightened, reveals his preoccupation with the criterion of expressivity (this is, after all, why he believes Artemisia incapable of the accolade of "genius") to the exclusion of others: for example, whether Judith and the maidservant look true to life. Garrard, on the other hand, is concerned with whether the female figures are represented as they might look in enacting the real event. Is it fair to compare works in terms of one property when critics themselves value properties to varying degrees? Even though these properties are cognitive properties—ones that are more highly valued by feminists in comparison to aesthetic properties—there seems to be an additional ordering of the two properties dependent upon individual critics. Since there seems to be no way to build some sort of hierarchy of properties into the matrix system, it leaves works like Artemisia's at a distinct disadvantage when assessed by critics like Haskell; he not only sees her work as failing to be expressive, but he embraces the bias of a critic who favors the criterion of expressivity over others.

Imagine, for instance, how different the matrix would look if instead of assessing the works in terms of the truth of the proposition about expressivity, our evaluators switched to a consideration of the truth of the proposition "This work of art is nonsexist." Designating the resulting value as (ICVb′), the following results would occur:

		Aesthetic and Cognitive Values					
		Complexity	Unity	Balance	RCV	ICVa	ICVb′
Garrard:	Artemisia	3	2	1	3	3	3
	Caravaggio	1	1	1	1	1	1
Haskell:	Artemisia	1	1	1	1	1	?
	Caravaggio	3	2	1	3	3	?

On this construal, Artemisia's work rates above Caravaggio's from Garrard's feminist viewpoint. But for Haskell, it is hard even to construct a complete matrix—not only because he would most likely believe this new proposition to be less important than the proposition asserting expressivity, but because he might think that the new proposition is not applicable at all. In this case, he could refuse to assign any value to (ICVb′) in a matrix system, leaving us with no basis of comparison between the two works with regard to the property of being nonsexist. A twofold question arises from this apparent dead end: namely, How do we determine which propositions are asserted by a work of art, and how do we determine their importance?

Extending Dickie's Matrix System

By means of a somewhat laborious route, we have come upon the most interesting and important aspect of Dickie's entire system. The complication with phrase (b), which captures imitative cognitive value, is the difficulty in determining just what types of propositions can be said to be asserted by means of a work of art. Consider some examples typical of art-critical statements:

(P1) The Mississippi River referred to in *Huck Finn* is the real Mississippi River.
(P2) *Tom Sawyer* confronts the issue of slavery.
(P3) *Fountain,* in flaunting the banal, refutes all previous definitions of art that rely on the notion of beauty.
(P4) Caravaggio's *Judith Beheading Holofernes* is sexist.
(P5) Gentileschi's *Judith Slaying Holofernes* confronts the issue of sexism.
(P6) *Judith Slaying Holofernes* was painted by a woman.
(P7) Artemisia's *Judith Slaying Holofernes* is typical of the poor quality of work by female artists and erodes all artistic standards.

Not even the second example, provided by Dickie himself, seems to be a case of *imitative* value, at least not in any clear way as is the first example intended to function as his paradigm of imitative cognitive value. Similarly, (P3) through (P7) seem to have nothing to do with what might be broadly construed as imitative value.

This is why Dickie has subsequently suggested the addition of another category of cognitive value: one called nonimitative cognitive value.[28] This category would *not* be subsumed under that of imitative cognitive value; in

28. This was suggested in personal correspondence with Dickie.

other words, the second disjunct (b) is no longer operable. Rather, there would be four kinds of cognitive value with nonimitative cognitive value—or what I propose to call propositional cognitive value—added to the other three.

What are the repercussions of adding a new type of cognitive value that can be assessed in all works of art? One distinct advantage is that works can be more thoroughly evaluated in terms of propositions they assert: propositions which are not restricted to imitative value alone. This, in effect, opens the floodgates for the consideration of a whole range of propositions by which critics can judge and compare. Assessing the many types of propositions available, as in the sampling of propositions (P1) through (P7), reflects more accurately the actual practices of art criticism. In fact, one might even go so far as to say that propositional cognitive value is the mode of evaluation most often used by contemporary art critics.[29]

In glancing over (P1) through (P7), it is clear that in all cases, except for the special case of (P6), the assignment of value for each proposition depends on whether a certain subpopulation holds the proposition to be true or false. Propositions (P4) and (P5), for instance, would be rated high in the matrix system for holding true for an audience of feminists, while it would simultaneously be rated low in the matrix system for holding false for misogynists (or for naive viewers whose consciousnesses are yet to be raised). Proposition (P7) would naturally be believed true by this same subpopulation of misogynists and false by the subpopulation of feminists. Given the numbers of possible propositions asserted by works of art, is there any way to sort through and make sense of them?

I would like to suggest a way, at least briefly before closing, that provides a means of organizing such propositions into useful categories. This method is inspired by William G. Lycan and Peter K. Machamer's 1969 article, entitled "A Theory of Critical Reasons."[30] In order to make sense of the aesthetic/nonaesthetic distinction, Lycan and Machamer speak of critical reasons asserted about works of art as "loaded" (i.e., nonfactual and context-dependent) or "detachable" (i.e., factual and not context-dependent). They

29. In the past, works were assessed more often in terms of imitative value or referent-centered value; but given the nature of twentieth-century art—works that are nonrepresentational or highly metaphorical—criticism has become concerned less with imitative and referent-centered value and more with propositional value.

30. This article is reprinted in W. E. Kennick's second edition of *Art and Philosophy: Readings in Aesthetics* (New York: St. Martin's Press, 1979), pp. 687–706. The paper was originally published in Benjamin R. Tilghman, *Language and Aesthetics: Contributions to the Philosophy of Art* (Lawrence: University Press of Kansas, 1973).

suggest arranging such reasons on continua ranging from the least context-dependent (being the lowest on the continuum) to the most context-dependent (located at the very top). Consider continuum no. 1, which captures Lycan and Machamer's theory of critical reasons adapted to Dickie's language (to be read from the bottom up, from (0) to (3)):

Continuum no. 1

(3) *P* has value or lacks value (with regard to *f*'s and *p*'s for a particular subpopulation, *S*). [Loaded; almost entirely context-dependent]

(2) Taking the *f*'s and *p*'s together, *P* is *a*, where *a* is a description of *P*. (Or *P* does *b*, where *b* is a predicate describing *P*.) [Requires lots of context]

(1) *p*, a property of *P*, is *a*, where *a* is a description of *p*. [Is descriptive, requires some context]

(0) *f* is a fact about *P* or the artist of *P*. [*f* is a detachable fact; requires no context for understanding the painting, *P*]

Category (0) captures facts about the work or artist (e.g., "The artist of *P* is a woman") and is an instance of cognitive value. These facts are detachable and, hence, *not* context-dependent because they require little background information on the part of the viewer to be understood. Category (1) cites properties of the work: properties which can be either aesthetic or cognitive, as in the case of "This narrow black line is exquisite" (aesthetic) or "The body language of Judith (in the Caravaggio version) is demeaning to women" (cognitive). Category (2) summarizes information contained in categories (0) and (1) and can also indicate either aesthetic or cognitive value. For example, propositions like "*P* is complex" or "*P* is unified" are propositions of type (2) indicating *aesthetic* value, but a claim like "*P* is nonsexist" would count as an instance of a proposition with *cognitive* import. Category (3) is the culmination of the process of listing reasons/propositions: the overall judgment of *artistic* value (not merely aesthetic value). Context-dependent statements, like those of category (3), are "loaded" in that "their significance depends upon a context *larger* than that provided by the painting itself": for example, the context of art education.[31] In moving up the continuum, each reason is ranked according to ease of comprehension; that is, "according to how much critical and historical background one must have in order to *understand* it."[32] The closer the propositions are to the top

31. *Art and Philosophy*, p. 697.
32. Ibid., p. 698.

of the continuum, the less defeasible, given that each higher level builds upon levels below. This, as will be discussed shortly, is the clue for feminists who seek to vindicate women's devalued works of art.

The connection between propositions listed in the continua and Dickie's matrix system should be apparent. Numerical values are assigned to propositions of categories (0), (1), and (2) in order to construct matrices that compare works in terms of specific properties or facts. (Remember that category (3) *cannot* be accommodated by the matrix system, since a work's overall value cannot be indicated on a matrix.) Thus, categories (0), (1), and (2) constitute instances of propositional cognitive value that can be schematized by means of Dickie's matrices. To return to our case study involving Artemisia Gentileschi and Michelangelo da Caravaggio, consider category (2) in continuum no. 2 and continuum no. 3:

Continuum no. 2

(3) *P* (Artemisia's *Judith Slaying Holofernes*) lacks value (for Haskell).
(2) *P* fails to express personal suffering.
(1) Judith does not express Artemisia's personal suffering (over being raped).
(0) The artist of *P* lacks the capacity for expressing personal suffering. (The artist of *P* is a woman.)

Continuum no. 3

(3) *P* (the work of Artemisia) has value (for Garrard).
(2) *P* is nonsexist.
(1) Both the maidservant and Judith escape the stereotypes of maiden, virago, and crone.
(0) The artist of *P* is a woman.

Continuum no. 3 represents propositional cognitive value from a feminist point of view that is explicitly intended to counteract traditional, male-oriented devaluations of women's works. Feminists see their task as filling in the continua in various innovative ways with propositions previously unrepresented. Determining which propositions a work of art asserts depends upon the perceptible as well as the nonperceptible features and, in the case of cognitive value, depends upon ways the work is tied to the world. Since the less defeasible propositions are nearer the top of a continuum, one strategy for feminists to pursue is arguing for the truth of those propositions in categories (1) and especially (2) in order ultimately to enlarge the subpopulation holding those propositions to be true. This move will counter criticism from those who devalue women's works by having feminists focus on the properties of the work itself and not on the gender of the artist. Those propositions focusing on the properties of the work, combined with facts about the artist, will ultimately count as reasons for a higher judgment of value of the work.

To summarize, testing the practicality of Dickie's matrix system focused on analyzing the critical commentary evaluating two works on a well-known theme by Michelangelo da Caravaggio and Artemisia Gentileschi. Modifications to Dickie's approach to cognitive value were explored, resulting in a more workable framework for understanding the type of critical statements traditionally used to devalue works by female artists as well as for accommodating innovative critical remarks used to (re)attribute value to works by women.

The analysis of Dickie's *Evaluating Art* and the amendments to Dickie's original insights are beneficial in several ways. The amendments expand prior philosophical discussions of aesthetic and artistic value beyond their former confines—forcing cognitive value to the forefront—thereby making the enterprise of evaluation much more open to the ways art is actually assessed. The notion of "propositional value," as developed in this essay, serves as a more practical means of evaluation for works like *Fountain* and *Piss Christ* than any criterion of aesthetic value or imitative cognitive value ever could. For, surely, the value of these works only minimally derives from the former's gleaming white surface and the latter's recognizable depiction of Christ on the cross. Regarding such works as trivial or blasphemous reinforces the way evaluations take shape in the form of propositions: propositions which capture the way a work of art is tied to the world, propositions which are ultimately judged to be either true or false.

Assessing a work via propositional value also ties in naturally with the feminist strategy of examining the neglected value of works by women and other undervalued artists. Karen Finley's performances can be judged aesthetically; that, of course, is why she wears costumes or assumes none—choosing to smear her unclothed body with chocolate or raw eggs and glitter. But the import of her work lies far beyond any aesthetic concerns one might discern. The force of her work stems from the combination of recited text, assumed persona, and direct confrontation of the audience: facets that cannot—as in the cases of Duchamp and Serrano—be captured by either aesthetic or imitative value. The notion of propositional value, as an aspect of Dickie's matrix system, fills a gap in our understanding of works like Finley's. What philosophers have long ignored, feminist critics and theorists can now capitalize upon.

Feminists are encouraged to consider accepting the amended matrix system as a move beyond the narrowness of past philosophical theories and as a bridge to more enlightening ways of isolating the unique values that artworks possess. In this way, critical commentary that conceals biases below the surface can be exposed and addressed. *Evaluating Art* is invaluable in its move toward that end.

Marcia Muelder Eaton

Evaluating More Than Art

In the final chapter of his book *Evaluating Art,* George Dickie purports to capture in a fairly formal way what art critics do in a more or less informal (perhaps even unconscious) way.[1] Specifically, he is interested in the role that *ranking* plays in critical assessment. I want to raise some questions with regard to the possibility of extending his method to another sort of aesthetic evaluation: namely, evaluation of landscapes.

In the last thirty or so years attention has increasingly been given to ways in which landscape values—scenic resources, for example—can be preserved in technological societies like ours where development and pollution threaten their existence. In 1969, for instance, the Environmental Policy Act stipulated that "aesthetic amenities" must be given due account in environmental

I am grateful to Ruth Wood for valuable editorial assistance in preparing this essay. I also benefited greatly from the opportunity, at an "Author Meets Critics" session at the Pacific Division Meetings of the American Philosophical Association in March 1990, to discuss George Dickie's *Evaluating Art* with Benjamin R. Tilghman, Bruce Vermazen, and Dickie himself.

1. George Dickie, *Evaluating Art* (Philadelphia: Temple University Press, 1988), pp. 157–82.

impact studies. We are told by people in the business of making such predictions, that the 1990s will be characterized by growing public concern with the environment. Assessment, preservation, maintenance, and creation of beautiful spaces and places—urban, rural, and wild—are likely to play a central role.

I would like to see whether Dickie's method for evaluating art can be applied to evaluating aesthetic resources of the environment. I have two goals here. First, if Dickie's project can be generalized, it will contribute significantly to the work of urban planners, landscape architects, forest managers, and the like. These people are faced with important decisions that must be made. Unlike most problems in philosophical debate, theirs require action, often within rather drastic time deadlines. Second, if the method does not withstand extension, we may learn something important about the differences between assessments of works of art and of landscapes (including cityscapes). Or we may discover weaknesses in Dickie's theory. If it does not serve adequately as a general theory of aesthetic evaluation, that may be because it does not serve adequately as a theory of artistic evaluation either. In seeing whether we can evaluate more than art, we may learn something about evaluating art itself.

A vast amount of work has been done in recent years in the area of landscape assessment. Much of it has had the obtaining of quantitative results as a central goal. Assuming that objectivity requires the assigning of numerical scores (a mistake I have called the "quantitative fallacy"),[2] an enormous variety of methods has been applied in order to attempt to discover whether a given landscape deserves, say, a 6 or a 7 on a ten-point scale. Sometimes based upon a particular legal, psychological, or economic theory, sometimes lacking any theoretical foundation, a continuum of mathematical methodology and sophistication is found in these studies. These range from the use of simple polling methods (reporting what percentage of a given population is bothered by power lines, for example) to complicated applications of linear regression theory (where, for instance, hypotheses concerning the weighting of various factors in preferences of a population are proposed).

One of the prevailing weaknesses of these assessment studies has been the failure of the investigators to prove that they are actually capturing *aesthetic* preferences. Answering the question "Are you bothered by power

2. Marcia Muelder Eaton, *Aesthetics and the Good Life* (Cranbury, N.J.: Associated University Presses, 1989), chap. 3.

lines here?" affirmatively or negatively does not ensure that the responder is reporting an aesthetic experience. He or she may be primarily concerned about ecological implications or may be impressed by construction efforts. Using statistical analysis, one may "discover" that a person prefers landscapes with trees over twenty feet high to those with trees whose height averages less than twenty feet. In fact, the aesthetic experience may be directed at the type of tree; the observer may not even have noticed the height. What is needed is a theory which will ensure that numbers, indecisive in themselves, are truly related to aesthetic response.

Dickie's method certainly fulfills this demand. He establishes clearly that rankings, when forthcoming, will be aesthetic rankings, and applied aestheticians whose task it is to produce rankings can learn much from him. "Better" or "worse" will be tied to those of an object's intrinsic properties which are valued within a community's aesthetic traditions. The properties he includes (unity, color, shape, etc.) and the context in which attention is given to them are central to aesthetic activity. People asked to rank works of art according to Dickie's method will know that they are being asked to rank them aesthetically. Since artworks and landscapes can be evaluated on many grounds (in terms of religious or economic value, for instance), simplistic questions will not yield results that clearly tell us anything about the basis of evaluation. "Do you give this a score of 6 or 7 on a scale of 10?" asked of the Mona Lisa or the Grand Canyon leaves itself open to a range of interpretations. However, "Score this in terms of unity, color, and proportion" demands aesthetic attention, and the rankings that result will assuredly be aesthetic rankings.

Even when these assurances exist, however, there are problems. Elsewhere I have discussed in some detail a specific landscape-assessment activity—a Jones & Jones evaluation of the Upper Susitna river basin in Alaska.[3] But I think that a summary will be helpful again here, for it highlights difficulties that accompany ranking and it will indicate vulnerable spots in Dickie's method for evaluating artworks.

In 1975, Jones & Jones, an engineering firm in Seattle, was hired by the Army Corps of Engineers to determine how the Upper Susitna River would be affected by the construction of four hydroelectric dams and their reservoirs. They mapped the watershed and viewshed of the river and described river segments in terms of channel characteristics (e.g., braided channel or looped meander channel), physical factors (e.g., glacial scars or patterned ground),

3. Ibid., pp. 67–72.

biological factors (e.g., presence of brush or mammals), landform factors (e.g., surface patterns or spatial definition), and cultural factors (e.g., presence of campsites or land ownership). These factors clearly are amenable to a variety of kinds of preferences—economic and ecological as well as aesthetic. The authors developed a formula, however, to ensure that genuinely aesthetic scores would be forthcoming:

$$\text{Aesthetic Value} = \frac{\text{Vividness} + \text{Visual Intactness} + \text{Unity}}{3} \div \text{Visual Uniqueness}$$

It is interesting to note how much these properties are like what Dickie and others call "standard aesthetic properties." The particular formula is not crucial. Jones & Jones divide by three in order to obtain an average. They make aesthetic value inversely proportional to visual uniqueness; other formulas might make the proportions direct. But the formula is already far more complicated than the simple scores we will find in Dickie's method—and one wonders whether his method might benefit from the work of applied aestheticians like Jones & Jones.

What I find most useful in the Jones & Jones study is the specific application they make to the problem of determining where dams should actually be built. For it is in the details of the application that serious problems arise, and I expect that similar problems might arise in specific applications of Dickie's methodology. What, for example, is involved in determining whether a landscape or work of art is "vivid"? Jones & Jones assert (without explanation) that thirteen factors are involved, and these range from watershed features to the presence of nonnatural structures. How will Dickie account for such a value—will it be a composite as it is for Jones & Jones, or will it be a primitive term? Jones & Jones believe that uniqueness can be expressed quantitatively. But as this factor figures in their formula, something uniquely ugly would weigh exactly as would something uniquely beautiful. How, one wonders, will Dickie deal with such a problem? Will uniquely ugly works of art be evaluated positively?

In their recommendations Jones & Jones suggest that "the construction of Devil Canyon Dam would have a very high effect on the aesthetic value . . . since the resources on which that value is based would be largely inundated: the gorge and its white water. The dam structure and its attendant facilities would also affect the visual intactness of the run adversely."[4] Reservoir dams evidently have less appeal than white water rivers. But why? Are they less vivid, less visually intact, less unified? The reader can, I believe, imagine analogous problems with respect to the actual evaluation of works of art.

Before we get to the details of Dickie's evaluative methodology, a short summary of the argument leading to its presentation will be helpful. Dickie follows a standard line of argumentation: he discusses existing (or possible) theories, locates their strengths and weaknesses, and builds a new theory in which he attempts to preserve the former and avoid the latter. Basically, he thinks, there are two kinds of theories of aesthetic value. The first maintains that artistic value derives from a single source.[5] The second maintains that it derives from many things.[6] Both of these are instrumental theories; that is to say, both locate aesthetic value as lying in the experience produced by a work of art. (The experience in turn is either itself intrinsically or instrumentally valuable.)

Dickie claims that eighteenth- and nineteenth-century rejection of imitation or representation theories of artistic value, Kant's theory of taste, and Schopenhauer's understanding of Kant's theory made the experience of beauty incompatible with the experience of representational properties. The cognitive or moral content of an object was taken to play no role in the aesthetic experience (and hence judgment) of it. This view has positively or negatively influenced a variety of twentieth-century aestheticians whom Dickie then discusses.

Paul Ziff has argued that a work of art is good if and only if action taken with respect to a particular work by a particular person under appropriate conditions is worthwhile for its own sake, with the work itself determining those actions and conditions.[7] Dickie believes that the actions Ziff has in mind are essentially noncognitive. In any case, all we can derive from Ziff's theory is that an object is "good to some degree"—depending on how worthwhile the experience is. Being "good to some degree" is extremely vague and will not provide what Dickie is ultimately after: a nonrelativistic way of evaluating artworks. One can strengthen it by adding "well worthwhile,"

4. Jones & Jones, *An Inventory and Evaluation of the Environmental, Aesthetic, and Recreational Resources of the Upper Susitna River, Alaska.* Report prepared for U.S. Department of the Army, Alaska District, Contract CADW85-74-C-0057, p. 170.

5. Dickie says that Monroe Beardsley and Nelson Goodman represent this view.

6. Paul Ziff, Frank Sibley, Nicholas Wolterstorff, Bruce Vermazen, J. O. Urmson, David Hume, and Dickie are representatives of this view.

7. Paul Ziff, "Reasons in Art Criticism," in *Art and Philosophy,* 2nd ed., ed. W. E. Kennick (New York: St. Martin's Press, 1979), pp. 669–86.

Dickie suggests, but still Ziff's view does not allow us to compare works, because some require one sort of act (e.g., contemplation) and others require a different sort (e.g., scanning). What Dickie wants from an evaluative methodology, then, is a nonrelativistic basis for comparing works of art. (This is also, of course, what applied aestheticians are after.)

Monroe Beardsley, located firmly in the Kant/Schopenhauer camp, takes aesthetic experience to be essentially relationless, according to Dickie.[8] It is detached from the rest of experience and is directed at an object's unity, intensity, and complexity. This trio constitutes the standard, primary goodmaking characteristics of something. All other positive features (balance or vibrancy, for instance) contribute to one of these three. Since moral value does not so contribute, it is irrelevant to aesthetic experience on Beardsley's view. Moral value is even detrimental to it, since it threatens to distract aesthetic attention. Dickie believes that this is wrong, and I agree with him. Unified, intense, and complex works will always "have some value"; of course, Dickie sees that this is much weaker than "is good." Weak principles (which get us to "has some value") may explain strong ones (those which allow us to conclude that something "is good"), but by no means do they imply them. And only strong principles allow for ranking works.

Nelson Goodman disagrees with Beardsley's view that aesthetic experience is detached.[9] He believes that art refers to the world, and that aesthetic experience is related to the rest of human experience. Cognitive features thus matter: value resides in how well something signifies what it signifies. Instead of putting the aesthetic burden exclusively on possession of properties (as Beardsley does), Goodman's theory puts the weight on exemplification. And though Dickie finds this view attractive, he is concerned that Goodman does not give a clear way of ranking cognitive efficacy. Nor does Goodman prove, Dickie argues, that all aesthetically relevant features exemplify or refer to something. It follows from Goodman's view that all uniformly colored paintings—both a square canvas simply painted bright green and a square canvas simply painted olive drab, for example—will have the same value. Dickie thinks this is wrong, and that it implies that more than exemplification is involved. Dickie concludes from this that both possession and exemplification count toward artistic value.

8. See Monroe Beardsley, *Aesthetics: Problems in the Philosophy of Criticism* (New York: Harcourt, Brace & World, 1958) and "On the Generality of Critical Reasons," *The Journal of Philosophy* 59 (1962): 477–86.

9. Nelson Goodman, *Languages of Art: An Approach to a Theory of Symbols* (Indianapolis: Bobbs-Merrill, 1968).

Dickie admires Nicholas Wolterstorff for moving in the direction of synthesizing the positions of Beardsley and Goodman.[10] Wolterstorff has a religious perspective which has led him to observe that some artworks have many purposes. He distinguishes, therefore, between artistic and aesthetic value, with aesthetic being only one kind of artistic value. Wolterstorff characterizes artistic excellence as serving well the purpose for which a work of art was made. This permits a "mixture" view—a view in which cognitive as well as perceptual features can be appreciated at the same time. But, Dickie thinks, more than the possibility of mixing is required. He argues that sometimes (as in *Huckleberry Finn*) there is actually a dependence of aesthetic on cognitive or moral features. At any rate, the aesthetic-as-detached view must be abandoned.

Borrowing from Hume's concept of a "competent judge,"[11] Dickie views such a judge as someone who can point out things in artworks that people do value. Instead of insisting as Hume did that qualified critics must attain an ideal combination of physical and mental acuity that will provide a standard for universal agreement among them, Dickie sees critics as performing a more modest task, I think. But he does not make explicit what the nature or significance of this task is. I shall have more to say on this point later. Wolterstorff is correct that people who engage in the assessment of art value many different things—too many to expect agreement. We can agree that a variety of things is valuable, but disagree about the relative value of each thing. This, of course, makes evaluating art—particularly ranking artworks—very difficult.

And now we come to Dickie's final chapter. Dickie begins this chapter by remarking on the inadequacy of the definition of positive and negative aesthetic value that he has arrived at in earlier chapters.[12]

> A property is a positive criterion of aesthetic value if it is a property of a work of art and if in isolation from other properties it is valuable.

and

> A property is a negative criterion of aesthetic value if it is a property of a work of art and if in isolation from other properties it is disvaluable.

10. Nicholas Wolterstorff, *Art in Action* (Grand Rapids, Mich.: William B. Eerdmans, 1980).
11. David Hume, "Of the Standard of Taste" (1757).
12. Dickie, *Evaluating Art,* p. 157.

He says that since aesthetic value is only one kind of artistic value, these definitions must be revised: we must substitute "artistic" for "aesthetic" in both cases.

Dickie agrees with Nicholas Wolterstorff that artistic and aesthetic value are distinct. Both believe that the value of art is not limited to the sort of value that Monroe Beardsley, in the tradition of Kant and Schopenhauer, identifies as *the aesthetic:* pleasure directed at intrinsic properties of a work and detached from other areas of human experience. Aesthetic value, on this view, is restricted essentially to pleasure or satisfactions of *perception*—to sensual pleasures. The importance of art extends beyond this; it has, for example, religious, historic, economic, political, moral, and social value as well.

I agree with Dickie and Wolterstorff that art has more than aesthetic value. And this point is also true, and important, for landscapes. The value of landscapes includes the capacities for recreation and wildlife habitat as well as the potential for aesthetic experiences. Where I disagree is in limiting the aesthetic to the perceptual. Dickie buys into the Beardsley view when he discusses cognitive properties. He writes: "As noted above, properties other than aesthetic properties can be of artistic value or disvalue. These *other* [emphasis added] valuable or disvaluable properties are cognitive properties."[13] I had up to this point thought that Dickie wanted a synthesis of the Beardsley and Goodman views—that he wanted to make room within *the aesthetic,* not just within the artistic, for both perceptual and cognitive value. Indeed, in his discussion of *Huckleberry Finn,* Dickie argued that one must abandon the view of the aesthetic as always isolated or detached from all other aspects of human experience. Did he really intend there to be speaking of *artistic* and not *aesthetic* value? What remains unclear is whether cognitive or moral values (and all other sorts of value, for that matter) simply *contribute* to aesthetic value or whether they can actually be themselves aesthetic.

When we turn to aesthetic landscape values, I think the inadequacy of a separatist view is reinforced. Cognition shapes and even creates the perceptual, and vice versa. Studies indicate that attention to matters of ecology, health and safety, and stewardship contribute to the aesthetic experience of a landscape.[14] What a landscape represents as well as what a landscape painting represents (a cognitive value in Dickie's view) may very

13. Ibid., p. 158.

14. For examples of such studies, see *Proceedings of Our National Landscape: A Conference on Applied Techniques for Analysis and Management of the Visual Resource.* U.S. Department of Agriculture, Forest Service, Pacific Southwest Forest and Range Experiment Station, General Technical Report PSW-35, Indian Village, Nevada, April 23–25, 1979.

well be a component of an aesthetic experience, I believe. In my own theory, the aesthetic is characterized as intrinsic features culturally identified as worth attending to and reflecting upon.[15] Since I think that reflection (cognition) is as truly a part of aesthetic experience as attention (perceptual), I would prefer that Dickie stick to an integrative view of aesthetic as well as artistic value.

This issue aside, Dickie worries about how we get from weak principles (such as "This work is valuable in some degree") to strong ones (such as "This work is good"). Ultimately he thinks that strong specific evaluations may not be possible. But he does think it is possible to compare and even to rank at least some artworks.

Dickie says, and I agree, that evaluative comparison or ranking of specific works "requires that there be a measure of something that the works have in common."[16] *Beauty* and, Beardsley's nominee, *capacity to produce aesthetic experience of high magnitude* are too restrictive (because there are other sources of artistic value). But views like Dickie's and Wolterstorff's that correctly recognize many sources of artistic value are so complicated that it is not readily apparent how comparisons or rankings will be forthcoming. If Jones says, "*P* is better than *Q* because it is more balanced" and Smith says, "*P* is better than *Q* because it is more elegant," they may not really be engaged in the same ranking process. That is, both are indeed ranking *P* and *Q*, and both give *P* a higher rank, but not with regard to the same features. Hence their rankings may be only coincidentally or superficially the same.

Dickie uses Bruce Vermazen's article, "Comparing Evaluations of Works of Art," as a first step in constructing his own ranking procedure.[17] Vermazen agrees that many things in art are valuable. Some are independently valuable (i.e., do not depend on other features) and some are dependently valuable. He argues that while it is generally possible to rank two works with respect to the degree of a single, independently valued property that they both possess (such as unity), it is not generally possible to rank them with respect to the degree of two different, independently valuable properties. It is hard to rate a vividly colored painting against a subtly colored one, harder still to compare vivid color with symmetry, and impossible to weight color in a painting against meter in a poem. The old apples/oranges problem seems to confront us at every turn.

15. Eaton, *Aesthetics and the Good Life.*

16. Dickie, *Evaluating Art,* p. 162.

17. Bruce Vermazen, "Comparing Evaluations of Works of Art," *The Journal of Aesthetics and Art Criticism* 34 (1975): 7–14.

Dickie extends Vermazen's observation. Even if two works have the same properties, comparisons may not always be possible. While a work that is very brightly colored, highly unified, and well balanced will easily be ranked above one that is very brightly colored, highly unified, but unbalanced, the ranking process breaks down, Dickie thinks, when one tries to compare a very brightly colored, highly unified, unbalanced work with one that is not so brightly colored, highly unified, and balanced. This indicates how limited Dickie's methodology will be, since art criticism rarely involves simply comparing works where the first sort of description fits neatly. Even apparently obvious rankings such as "Monet's *Water Lilies* paintings are better than Walt Disney's Mickey Mouse paintings" will not be supported. Suppose Mickey Mouse gets a higher score for *cuteness* than *Water Lilies.* Even if its score on all other properties is lower, Mickey Mouse and *Water Lilies* will remain incomparable.[18]

Nonetheless, Dickie thinks that at least (perhaps at best) a method of ranking can be worked out by comparing works which share independently valuable properties. Once one has identified works where the same sort of coloration, organization, and so on seem to matter most for their overall value (i.e., once one has limited oneself to just oranges or just apples), one can proceed rationally to compare them. The first step is to evaluate a single work with respect to its own independently valuable properties. Then that work can serve as a base which can be used to rank the work with respect to a set of other actual or possible works.

Suppose we evaluate a single work with respect to the degree of bright color, unity, and balance that it displays. On a three-point scale, suppose the work gets 1 for bright colors, 2 for unity, and 3 for balance. A matrix can be constructed in which works scoring differently with respect to these three properties can be compared:

3,3,3
3,2,3–2,3,3
2,2,3–1,3,3
* 1,2,3 *
1,2,2–1,1,3
1,2,1–1,1,2
1,1,1

18. I am grateful to Luc Bovens for this example.

Works on the same level (connected by a dash) cannot be compared, says Dickie. (Like the *Water Lilies*/Mickey Mouse problem, this shows another serious limitation to Dickie's methodology.)

How well might this process work in landscape assessment? Suppose our task is to evaluate a stretch of forest along a river in order to determine where to build a bridge. Suppose we determine that the scenic value of the area is owing to the thick growth of many species of trees found there during the growing season. We want to choose the site where a bridge will have the least negative impact on scenic (aesthetic) values. Choose a particular point along the river and score it on a three-point scale with respect to variety of trees, density (number) of trees, and pleasing color of foliage during the summer months. If we get a 1,2,3 score we can, using Dickie's method, construct the necessary matrix. Any point along the river whose score is at a position on the matrix below 1,2,3 will be a better place to build the bridge than the point first assessed. Clearly the place that gets a 3,3,3 will be the best construction site.

So far, so good. Numerical scores are assigned via a "greater-than/lesser-than" method, both for works of art and for landscape sites. Dickie acknowledges that we may need, say, a five-point scale for adequate assessment of some properties, whereas a three-point scale will suffice for others. In a parenthetical remark he says that these are ordinal scales only, not cardinal—that is, a score of 3 is not necessarily three times better than a score of 1.[19] But restriction to ordinality creates serious problems—both for art and landscapes. In fact, I believe it is impossible to account for ranking without considering cardinality. As soon as one begins to think in terms of "greater-than/lesser-than," quantity, not just order, matters. "Has more value" implies cardinal as well as ordinal location within a grid or matrix. Having once settled that *Huckleberry Finn* has more value than *Tom Sawyer,* it makes sense to ask where one should put *Life on the Mississippi.* As soon as we begin to worry about whether it should go closer to *Huck* or to *Tom,* cardinality enters. Like deciding whether a student deserves an A-minus or a B-plus, we immediately begin to think in terms of one-half or twice as good. And thus the claim that we have a strictly ordinal ranking is proven wrong.

If the number of trees and color of foliage are weighted less strongly than the variety of trees, then a 2,1,1 score would not necessarily be ranked higher than a 1,3,2 score. All independently valuable properties do not have

19. Dickie, *Evaluating Art,* p. 172.

the same weight, either in landscapes or artworks. Color may be more important than unity in some works, unity more important than color in others. But quantifying how much more—which is required if the determination of relative value by position in a matrix is to be preserved—is very difficult. In fact, in some of the environmental studies I have read, where this sort of quantification is attempted, the results are often absurd. And I expect that the same difficulties would attend cardinal assignments in works of art. Even if one were able to say that in a particular landscape (the painting or the real thing) color is three times more important than unity, it is unlikely that it would matter in the same proportion in other colored and unified landscapes.

What Dickie is surely right about, I believe, is that many things are valued in aesthetic objects. Incidentally, I am not as convinced as he is that there are any "standard" features—and I do not think that his system requires them. At most, as Lycan and Machamer argue, there are some terms which name features and at the same time play an evaluative role.[20] "Beauty" is one of these; "symmetry" is not (or is less so). "I don't like beauty" is much odder than "I don't like symmetry." And perhaps because "unity" is more like "beauty" in this respect, it is picked out as *standard* by Dickie (and others). Still, this quibble aside, in attempting to describe what critics do when they evaluate, Dickie is right, I think, that a variety of things are positively and negatively influential. Even a cursory investigation of discussions of such critical favorites as *Hamlet* or the ceiling of the Sistine Chapel or Mozart's Symphony no. 39 shows this.

What I am not so clear about is the role of *ranking* itself in criticism. Why does Dickie think this is such a crucial component of evaluation? It is true that critics use comparatives and superlatives. In order for a critic to assert that a recent release is "one of the year's ten best," something like ranking does seem to be required. Reviewers of the arts obviously engage in ranking when they make recommendations about when and where we should spend our time and money. But how much of what critics do is this sort of thing? Or, when they do it, how important a role does it play? Are not critics more often engaged, as Arnold Isenberg and others have said, in pointing to characteristics of particular works—comparing them to others—in order to draw attention to special properties rather than in order to rank them per se?[21]

20. William C. Lycan and Peter K. Machamer, "A Theory of Critical Reasons," in *Language and Aesthetics,* ed. B. R. Tilghman (Lawrence: University Press of Kansas, 1973), pp. 87–112.

21. Arnold Isenberg, "Critical Communication," *Philosophical Review* 58 (1949): 330–44.

In the area of landscape assessment there is a vital role for ranking. Decisions about where to build bridges, which regions to preserve in their natural state, and so on usually do require explicit ranking. A problem in this realm that creates serious difficulties for landscape planners and managers may also be a problem for the evaluation of artworks. If it is, that will tell us something about the strength of Dickie's proposal. If it is not, it may point to important and distinctive characteristics of artistic evaluation.

The problem is that of the aggregation of preferences: How do we go from individuals' rankings to a single aggregate ranking? (This is sometimes referred to as the search for a social welfare function.) In the case of environmental aesthetic decisions, it is obvious that such aggregations are necessary. Though there seem to be areas of general agreement (everyone seems to like water and trees), there are dramatic disagreements about which properties are pleasing. Some studies, for example, show that power lines are not universally disvalued—some rural dwellers think their shape and size improves otherwise unobstructed, "boring" views. Industrial tycoons in Ayn Rand's *Atlas Shrugged,* I am told, also love to see power lines when they drive through the countryside. Whether one considers only the preferences of experts or people of established taste and sensitivity or is more democratic (consults all the people or all the people who will be most affected by a particular decision), it is still rarely the case that a single individual's rankings settle choices of construction sites, land preserves, and so forth.

Suppose that each of several individuals has his or her own Dickie matrix for spots along a river ranked in terms of unity, color, and variety. How do we get to an overall group matrix?

The most common way in our culture to get from many individual preference rankings to a single aggregate ranking is via voting. This, in fact, is the way that some public aesthetic environmental decisions are made. Commissions or city councils or entire local populations vote to determine, for instance, where along a river stretch a bridge should be built. Obviously such elections are never purely aesthetic—that is, factors other than the aesthetic enter. But though in actuality a variety of considerations are enmeshed, for our purpose we can imagine a purely aesthetic plebiscite. Even granting this, however, voting procedures are notoriously problematic.[22] Often they

22. For an excellent discussion of problems with voting, see Iain McClean, *Public Choice* (Oxford: Basil Blackwell, 1987); in what follows I am greatly indebted to the clarity of his remarks. I am also grateful to Luc Bovens, who, in private conversation, has helped me to understand Arrow's theorem and other issues relating to rational choice.

result in decisions that are clearly irrational or obviously unfair. Or they result in choices that fail intuitively to reflect a group's actual preferences.

In Condorcet voting, for example, the best outcome is that which no other outcome could defeat in a straight, "one-on-one" vote—that is, a vote in which each option is viewed with respect to only one of the other options at a time. Borda votes (where overall ranking is determined by taking the number of voters, *n*, and assigning a score of $n-1$ to each individual's first choice, $n-2$ to the second choice, down to 0 for the last choice) put a higher premium on ensuring that an outcome will have the highest ranking overall. Typically where there are more than two options, it is not possible for both a Condorcet and a Borda criterion to be fulfilled. Consider this example in which eleven voters rank four options.[23]

Number of Voters	3	3	3	2
Ranking	b	b	a	a
	a	a	c	d
	c	d	d	c
	d	c	b	b

Borda outcome: a gets 27, b gets 18, c gets 11, d gets 10; a wins.
Condorcet outcome: though a can win against c and d, b can win ("one-on-one") against a, c, and d; b is the winner.

Depending on which voting procedure is applied, two different river sites will be chosen—neither capturing the genuine will of the people perhaps.

Currently the most widely discussed aggregation problem is that raised by Kenneth Arrow.[24] According to Arrow's theorem, there is no way (via voting or otherwise) to get from individual rankings to a social ranking that satisfies certain apparently reasonable and unrestrictive conditions—conditions that seem necessary for the existence of democratic systems. He gives these four conditions:

U: Universal or unrestricted scope: no matter how many people present rankings and no matter how they rank the same options, the aggregation function should work.

P: Pareto principle: when every individual prefers x to y, the aggregation principle must also do so.

23. This is an example of Lewis Carroll's quoted in McClean, *Public Choice.*

24. See, for example, Kenneth Arrow, *Social Choice and Individual Values* (New York: John Wiley, 1951; 2nd ed., 1963).

D: Nondictatorship: no single individual's preferences should automatically determine the final outcome.

I: Independence from irrelevant alternatives: the aggregation function will take into account only the set of alternatives used by the rankers.

Arrow proves (though not without controversy) that one or more of these principles always breaks down as we go from the preferences of many to a single ranking. For instance, many procedures result in a ranking that either defies the Pareto principle or makes the rankings of a single individual the winner, thus creating a dictator. Or outcomes are irrational. Consider:

Number of Voters	1	1	1
Ranking	y	x	w
	x	w	z
	w	z	y
	z	y	x

x is preferred to w (2 votes to 1); y is preferred to x (2–1); z is preferred to y (2–1). So if transitivity of preferences is to hold, as it must if a procedure is rational, z should be the winner. But all the votes prefer w to z, so Pareto is flouted.

It is clear, I think, that a great deal of work remains to be done before Dickie's ranking method can get us to a public aesthetic policy. But, it may be objected, who cares? Specifically, should Dickie care? Even if it is true that some political, social, and economic bureaucracies require democratic strategies for aggregation of landscape preferences, surely Dickie is under no obligation to worry about this, it might well be argued. His is an attempt to provide a formal analysis of qualified individual rankings of artworks, no more, no less. To criticize him for doing less is surely unfair.

I agree that it is unfair if this is really all Dickie wants to do. But the significance of his analysis is surely more profound if its implications are wider. Explaining how individual ranking works will really matter, I think, if it can be shown that the activity itself really matters. In other words, why do we as individuals rank artworks at all? My hunch is that we would not bother with ranking them if there were no social implications. Two social activities and their associated institutions, practices, and rituals do make rankings meaningful: public artistic assessment and art criticism.

There certainly are public evaluations of art: funding decisions, public museum purchases, choices about sculptures for public spaces, and so on.

Even if we restrict the "rankers" to persons recognized as qualified or competent judges, there is notorious lack of agreement with regard to these matters. What aggregation functions might we use for committees of disagreeing experts? I do not see how Dickie's analysis sheds light on this social problem.

Does individual ranking (and hence the explanation of it) derive significance from being part of the social activity known loosely as "art criticism"? This activity rarely amounts to a simple statement of individual preference. If it did, then saying that *Hamlet* is good (or has some value) would be like saying that oysters taste good (or have some taste value). Even some subjectivist theories of aesthetic value (like Kant's) reflect a drive to universalize artistic judgments. Undoubtedly some critics assume confidently that their own individual preferences should settle questions about which works have value. But others attempt to universalize—they imply that their preferences will be shared by others. Voting may be obviously inappropriate, but are all aggregation procedures totally irrelevant? Do critics ever consider the rankings of others in arriving at their own judgments? If they do, Arrow's warning that no procedure is guaranteed to get us from the many to the one again may be relevant to the evaluation of art. At the very least, Dickie's analysis will be more important if he shows what role individual ranking plays in the collective aspects of criticism. How, for example, is it related to what I have suggested is the more central function of criticism: namely, drawing attention to certain properties of works of art? If Dickie hopes to explain evaluation of art because it is a core function of art criticism, then more than individual matrices must be provided. Problems of aggregation make it very difficult to go from individual to group rankings. What is needed is a social matrix. If Dickie could prove that there are standard properties collectively valued, then perhaps he could provide a basis for arriving at group matrices.

Dickie's correct claim that art's value arises from a variety of factors provides a much more adequate account of the reasons that cultures take art to be important than any single-valued theory. The "matrix procedure" may be an important first step for explaining how some rankings escape the charge that all evaluation is relativistic. But the necessity of restricting the construction of matrices to those cases where the relevant features are agreed upon and equally weighted results in a method that will have, I fear, very narrow application even within the artworld. The complexity of human aesthetic valuings which Dickie so clearly portrays acts against the discovery of a simple decision procedure for determining which things are best.

3

RECONSIDERING THE HISTORY OF AESTHETICS

Peter Kivy

From Literature as Imagination to Literature as Memory: A Historical Sketch

We are currently experiencing an extended revival of interest in aesthetics and the philosophy of art that is still at full tide. It began in the 1960s with the work of Monroe Beardsley, Arthur Danto, and Nelson Goodman, to name just a few of the principal movers; and it was given added impetus, early on, by George Dickie, first in his influential criticism of "aesthetic attitude" theories and later in his much-discussed institutional theory of art.

It is no accident that the aesthetic revival led also to a renewed interest in "roots" and, furthermore, no accident that the historical period most thoroughly canvassed in this revival was the Enlightenment. For, like others who thought of themselves as "analytic" philosophers in an empirical tradition, philosophers of art naturally saw Locke, Berkeley, Hume, Kant, and the rest as their spiritual forebears. Add to this the fact that the philosophical study of the arts, as an autonomous branch of philosophy, was given both its

I am most grateful to Robert Yanal for his careful reading of an earlier version of the present essay and for a number of helpful suggestions leading to its improvement.

subject matter as well as its very name in the early modern period, and it seems quite inevitable that the aesthetic revival of the sixties should have looked to the Enlightenment for its historical sources.

Dickie, too, has been drawn to the study of eighteenth-century aesthetics; and, like many others, he has been particularly (though not solely) concerned with the concept of "aesthetic disinterestedness"—not surprising, given his early critique of modern "aesthetic attitude" theories. It is in the spirit of this concern of Dickie's that the present essay is offered.

But, I must add, it is to *other* aesthetic doctrines of the Enlightenment that I will turn here. Nevertheless, as I will suggest at the very end, the topic of "aesthetic disinterestedness" is far from irrelevant to my topic and (hence) to Dickie's own work in Enlightenment philosophies of art and beauty.

1

In the second book of the *Advancement of Learning* (1605), Francis Bacon parceled out the disciplines of history, poetry, and philosophy, respectively, to the faculties of memory, imagination, and reason. He then went on to define poetry in the following way:

> Poesie is a part of Learning in measure of words for the most part restrained, but in all other points extremely licensed, and doth truly referre to the Imagination, which, being not tyed to the Lawes of Matter, may at pleasure ioyne that which Nature hath seuered, & seuer that which Nature hath ioyned, and so make vnlawfull Matches and diuorses of things.[1]

Some two hundred years later, in the preface to the *Lyrical Ballads,* William Wordsworth gave another definition of poetry—by far the more quoted one—to the effect that poetry "takes its origin from emotion recollected in tranquillity."[2]

At the risk of putting more weight on these utterances than, perhaps, they were ever meant to bear, I will call Bacon's view the theory of "literature as constructive imagination," and Wordsworth's I will call the theory of

1. In *Critical Essays of the Seventeenth Century,* ed. J. E. Spingarn (London: Oxford University Press, 1957), 1:4–5.

2. William Wordsworth, preface to the *Lyrical Ballads* (version of 1802).

"literature as imaginative memory." My argument will be that the route from Bacon to Wordsworth in this regard was, at least in part, traveled because of crucial changes in the philosophical concepts of memory and imagination, wrought during the eighteenth century: changes which turned imagination of the kind Bacon had in mind from a faculty seemingly well suited to house the literary impulse into a faculty quite alien to it; and, conversely, changes which transformed the seventeenth-century concept of memory, a philosophically barren one, into one capable of bearing literary fruit. My argument is admittedly a broad one, and it runs roughshod over all sorts of nice distinctions. However, I suggest it merely as the most conjectural of working hypotheses and do not pretend I can here and now give it the kind of historical documentation that would be needed to make it anything more. I will, in other words, take advantage of my philosophical prerogative, which has, to appropriate a phrase from Bertrand Russell, all the advantages of theft over honest toil.

2

My argument, to begin with, is based on a belief—which I will not attempt to substantiate here—that seventeenth-and eighteenth-century writers shared with each other (and with us) two basic premises about literature: first, that literature is "creative" and, second, that creation is a paradigm case of activity—that is to say, creating is something you *do*, not something that happens to you.

If I am allowed to impute these two implicit premises to the seventeenth- and eighteenth-century writers with whom I shall be dealing, then my argument will be that the imaginative theory of literature was supported in the seventeenth century by a view of the constructive imagination which construed it as active and, therefore, fulfilling a necessary condition for being creative; whereas the theory of literature as memory was not a real option because the philosophical analysis of memory—exemplified by Locke's chapter "Of Retention," in the *Essay Concerning Human Understanding*—was, quite simply, too philosophically unsatisfactory to bear any weight of theory at all. Conversely, the argument will be that during the eighteenth century, the kind of imaginative faculty which such writers as Bacon, Hobbes, and Dryden took to be the seat of poetry became more and more passive and deterministic, hence unacceptable as a faculty of literary creation; whereas the Lockean concept of memory was rejected, at least by some, for a more philosophically respectable one, thereby making it available as a literary faculty.

I will identify three stages in this road from literature as constructive imagination to literature as imaginative memory: first, the stage at which the imagination is active, the memory lacking a plausible account; second, the stage at which imagination congeals; and third, the stage at which memory receives at least an initially plausible treatment. That there are gaps in this historical schema I will not deny. Whether they can be filled in satisfactorily I leave an open question.

3

It takes no profound gift for textual interpretation to see what made the seventeenth-century concept of constructive imagination a suitable one for a theory of literature. The imagination was, for Bacon, a creator: not, to be sure, a creator in the Old Testament sense of someone who brings something into being from nothing, but rather more like the Platonic demiurge who builds anew from what already exists. Nevertheless, what the constructive imagination achieves is creation of the new and the novel, for it takes ideas that through perception we have found to go together, and pulls them apart; or joins together what we know, from experience, can never exist that way. So the imagination can make a unicorn by giving a horse what it cannot in nature have; or make an invisible man by taking from a man what in nature he must have. The imagination is forever the doer, the creator, that will not take things as they come, but must re-form them to its ends. "And therefore it is," Bacon says, that poetry, the child of imagination, "was euer thought to haue some participation of diuinesse, because it doth raise and erect the Minde, by submitting the shewes of things to the desires of the Mind, whereas reason doth buckle and bowe the Mind vnto the Nature of things."[3]

In a similar vein, Hobbes writes in 1650:

> For memory is the World (though not really, yet so as in a looking glass) in which the Judgment, the severer Sister, busieth her self in a

3. *Critical Essays,* 1:6.

> grave and rigid examination of all the parts of Nature, and in registering by Letters their order, causes, uses, differences, and resemblances; Whereby the Fancy [i.e., the imagination], when any work of Art is to be performed, finds her materials at hand and prepared for use, and needs no more than a swift motion over them, that what she wants, and is there to be had, may not lie too long unespied.[4]

For Hobbes, as for Bacon, the fancy (or imagination) takes what it is given by perception and memory, and freely reformulates it in the literary act. But although Hobbes, too, emphasizes the free activity of the imagination, he clearly is afraid that freedom will become licence. Thus, he writes, "There are some that are not pleased with fiction, unless it be bold, not only to exceed the *work,* but also the *possibility* of nature," and he warns against such excesses: "Beyond the actual works of nature a Poet may now go; but beyond the conceived possibility of nature, never."[5] Nevertheless, one can clearly make out in Bacon and Hobbes, despite such differences, both the theory of literature as constructive imagination and the active, creatively constructive concept of imagination they both shared, which made such a theory possible, under the assumptions that literature is creative, and creation a paradigm case of activity.

It is, of course, this kind of imagination—what I have been calling the "constructive imagination"—that Locke in part had in mind when he described that activity of the mind which he called "compounding" or "composition," whereby the mind "puts together" the simple ideas "it has received from Sensation and Reflection, and combines them into complex ones."[6] More important for our argument, it is to Locke that we turn for the inaugural account in the British empiricists of the concept of memory, an account, I have suggested, that essentially closed the door on the theory of literature as memory, thus reinforcing the already well-formulated theory of literature as constructive imagination. And to complete the first stage of our historical schema we must look briefly at that account.

In the tenth chapter of book II of the *Essay Concerning Human Understanding,* Locke isolates "The . . . Faculty of the Mind, whereby it makes a farther Progress towards Knowledge . . . which I call *Retention,* or the keeping of those simple *Ideas,* which from Sensation or Reflection it hath

4. Thomas Hobbes, answer to Davenant's preface to *Gondibert,* ibid., 2:59.

5. Ibid., 2:61–62.

6. John Locke, *An Essay Concerning Human Understanding,* ed. Peter H. Nidditch (Oxford: Clarendon Press, 1975), p. 158 (II.xi.6).

received. This is done," Locke continues, in "two ways. First, by keeping the *Idea,* which is brought into it, for some time actually in view, which is called *Contemplation.* The other way of Retention," Locke concludes,

> is the Power to revive again in our Minds those *Ideas,* which after imprinting have disappeared, or have been as it were laid aside out of Sight.... This is *Memory,* which is as it were the Store-house of our *Ideas.*[7]

Now Locke thought of remembering as occurring in two ways: 1) intentionally, as where I try to recall, say, what the formula is for the area of a circle and arrive at the (correct) conclusion that it is πr^2; or 2) unintentionally, as where something just pops into my head—say, the recollection of my first pitcher of legal beer in Ann Arbor. What we have, then, is a distinction between the active and the passive aspects of the memory:

> In... viewing again the *Ideas,* that are lodg'd *in* the *Memory, the Mind is oftentimes more than barely passive,* the appearance of those dormant Pictures, depending sometimes on the Will. The Mind very often sets it self on work in search of some hidden *Idea,* and turns, as it were, the Eye of the Soul upon it; though sometimes too they start up in our Minds of their own accord, and offer themselves to the Understanding; and very often are rouzed and tumbled out of their dark Cells, into open Day-light, by some turbulent and tempestuous Passion; our Affections bringing *Ideas* into our Memory, which had otherwise lain quiet and unregarded.[8]

As it stands, Locke's notion of memory seems unexceptionable (as well as uninteresting). The problem is that it is so out of phase with his own philosophy of mind as to render it, in context, something of a philosophical embarrassment.

The source of the difficulty lies at the very foundation of Locke's theory of knowledge and philosophy of mind: namely, his belief that, for ideas, *esse est percipi;* in other words, that the whole being of an idea lies in its being perceived and that the notion of an unperceived idea is an unintelligible one. For if that is the case, how can there be a "Store-house of our *Ideas,*" where they have been "as it were laid aside out of Sight"? With regard to

7. Ibid., pp. 149–50 (II.x.1–2).
8. Ibid., pp. 152–53 (II.x.7).

ideas, for Locke, out of sight is literally out of mind. *Retention,* if Locke is steady to his text, can only be of the first kind: that is, contemplation. If ideas cease to be when we cease to perceive (i.e., attend to) them, then there can be *retention* only where there is *attention.*

This difficulty in Locke's account of memory was perceived straightaway by one of his earliest critics, James Norris, in his *Cursory Reflections upon a Book Called an Essay Concerning Human Understanding* (1690). And to later editions of the *Essay* Locke added the following disclaimer:

> But our *Ideas* being nothing but actual perceptions in the Mind, which cease to be any thing, when there is no perception of them, this *laying up* of our *Ideas* in the Repository of the Memory, signifies no more but this, that the Mind has a Power, in many cases, to revive Perceptions, which it has once had, with this additional Perception annexed to them, that it has had them before. And it is in this Sense it is, that our *Ideas* are said to be in our Memories, when indeed, they are actually no where.[9]

It is pretty obvious, however, that this bit of patchwork is not going to be of much help. For one would think it is a *necessary* condition for being a memory that something actually have been experienced or perceived before. But now consider the following two possible interpretations of what Locke means by a perception that I have had some idea before. If he means merely that I have a conviction, no matter how strong, of having had the idea before, then that is consistent with my being mistaken, and with this not being a case of memory at all. So Locke must be using "perception" here in the strong epistemic sense, such that "S perceives that *p,*" only if *p.* In that case, I can perceive that I had some idea before only if I really did have the idea before. This would allow Locke's definition to fulfill the necessary condition for memory stated above. But then a further problem arises. For it is *not* a necessary condition for something's being a memory that it *be* accompanied by the conviction of its having been perceived or experienced before. It is quite possible to be remembering something without knowing that you are remembering it. I may be thinking of something, and yet not know whether it is imagined or remembered; but that does not mean it is not a memory, as Locke's account would seem to suggest. In any case, surely part (at least) of what we mean by remembering is recalling to attention what still exists in our minds but is not at the moment attended to; and on Locke's view there can be no such thing.

9. Ibid., p. 150 (II.x.2).

There is, then, no real philosophical basis at all for the concept of memory in Locke's *Essay*. And this, it must be emphasized, was the very best that empiricism could do for the concept of memory in the seventeenth century. It cannot be any wonder, then—and this is my argument here—that the memory provided no real option in the seventeenth and early eighteenth centuries for theory of literature, even if the time had been ripe; whereas the constructive imagination, active, creative, and seemingly well understood, provided the essential requirements for a literary faculty. Endorsed by tradition, "common sense," and contemporary philosophy of mind, it could not fail to be seen as the seat of literary inspiration.

4

How, then, did the constructive imagination lose its literary credentials? This is the second phase in my historical schema; and the story is easily and briefly told, for it will be a familiar one once the constructive imagination is seen in a slightly different light.

Suppose we ask the friends of the constructive imagination a few hard questions. To begin with: What made you, just now, think of a man made entirely of glass? The answer, let us suppose, is something like this: Nothing *made* me: I did it of my own free and active will; I just chose to join the idea of a man to the idea of glass, and the result was the idea of a man made entirely of glass—something which does not occur in nature but which can occur "in the imagination."

But we will not let our friend off the hook so easily. What do you mean, we ask, that you did it of your own "free will"? Does that amount to anything more than just the disguised admission that you don't *know* why just now you thought of a man made entirely of glass? You might just as well say that heavy bodies fall to earth "of their own free will," merely because you don't know *why* they fall to earth. Then along comes Newton and tells you why. As Spinoza says:

> [M]an is born ignorant of the causes of things.... From this it follows... that he thinks himself free because he is conscious of his wishes and appetites, whilst at the same time he is ignorant

> of the causes by which he is led to wish and desire, not dreaming what they are.[10]

I think you will have guessed, by now, what is coming down the pike. For if all that supports freedom of the imagination is the absence of psychological explanation, that support was removed, in the mid-eighteenth century, at least to the satisfaction of those who mattered, by the rise of the associationist psychology, with all its deterministic implications. I will not quote David Hartley in this regard, although he is, of course, the one most responsible for the enshrinement of the doctrine, but Hume instead, because he recognized so clearly the true significance of the doctrine for his contemporaries and summed it up so pithily in the *Enquiry Concerning Human Understanding.* "It is evident," Hume wrote,

> that there is a principle of connection between the different thoughts or ideas of the mind, and that, in their appearance to the memory or imagination, they introduce each other with a certain degree of method and regularity. In our more serious thinking or discourse this is so observable that any particular thought which breaks in upon the regular tract or chain of ideas is immediately remarked and rejected. And even in our wildest and most wandering reveries, nay, in our very dreams, we shall find, if we reflect, that the imagination ran not altogether at adventures, but there was still a connection upheld among the different ideas which succeeded each other. Were the loosest and freest conversation to be transcribed, there would immediately be observed something which connected it in all its transitions. . . . Among different languages, even when we cannot suspect the least connection or communication, it is found that the words expressive of ideas the most compounded do yet nearly correspond to each other—a certain proof that the simple ideas comprehended in the compound ones were bound together by some universal principle which had an equal influence on all mankind.[11]

The significance of Hume's statement is quite clear. What is being described is a strict psychological determinism in which every sequence of ideas, no matter how seemingly fortuitous, or "willful," is governed by psychological

10. Appendix to pt. 1 of the *Ethics,* ed. James Gutmann (New York: Hafner, 1949), pp. 72–73.
11. David Hume, *An Enquiry Concerning Human Understanding,* sec. 3, "Of the Association of Ideas" (opening paragraph).

"laws" that give evidence (if one is not a Humean) of underlying psychological "causes." On such a view, the constructive imagination must lose all pretense of "freedom"; and its productions become, to appropriate Charles Darwin's phrase, just another secretion of the brain, no more the result of human activity than a runny nose. And with the evaporation of freedom, creativity also goes up the spout. One should no more be praised or admired for imagining a knight tilting windmills than for breaking out in hives. In this way, I suggest, the constructive imagination lost its literary credentials in the eighteenth century: not all at once, needless to say, but gradually, as the implications of psychological determinism became more and more apparent.

5

The story of the reconstitution of the memory—the final phase in my historical schema—is not so easily told. I am sure we are not to look only to the philosophers; and I strongly suspect that the novelists have a hand in it. What I want to do here—indeed, all I think I really can do—is to point to what I take to be a crucial breakthrough for the theory of literature as memory. For what associationist psychology took away from the faculty of constructive imagination—namely, its *freedom*—was bestowed on the memory, I shall argue, by Thomas Reid in his later work, not perhaps explicitly but certainly by implication.

I can take time now only to summarize Reid's position on memory, so that I can move on immediately to the relation of memory to freedom. For Reid, in brief, there can essentially be no "account" of memory. It is one of those faculties of mind which are innate. As Reid concludes at one point: "Our original faculties are all unaccountable. Of these memory is one. He only who made them, comprehends fully how they are made, and how they produce in us, not only a conception, but a firm belief and assurance of things which it concerns us to know."[12]

Now it is perfectly obvious that Reid has not really solved the problem that Locke's account of memory left in its wake. Rather, he has, in a sense, simply changed the subject: from "account" to "justification." Since the faculty of memory, like all the "original faculties," as Reid calls them, is

12. Thomas Reid, *Essays on the Intellectual Powers of Man,* ed. Baruch Brody (Cambridge: MIT Press, 1969), p. 332.

"unaccountable," what has been substituted for an account of memory is a *justification* of it—quite another matter, of course. But at least in a broad sense of "giving an account," Reid has, I suppose, given an "account" of memory in claiming that no account is possible in the way of laying bare the machinery, the faculty being simple and innate, with no "machinery" to lay bare and no justification possible, the memory being more certain than anything which might be brought forward in its rational support.

Thus baldly stated, out of the context of Reid's fully worked out theory of knowledge, this sounds like the most naive of attempts simply to assume what is at issue. But that is far from the truth of it. Reid's point, not by any means a trivial one, is something like the following. An argument always goes from the direction of the more certain to the direction of the less, with the object in view, of course, of transferring to the less certain conclusion whatever degree of certainty attaches to the premises. But if the certainty of a claim is as great as is possible in this life, then that claim can never sensibly serve as the conclusion of an argument, only as a premise; for as a conclusion it would defeat the purpose of argument, which is to go from the more certain to the less. And it is just Reid's contention that the evidence of memory is as strong as any other evidence we have. Hence, we cannot derive it from any evidence more certain: which is to say, we cannot argue for it. As Reid puts the case: "This belief, which we have from distinct memory, we account real knowledge no less certain than if it was grounded on demonstration; no man in his wits calls it in question, or will hear any arguments against it. The testimony of witnesses in causes of life and death depends upon it, and all the knowledge of mankind of past events is built on this foundation."[13]

The process which produces remembrance Reid divides, as had Locke, and as does common sense, into the active and the passive, making along the way some nice distinctions which, for lack of time, I will have to pass over. The active memory, "when we cast about and search for what we would remember, and so at last find it out," Reid calls "reminiscence," which therefore, he points out, "includes a will to recollect something past, and a search for it. But here," Reid continues, "a difficulty occurs." And what this difficulty turns out to be is something very much like the Socratic "paradox of inquiry." As Reid states the problem:

> what we will to remember we must conceive, as there can be no will without a conception of the thing willed. A will to remember a thing,

13. Ibid., p. 326.

> therefore, seems to imply that we remember it already, and have no occasion to search for it.

That is to say, in order to try to think of *X,* I must set *X* before my mind as what I am trying to think of, and then try to think of it. But if I *can* set *X* before my mind, then I *am* thinking of it—and there is no sense in trying to do that very thing. Reid answers:

> But this difficulty is easily removed. When we will to remember a thing, we must remember something relating to it, which gives us a relative conception of it; but we may, at the same time, have no conception of what the thing is, but only what relation it bears to something else.... By applying my thought to what I remember concerning it... I am led, in a train, to the very thing I had forgotten.[14]

So, for example, if I remember that you told me something while we were standing under the clock in Grand Central Station, but cannot remember what it was, I may picture to myself the scene in my mind's eye, and a train of associations will be started up which, it is to be hoped, will lead to the idea of what it was you told me.

I will not raise the question here of whether this is a successful resolution of Reid's Socratic paradox. Rather, I want to lay bare another, more relevant problem this use of the association of ideas raises for us: namely, that it puts the *memory* under the same cloud of psychological determinism which hovers over the concept of the constructive imagination—a conclusion already explicitly suggested in Hume's first *Enquiry.* For, we might well ask Reid, if what you imagine to yourself sets up a train of (we must assume) strictly determined ideas, why should we think that the imagining to yourself is any more a free act than any of the subsequent images in the train it sets up? Why should we not believe that what preceded it determined it to occur, just as it determined what was to follow? Hence, there would be no more freedom, no more "willing," in what Reid calls "reminiscence" than there would be in the passive memory or constructive imagination. All would be hostage to the association of ideas.

Now if we were to restrict ourselves to the work in which Reid's doctrine of the memory is put forth, and from which I have been quoting—that is, the *Essays on the Intellectual Powers of Man,* published in 1785—no answer to

14. Ibid., p. 381.

this charge of psychological determinism would be found. But two years later, in the *Essays on the Active Powers of the Human Mind* (1787), Reid gives a spirited and insightful defense of the freedom of the will: a defense which is still looked upon with respect by contemporary philosophers. And if Reid's account of the active memory in the *Essays on the Intellectual Powers* is read in the light of his defense of freedom of the will in the companion work, a theory of the freedom of the memory emerges which, I would suggest, makes the memory a very real option for literary theory.

What Reid espouses is a doctrine known as "agent causation." And to get right to the heart of the matter, I will not tease the doctrine out of Reid but, instead, will quote from a recent defense of his view by Roderick Chisolm. "We must not," Chisolm explains, "say that every event in the act is caused by some other event," for that, of course, would amount to strict determinism and denial of freedom; "and we must not," he continues, "say that the act is something that is not caused at all," for that would suggest that the act is capricious or accidental—the responsibility of no one. "The possibility that remains, therefore, is this," Chisolm concludes, giving a possibility which is essentially that envisaged by Reid:

> We should say that at least one of the events that are involved in the act is caused, not by any other events, but by something else instead. And this something else can only be the agent—the man. If there is an event that is caused not by other events, but by the man, then there are some events involved in the act that are not caused by other events. But if the event in question is caused by the man then it *is* caused and we are not committed to saying that there is something involved in the act that is not caused at all.[15]

With this penetrating statement of agent causation before us we can quickly comprehend Reid's conception of human freedom. Of our own abilities, as agents, to initiate acts, both mental and physical ones, we have, according to Reid, a direct awareness: "in certain motions of my body, and directions of my thought, I know not only that there must be a cause that has power to produce these effects, but that I am that cause; and I am conscious of what I do in order to the production of them."[16] In this (our

15. Roderick M. Chisolm, "Human Freedom and the Self," in *Freedom and Morality,* ed. John Bricke (Lawrence: University Press of Kansas, 1976), p. 27.

16. Thomas Reid, *Essays on the Active Powers of the Human Mind,* ed. Baruch Brody (Cambridge: MIT Press, 1969), p. 36.

active power as agents) lies our freedom. "Every man is led by nature to attribute to himself the free determinations of his will, and to believe those events to be in his power which depend upon his will."[17] And although motives influence our free acts of will, "the influence of motives is of a very different nature from that of efficient causes.... Motives, therefore, may *influence* to action, but they do not act. They may be compared to advice, or exhortation, which leaves a man still at liberty."[18]

If we return now to the problem of active memory, and apply the concept of agent causation to it, the problem dissolves. The chain of associations which *I* initiate, when I attempt to remember something, is indeed psychologically determined from beginning to end. But its *initiation* is a free act of mine: as we have seen, not only "motions of my body," but "directions of my thought" as well, are under my control. The chain of associations which I set up by my free causal agency is not itself uncaused: on the contrary, it is caused by *me.* But it is not caused by some other mental event, part of some other deterministic chain of associations; hence, psychological determinism is avoided. The active memory, though not inconsistent with the association of ideas, is no longer hostage to it. This concept of free and active memory, I suggest, is Reid's contribution to the theory of literature as memory. It provides for the active memory the necessary conditions of a literary faculty: freedom and (hence) creativity.

It might, perhaps, be objected here that it is not at all clear why creativity should require freedom. Indeed, there is a very old "theory" (if that is the right word for it) that suggests just the opposite. The ancient "theory" of "inspiration," after all, which finds its mature philosophical expression in Plato's *Ion,* suggests that far from being an act of "free will," the occurrence of original ideas is simply something that happens to you; and it does not much matter, I suppose, from the point of view of freedom, whether what happens to you is imposed by the gods or by antecedent natural causes, since *you* are not the agent-cause in either case. Indeed, if one school of thought in the seventeenth century (as represented by Descartes) had the constructive imagination as free, another school (represented by Hobbes and Spinoza) had it no less determined than did the eighteenth-century associationists (although Hobbes, as we have seen, saw it as "free" in another sense).

The point is well taken but, I think, beside the point as well, as regards what I am suggesting here. For what I maintain is a matter more of emphasis,

17. Ibid., p. 37.
18. Ibid., p. 283.

so to speak, not of hard doctrine. And the emphasis, in early modern as well as nineteenth-century aesthetics, is on the faculty of creation—whether the constructive imagination of the seventeenth century or the imaginative memory of Wordsworth—as free in some sense or other, with the analogy very much present of the freedom of the artist, vis-à-vis the creation of his work, to the freedom of the Divine Creator in the creation of His. And, after all, the latter is, for all but the Spinozists, the paradigm of "free cause" in the agent causality sense.

6

Let me press on now by answering, quickly, three possible objections.

It might be argued that philosophers are only just now in the process of rescuing Reid from obscurity; and that such a little-known philosopher, in the backwaters of the Scottish Enlightenment, could hardly have influenced the likes of Wordsworth. But the fact is, as is well known, that while Reid flourished, and for a hundred years after, he was far from being an obscure figure in the history of philosophy. On the contrary, his philosophy was well known, respected, and highly influential. Reid's obscurity is a recent phenomenon, not an eighteenth-century one.

But even granted that Reid enjoyed a considerable reputation in his time, surely it is a mistake to think that someone who was admired mainly for his epistemology and philosophy of mind, and who contributed little to aesthetics, criticism, or the philosophy of art, could have been a substantial force in the development of literary theory. Here again, however, we must recall Reid's situation in his own time. The Scottish Enlightenment, of which he was a leading light, was a crucible for important and influential movements in the theory of criticism and aesthetics. And although Reid did not produce extensive work in those areas,[19] his other philosophical ore was as much a part of that mix as were the aesthetic theories of Lord Kames, Alexander Gerard, or Archibald Alison.

Finally, and most important, it might be argued that Reid's version of

19. On Reid's contribution to aesthetics and the philosophy of art, see my *The Seventh Sense: A Study of Francis Hutcheson's Aesthetics and Its Influence in Eighteenth-Century Britain* (New York: Burt Franklin, 1976), chap. 9; "The Logic of Taste: Reid and the Second Fifty Years," in *Thomas Reid: Critical Interpretations,* ed. Stephen F. Barker and Tom L. Beauchamp (Philadelphia: Philosophical Monographs, 1976); and "Thomas Reid and the Expression Theory of Art," *The Monist* 61 (1978): 167–83.

agent causation can just as well restore freedom and (hence) the possibility of creativity to the imagination as it can bestow them on memory. For if a chain of ideas can be freely initiated in an effort to remember, it can also be freely initiated in what I have called the constructive imagination. So, the claim that a deterministic imagination and a free memory led to a theory of literature as recollection must fail.

This is, of course, altogether true. And *if* my claim were that the necessary and sufficient conditions for a theory of literature as recollection are a deterministic imagination and a free memory, and that those conditions obtained in the wake of Reid's philosophy of mind, then my claim would be defeated as surely as God made little apples. But my claim, as I hope was clear from the outset, is a much weaker one than that. Indeed, anyone who made such a strong claim, based on necessary and sufficient conditions in the history of ideas, or the history of anything else, for that matter, would be rash in the extreme and headed for inevitable disaster. What I *am* claiming is that at a time ripe for a theory of literature as imaginative memory—a time in which other factors, cultural, literary, aesthetic, and philosophical, were pushing literary theory in that direction—a theory of memory as free and (hence) potentially creative was, as it had not been before, an available addition to the vector of forces: not, of course, a sufficient condition, but certainly a necessary one.

7

I promised, at the outset, that I would at least suggest, in my conclusion, the relevance of "aesthetic disinterestedness" to my topic, thus closing the circle and, I hope, making legitimate the connection between what I have outlined here and Dickie's interest in the Enlightenment origins (if such they were) of the modern "aesthetic attitude." This can be accomplished quite simply by posing the following question: Given the historical fact that seventeenth-century theories of poetic imagination gave way, in the late eighteenth and early nineteenth century, to theories of the poetic memory, are we to see this historical process as being in step with the parallel development of the concept of "aesthetic disinterestedness"?

Well, we need only reconsider briefly Wordsworth's famous definition of poetry, which I take to be the culmination of the evolution from poetic imagination to poetic memory, to see that, far from being out of step with the doctrine of the "aesthetic attitude," it is indeed a special case of that very doctrine. For what else would it be for poetry to constitute "emotion recollected in tranquillity" than for it to be emotion recollected in the attitude of "aesthetic disinterestedness"? In fact, I imagine it is just that achievement of *tranquillity* toward our emotions, the tranquillity that divests them of "practical" significance and consequences, which the doctrine of "aesthetic disinterestedness," at least in some of its versions, was trying to formulate—not, of course, just as an attitude toward *emotions,* but as an attitude toward any "object" whatever of aesthetic contemplation and appreciation.

The emergence of *emotions* as a favored "object" of the "aesthetic attitude," and hence of aesthetic contemplation and appreciation, requires, to be sure, another whole story to tell—a story which involves, among other things, the rise of romanticism. That story, however, I do not propose to enter upon here.

Nevertheless, the story I have already told may well, for all I know now, be fiction rather than history. If so, I believe it is at least the kind of fiction of which Hobbes approved, namely the *possible* kind. I must leave for another occasion (or occasions) the details (if such there be) required to make it anything more than that.

Ted Cohen

Partial Enchantments of the *Quixote* Story in Hume's Essay on Taste

Hume's "Of the Standard of Taste," which appeared in 1757, brought the theory of taste closer to success than any other attempt before or after.... In his essay, Hume... finesses the difficulties of Hutcheson's less sophisticated theory and... avoids the obscure wrong-headedness of the third Critique.
—George Dickie, *The Century of Taste*

For more than thirty years George Dickie has pursued his clear, steady work in the philosophy of art and in the history of the philosophy of art. His earliest work was on Francis Hutcheson, and now, after many years spent formulating his own views, Dickie has turned again to the eighteenth century. My own earliest work concerned the institutional theory of art, inspired by Dickie's work; and now, after my own years spent working on Kant's aesthetics, I find myself again following Dickie. Dickie has decided that Kant represents not the profundity usually attributed to him, nor any depth greater than Hume's, but a descent into obscurity. I am not yet quite ready to second that assessment, but I am now fully persuaded that Hume's essay is a treasure and that its riches are lost in Kant. This essay is an

I first presented this material as the Gail Stine Memorial Lecture at Wayne State University in February 1992. It was an honor and my personal pleasure to be able to speak as a memorial to my friend Professor Stine. It is a further satisfaction now to have this work permanently in print, especially in a volume edited by Professor Stine's colleague, Professor Yanal.

attempt to expose some of the wonders awaiting those who will dig into Hume's essay on taste.

One of the most engaging passages in Hume's essay is also the most intractable section in the piece. Hume says this:

> And not to draw our philosophy from too profound a source, we shall have recourse to a noted story in DON QUIXOTE.
>
> It is with good reason, says SANCHO to the squire with the great nose, that I pretend to have a judgment in wine: This is a quality hereditary in our family. Two of my kinsmen were once called to give their opinion of a hogshead, which was supposed to be excellent, being old and of a good vintage. One of them tastes it; considers it; and after mature reflection pronounces the wine to be good, were it not for a small taste of leather, which he perceived in it. The other, after using the same precautions, gives also his verdict in favour of the wine; but with the reserve of a taste of iron, which he could easily distinguish. You cannot imagine how much they were both ridiculed for their judgment. But who laughed in the end? On emptying the hogshead, there was found at the bottom, an old key with a leathern thong tied to it. [pp. 234–35][1]

And then Hume goes on to explain the point of this story:

> The great resemblance between mental and bodily taste will easily teach us to apply this story. [p. 235]

In fact it seems to me impossible to find a compelling, consistent application of the story. The only explicit clue Hume gives is this:

> Where the organs are so fine, as to allow nothing to escape them; and at the same time so exact as to perceive every ingredient in the composition: This we call delicacy of taste, whether we employ these terms in the literal or metaphorical sense. Here then the general rules of beauty are of use; being drawn from established

1. All references to Hume's essay are to David Hume, *Essays Moral, Political, and Literary* (Indianapolis: Liberty Classics, 1985).

> models, and from the observation of what pleases or displeases, when presented singly and in a high degree: And if the same qualities, in a continued composition and in a smaller degree, affect not the organs with a sensible delight or uneasiness, we exclude the person from all pretensions to this delicacy. To produce these general rules or avowed patterns of composition is like finding the key with the leathern thong; which justified the verdict of SANCHO'S kinsmen, and confounded those pretended judges who had condemned them. Though the hogshead had never been emptied, the taste of the one was still equally delicate, and that of the other equally dull and languid: But it would have been more difficult to have proved the superiority of the former, to the conviction of every by-stander. [pp. 235–36]

Hume says that finding certain rules of composition is like finding the key with the leathern thong, and I am embarrassed to say that I tried for a very long time before I could find even one respect in which finding such a rule might be like finding the key and thong. I will tell you what I found presently. First I will lay out what seems to be an outline of Hume's theory of taste.

It is clear that this essay is meant to be support for Hume's assertion that there is what he calls "a standard of taste." Nothing else is this clear, not even what a standard of taste is, or would be. Hume introduces the idea in this sentence:

> It is natural for us to seek a *Standard of Taste;* a rule, by which the various sentiments of men may be reconciled; at least, a decision, afforded, confirming one sentiment, and condemning another. [p. 229]

It is difficult to reconcile this remark with other things Hume says about the standard of taste, but the remark itself, already, is problematic. The standard is, he says, a rule. What does this rule do? What is it used for? He says that it may reconcile conflicting sentiments, but he also says it may simply afford a decision which confirms one of the conflicting sentiments and condemns another. Is this confirmation/condemnation a kind of reconciliation, or is it something done with the rule when reconciliation cannot be achieved?

Before I expose the other difficulty, the one encountered when this description of the standard is compared with another, let me set out the outline.

Beauty, according to Hume, is not a quality of objects. It is, rather, a feeling inspired in a person by the object. It is, thus, what Hume calls "a sentiment." Specifically, the sentiment is a feeling of pleasure. To the extent that one single object inspires pleasure in you but not in me, you will find the object beautiful and I will not; and to that extent, neither of us is right or wrong. Sentiments in themselves are not right or wrong, true or false, and it is simply a fact that the object produces pleasure in you but not in me.

Hume's extrication from this seeming impasse is by way of a version of what I call "ideal creature" theories. The leading idea is this: although it is true that the object pleases some of us and not others, it remains to determine *whose* feeling is fit to count as a standard. That is, if the object pleases you but not me, and that is all there is to it, then neither of us is right or wrong; but if you are a certain kind of person, then the feeling inspired in you is, in a sense, the proper and correct response, and I am deficient in having a different response.

As always with ideal creature theories, the problem then is to specify what it is to be the kind of person whose responses are norms. In his moral philosophy Hume calls such creatures "impartial spectators." He has no comparable term in the essay on taste, but he uses the term "true judge" and I will appropriate it in his name. Hume's problem is to tell us what makes someone a true judge.

His solution is to stipulate five characteristics a person must possess in order to be a true judge: a true judge must have delicacy of taste, must have strong sense, must be unprejudiced, and must have experience of practicing with the relevant kind of object and comparing such objects with one another. The formal success of Hume's solution depends upon his being able to say what a true judge is without therein supposing that he could say what beauty is. The project is to move from questions about putative objects of beauty to questions about the qualifications of auditors; if the putative auditors were tested against objects of beauty, the theory would be circular.

Hume sees the issue with great clarity. He says:

> But where are such critics to be found? By what marks are they to be known? How distinguish them from pretenders? These questions are embarrassing; and seem to throw us back into the same uncertainty,

> from which, during the course of this essay, we have endeavoured to extricate ourselves.
>
> But if we consider the matter aright, these are questions of fact, not of sentiment. [pp. 241–42]

Hume's claim is that the question "Is the object beautiful?" is a question of sentiment, as he calls it, while the question "Is the person a true judge?" is a question of fact. To make his point he will have to persuade readers that it is indeed a question of fact, a tractable empirical question, whether someone is a true judge, and this means being able to establish as an empirical proposition that someone has delicacy of taste, strong sense, lack of prejudice, and the rest. Accordingly Hume undertakes to show that this can be done, discussing each of the five characteristics separately, attempting to show of each both (1) that the characteristic is indeed a constituent trait in a true judge and (2) that the characteristic can be identified in empirical investigation.

All of this will be familiar to you, as will the fact that the *Don Quixote* story is related as part of Hume's treatment of delicacy of taste. It is troublesome enough to have to understand the story in that respect, and it is yet a greater bother to realize that Hume actually treats Sancho's kinsmen not only as exemplars of delicacy of taste but, in fact, as complete "true judges." I am just about ready to introduce you to the exquisite difficulties in understanding the story, but I make one last detour in order to complicate the question of what Hume thinks the standard of taste is; that is, what kind of thing he supposes it to be. Immediately before he faces up to the question of circularity, Hume says this:

> hence a true judge in the finer arts is observed, even during the most polished ages, to be so rare a character: Strong sense, united to delicate sentiment, improved by practice, perfected by comparison, and cleared of all prejudice, can alone entitle critics to this valuable character; and the joint verdict of such, wherever they are to be found, is the true standard of taste and beauty. [p. 241]

You recall that Hume began by saying that a standard of taste is a rule. Now he tells us that it is the joint verdict of true judges.[2] Does he think

2. To my knowledge, the first clear articulation of the problem set by Hume's two descriptions of the standard was given by Jeffrey Wieand in his exceptionally useful "Hume's Two Standards of Taste,"

this joint verdict is a rule? Perhaps, but I think he should not. I will be saying later that I think Hume's theory is strongest if all he requires of the true judges is their *feelings.* For now, let us look into this rule business. What kind of rule would this be, a rule that could function as a standard of taste? The best guess, I think, is that it would be a causal law (Humean, of course), linking certain properties of the object—properties that really are in the object—with certain feelings, sentiments that occur in an observer. The form of such a rule would be just this: Property *P* causes feeling *F.*

Now in the case we imagine, the one in which the object pleases you but not me, the rule shows us that if property *P* is present in the object, then in fact it *should* lead to the feeling of pleasure, and so you are right and I am wrong. How do we discover that property *P* is present; and, in particular, how do you persuade me of that, so that I might regret my failure to be affected by *P?* Ah yes, that is one good question. Before we take it up, let me, finally, get the *Don Quixote* story into this. When he tells the story, Hume plainly is thinking of the standard as a rule: he says that finding the key and thong is like finding what he calls "a rule of composition."

Let us get back to the wonderful story about Sancho.

The first question: Exactly why does the discovery of the key and thong have its effect upon the townspeople? How does this work? Surely the first point is this: the discovery of the foreign objects persuades the townspeople that the wine really does embody the tastes of iron and leather; and this leads them to suppose that the wine was having, we might say, its proper effect upon Sancho's kinsmen, though not upon anyone else. So far this fits the "*P* causes *F*" model.

But does it? The finding of the key plus thong cannot be the occasion for learning "*P* causes *F,*" because unless the townspeople *already believe* that *P* causes *F,* the discovery of the foreign objects in the wine will have no force. That is, unless they believe that a key and thong cause tastes of iron and leather, the finding of the key and thong will not vindicate Sancho's kinsmen. What the townspeople are compelled to believe, upon discovery of the key and thong, is not some rule of composition, but that a rule *they already know* applies in the case at hand. This seems the most natural way to understand the force of the story, despite Hume's own indication of what the force is.

Then is Hume simply wrong when he says that finding the key is like finding a general rule? Perhaps not, or not quite. He says that finding the

---

Philosophical Quarterly 34 (1983): 129–42. The most resourceful and subtle attempt to reconcile the two descriptions is James Shelley's "Hume's Double Standard of Taste," presented at the 1992 meeting of the Hume Society and not yet published.

key is like "[producing] these general rules or avowed patterns of composition." By "avowed" perhaps he means something already known and accepted, which suggests that what has been found is indeed like the key: namely, what has been found is that the (avowed) rule has application in this case.

There is a pervasive unclarity in Hume's essay as to just what it is the "true judge" does. Does he present us with a rule, or does he show us that a known rule is relevant in the case at hand? The *Don Quixote* story is offered, explicitly, as an illustration of delicacy of taste, and that talent is described by Hume as the ability to detect subtle ingredients; and that is exactly what Sancho's kinsmen prove able to do. And yet the story also seems to illustrate the capacities of a true judge, someone who possesses not only delicacy of taste but the other four characteristics as well, and it is, after all, only a complete true judge who can be used as a standard.

Notice how subtly the story illustrates a Humean true judge. First, there is the held-over question: Exactly how is it that finding the key is like discovering a standard? Well, in just this blunt way: it *settles* things. Hume said near the outset that a standard of taste, if there were one, would be something whereby "the various sentiments of men may be reconciled; at least, a decision, afforded, confirming one sentiment, and condemning another." I have said that it is not clear how reconciliation is related to confirming-and-condemning; but in the *Don Quixote* story we have everything. There are three sentiments. One kinsman tastes iron, one kinsman tastes leather, and, we may suppose, one of the townsmen tastes neither. The discovery of the key and thong *explains* the discrepancy exhibited by Sancho's relatives: because both a key and a thong were there, the wine contained faint trace tastes of both iron and leather. This is reconciliation. And both kinsmen's sentiments are at least partially confirmed, while the dull and languid townspeople, as Hume calls them, have theirs condemned.

And yet another thing. Hume tells us that what we require is not just one true judge, but a multiplicity. He says, with regard to true judges, that "the joint verdict of such . . . is the true standard of taste and beauty." In the *Don Quixote* story we have an exhibition of the utility in having not just one kinsman. There is another, more interesting reason for requiring a multiplicity of judges, and I will get to that as soon as I have finished the little bit of unpacking left to do.

When Hume discusses delicacy of taste, as when he discusses the other four characteristics, his logical goal is to show that the possession of this characteristic may be discovered as an empirical matter, a "matter of fact," as he calls it. In the *Don Quixote* story, the proposition that the kinsmen have delicate taste is confirmed by the discovery of the key and thong. But it is easy to imagine testing wine tasters, given the example of Sancho's relatives. You pretend to delicacy. We put you to the test. We pour out, say, a quart of wine, and we put a large iron key and a pliable, foot-long leather thong into the container along with the wine, and we let the whole thing sit for a week or so. Then we remove the key and thong and ask you to sip the wine and to report. You pass the test. Then we try again—this time, say, with two quarts of wine, a smaller key, and a short shoelace, the whole mixture left standing for only a few hours. What Hume is banking on is this: if you pass all these tests, then one day you imbibe from a huge container (perhaps a hogshead, as in Hume's version of the *Quixote* story) and tell us that the wine tastes of leather and iron, we will be inclined to take your word for it even if nothing but wine is found when the container is emptied.

And, finally, what might be called "the rhetorical point" of the story. No doubt in the future the townspeople will take the kinsmen's word for it when it comes to pronouncing on otherwise undetected flavors in wine; but they will also defer to the kinsmen in estimations of the quality of the wine. Recall the story: "One of them tastes it; considers it; and after mature reflection pronounces the wine to be good, were it not for a small taste of leather, which he perceived in it." In this fillip Hume departs from Cervantes. In the original, Sancho's kinsmen say nothing whatever about how good the wine is. But Hume's Spaniard does, and the point is clear: the discovery of the thong vindicates this man's sense of leather, and it also is meant to vindicate his pronouncements on the goodness of the wine. Those with a keen eye for some fact/value distinction may balk at this second vindication, but we should recall that it was no one if not David Hume who told us to take note of such distinctions.

What do you think? If one person has greater delicacy of taste—in this sense, a greater ability to detect ingredients—are you likelier to defer to his estimates of the quality of a work? Let us have an example. Suppose you think Hitchcock's *North by Northwest* is a wonderful movie, but I am not very fond of it. Suppose, that is, exactly in Hume's terms, that the movie inspires the sentiment of beauty (a feeling) in you but not in me. Suppose that my comprehension of the movie is feeble, and I do not follow you when you cite the movie's external references to *Hamlet,* or its internal connections between the faces atop Mount Rushmore, Cary Grant's lathered face, and the Cary Grant figure when it appears headless, with no face at all. You subscribe to a judgment—that *North by Northwest* is a comparison of faces, animate and inanimate, exposed and covered, authentic and fraudulent—

and I do not. If these descriptions of yours are accurate (and surely they are), then does your greater acuity in being able to give them lend support to your estimate of the movie and give it a preference over mine? Hume thinks so. I think he is right. Can we explain the logic of this connection between delicacy of taste and a greater authority in estimating?

Finally, a word about Hume's requirement of a *joint* verdict. Hume's moral theory is much better known than his theory of taste, and I am sure you know that in his moral theory Hume explains the difference between virtue and vice in terms of the feelings of an "impartial spectator." In this regard, his moral theory is formally the same as his theory of taste. He regards the relevant judgments as being, essentially, a matter of feeling, and not, in the first instance, an identification of external properties. He avoids the threatened relativism by insisting on the priority of those feelings arising in peculiarly qualified judges. The difference is that in the moral theory he refers to the feelings of only an individual person, one impartial spectator; while in the theory of taste he says that the standard of taste is the joint verdict of judges, thereby requiring more than one. Why this difference? I believe that Hume (probably) had two related things in mind.

(1) He supposes that everyone can, at least potentially, and given appropriate circumstances, convert himself into an impartial spectator, and thus he is telling us how each of us does in fact make moral judgments. Not only can we not all convert ourselves into true judges on the spot, or soon after, but Hume believes that such judges can be very hard to come by. He says:

> Under some or other of these imperfections [the absence of some of the five requisite characteristics], the generality of men labour; and hence a true judge in the finer arts is observed, even during the most polished ages, to be so rare a character. [p. 241]

When you need a true judge, therefore, you will almost certainly have to look for one (not being one yourself), and it is prudent to collect as many as you can, to compensate for the fact that with each of them there is only a probability that you have actually found one.

(2) It is possible to construe the true judge to be an idealized figure; and if so, then the only good way to discover how one would react is to assemble a multiplicity of near-true judges in an effort to find their asymptotic consensus. This is, perhaps, the most natural way to read the *Quixote* story if we

suppose Sancho's kinsmen to stand not only for the possession of delicacy of taste but for true-as-possible judges.

I think that (1) is Hume's main reason, for I do not think Hume regards the true judge as an idealization; but (1) and (2) are alike in implying the need for many true judges. Let me suggest another reason for requiring a multiplicity of judges, a reason probably not explicitly in Hume's mind, but one which his theory presciently provides for. Not every case in which an object pleases you but not me is a case in which one of us is exhibiting superior taste. Perhaps our tastes are just *different.* Hume says:

> It is sufficient for our present purpose, if we have proved, that the taste of all individuals is not upon an equal footing. [p. 242]

But sometimes differing tastes *are* upon an equal footing. The problem is to distinguish cases in which tastes differ from those in which the difference exhibits an "inequality," as Hume calls it. Suppose that you are pleased and I am not, and suppose also that you are a true judge. Is my difference from you *eo ipso* a manifest inferiority? I think not. If we differ about *North by Northwest,* that is one thing, but what if we differ about the television program *Law and Order*?

A true judge will be pleased and pained by things throughout the range of his experience. He may be pleased by a picture of his mother, pained by the sight of a woman who once slighted him. He will know pleasures and pains which are not the marks of beauty and ugliness. In order to know whether to count his feelings as part of a standard, we will have to know whether they come to him in his true judiciary or only in his condition as a human being. This is all to say, simply, that sometimes the true judge's feelings have force and sometimes they do not.

I submit that Hume's theory has a mechanism for distinguishing such cases, whether or not Hume had this in mind. My divergence from you is a sign of an inequality (and my inferiority) only if your reaction is not only the reaction of a true judge but is also congruent with the reactions of other true judges; that is, only if my response is at odds with *a joint verdict.* If you and your true judge pals do not agree in your responses, even among yourselves, then my disagreement with any one of you is not culpable. In his moral theory Hume is stuck with the problem of identifying those cases in which the pleasure of an impartial spectator is a sign of virtue, and he resorts to a not completely satisfying reliance on introspection, virtually a commitment to a belief in qualitatively different kinds of pleasure; and Hume's own list of virtues and vices is strikingly unconvincing to twentieth-century readers.[3] His theory of taste requires no such retreat. It can be read as a thoroughgoing, utterly non-*a priori* empirical theory, letting things sort themselves out however they wind up. This makes it the most appealing, and most defensible, theory of taste I know or can imagine.[4]

The theory does, however, leave one insidious question. I will raise it and then leave it. The proto-question is this: In what sense is the response of a true judge *correct?* The correlative question, which seems to me to be the unpleasantly deep and corrosive question, is whether one *should* be a true judge. Would one be *better* to be a true judge? What do you think?

Hume's essay is a marvelous piece of literature. It is a favorite idea of mine, and perhaps a fanciful one, that Hume not only knows this but intends to use it as such in a dialectical (shall we say "reflexive"?) encounter with the reader. In my intoxication with the *Don Quixote* story I have endeavored to

3. John Rawls faces the same problem in the theory of his "Outline of a Decision Procedure for Ethics," *Philosophical Review* 60 (1951): 177–97. He aims to uncover moral principles by determining what principles explicate the "considered moral judgments" of a group of "competent moral judges." But Rawls does not intend to submit every conceivable question to these moral judges (the equivalent of Hume's impartial spectators and true judges). Instead, he determines by himself, in advance, just what (kind of) questions will be submitted. Rawls's sense of what questions are relevant is more palatable to twentieth-century readers than Hume's list of virtues (in his moral theory), but it involves the same kind of *ad hoc* restrictions. It is just this kind of restriction which Hume does not need in his theory of taste.

4. It is defensible, in particular, against the kind of criticism made by Richard Shusterman in "Of the Scandal of Taste: Social Privilege as Nature in the Aesthetic Theories of Hume and Kant," *Philosophical Forum* 20 (1989): 211–29. Shusterman argues that Hume means the standard of taste to be "natural"; but in locating that standard in certain members of society, says Shusterman, he has not only rendered it natural, and thus non-normative, but he has guaranteed it will be at least in part a product of the social influences at work on those members. Now Hume surely does regard the standard as natural, in some sense, and there is no doubt that he expects the true judges to reach certain joint verdicts; and Hume is confident in stating some of the judgments that these verdicts will warrant—for instance, that Milton is better than Ogilby. But the theory itself, at its philosophical core, does not require any of this. There is only this question: Do the true judges deliver a joint verdict in the case at hand? If not, there is no standard, whatever Hume might have expected. If so, it is binding, at least with (empirical) probability. Critics like Shusterman are sure there is no (Humean) standard. Their certainty is philosophically as obnoxious as the certainty they identify in Hume that there is such a standard. Why not take Hume's best instinct and concede that it is an empirical question whether such a standard emerges? Marxism is an empirical theory, is it not? If so, then let us at least imagine testing it. If not, then this carping against Hume in the name of our superior awareness of economic, political, and social influences is itself only one more dogma.

find every ingredient in the composition. I would not bet that I have found them all, but I have found many more than I once detected. Do I have delicacy of taste in at least this kind of literature? Does my response of delight show that the essay is beautiful? And if it is beautiful, what does that have to do with the soundness of its *philosophy?*

Good questions. I bequeath them to you.

Robert J. Yanal

Kant on Aesthetic Ideas and Beauty

Readers of Kant's *Critique of Judgment* (1790) have understandably been stumped trying to decipher Kant's views on the relation between beauty and art.[1] At §43 Kant ends his discussion of "free natural" beauties such as flowers and birds of paradise and begins to formulate a theory of fine art, according to which fine art has as its purpose the expression of "aesthetic ideas." This theory of fine art, perhaps because it is saddled with examples of second-rate art (including a poem by "the great king" Frederick) and is sketchier than the theory of beauty, has not been given the attention accorded the four "moments." However, Kant's theory of fine art is not as

1. The translation and English terminology I have used is from Immanuel Kant, *Critique of Judgment,* trans. Werner Pluhar (Indianapolis: Hackett Publishing Co., [1790] 1987). References to quotes are given by citing section number (where Kant gives one), followed by the page reference to the *Akademie* edition of the collected works—e.g., §44, 305. Italics, *Akademie* pagination, and text within square brackets are as given by Pluhar.

"unsophisticated" and "unenlightening" as one commentator thinks.[2] It is rough and unfinished; but even so, it lays claim to being, along with Aristotle's account of the "philosophical" implications of literature, one of the great pre-Hegelian statements on the capacity of art to express ideas. At least, the fact that the *Critique of Judgment* contains such a theory should stand as a warning to those who blame Kant for "neutering" the capacity of art to have any practical effect by reducing art to a contrivance for producing an enemic "disinterested" pleasure.[3] On the contrary: Kant himself may in fact have thought his theory of fine art to be the capstone of his aesthetics. For at §51 he writes: "We may in general call beauty (whether natural or artistic) the *expression* of aesthetic ideas." And here is where the puzzle begins, for it is not at all clear how or why beauty should even apply to the expression of aesthetic ideas—let alone apply in a way such that "we may *in general* call beauty . . . the expression of aesthetic ideas."

The puzzle, in slightly more detail, concerns how the reader is to understand the application of the predicate "beautiful" to items of meaning (i.e., to works of fine art insofar as they express aesthetic ideas), given that the theory of beauty as drawn out in the pre–§43 portions applies the predicate almost entirely to items lacking meaning: namely, natural beauties and instances of pure design. The following passage is typical of Kant's pre–§43 exposition:

> Many birds (the parrot, the humming-bird, the bird of paradise) and a lot of crustaceans in the sea are [free] beauties themselves [and] belong to no object determined by concepts as to its purpose, but we like them freely and on their own account. Thus designs *à la grecque,* the foliage on borders or on wallpaper, etc. mean nothing on their own: they represent [*vorstellen*] nothing, no object under a determi-

2. "Unfortunately, Kant's theory of symbolism is relatively unsophisticated. He assimilates metaphor, personification, synecdoche, and other tropes, and he does not distinguish them from other forms of symbolism. Nor does he argue for his stated view that such symbols are ineffable. . . . Consequently, many of the details of Kant's view are unenlightening." Donald W. Crawford, "Kant's Theory of Creative Imagination," in *Essays in Kant's Aesthetics,* ed. Ted Cohen and Paul Guyer (Chicago: University of Chicago Press, 1982), pp. 173–74.

3. I have in mind an essay in which Danto seeks out "the political subtext" of both Plato's attack on art in the tenth book of the *Republic* and what Danto sees as a parallel attack by Kant in his third *Critique:* "So art is systematically neutered, removed from the domain of use on one side (a good thing if artists lack practical intelligence they merely can give the appearance of having) and, on the other side, from the world of needs and interests." Arthur C. Danto, "The Philosophical Disenfranchisement of Art," in his book of essays, *The Philosophical Disenfranchisement of Art* (New York: Columbia University Press, 1986), p. 10.

> nate concept, and are free beauties. What we call fantasias in music (namely music without a topic [*Thema*]), indeed all music not set to words, may also be included in the same class. (§16, 229)

This occurs in a section in which Kant distinguishes "free" from "accessory" beauty, a distinction we will come back to later. Suffice it to say that free beauty is the sort of beauty Kant is interested in explaining—that is, free beauty is beauty proper, and his purports to be a theory of free beauty. I have called the preceding passage typical, yet it seems more than that: it seems nearly definitional of his theory of beauty. Insofar as there are few examples given of the beauty of ordinary artifacts, let alone works of fine art,[4] it begins to seem as if Kant thought "beauty" applied not just in its most ordinary instances or even paradigm cases but *exclusively* to items lacking meaning.

It is arguable that our earliest, childhood experiences of beauty are of the beauty of flowers and wallpaper; and so it might be a kind of didactic strategy to introduce a theory of beauty that draws on such examples, then to go on later to discuss the beauty of fine art which we not only experience later in life but which also seems a more complex beauty. Yet there is more than an expository strategy going on, for the up-front formalism of the theory up to §43 makes it difficult to see how beauty can be applied to content; that is, to the expression of aesthetic ideas. It is our intuition, with which Kant never disagrees, that flowers as found in nature do not express or communicate anything. How, then, does the expression of aesthetic ideas turn out to be beautiful?

1

Kant's theory of beauty is in part motivated, at least in the two introductions Kant wrote for the *Critique of Judgment,* by a problem left over from the first *Critique.* That problem is how concepts apply to percepts. The problem subdivides further. There is what we can call the big-picture problem: How

4. At §7 Kant admonishes us that "it would be ridiculous" to say that "this object (the building we are looking at, the garment that man is wearing, the concert we are listening to, the poem put up to be judged) is beautiful *for me.*" Kant's intent here is to put forward an intuition about the beautiful: namely, that the beautiful is universal in a way that the agreeable is not. We should note that he is here at least comfortable in speaking of the beauty of poems and concerts; that is, of artworks.

does the world turn out to be receptive to the activities of the mind, which, after all, is imposing its creations (concepts) on something that might be entirely unconceptualizable? Then there is a problem arising out of Kant's mental mechanics. How does the imagination (understood roughly as the faculty of imaging, or that which is acquainted with though does not comprehend perceptions) manage to interact with what in the third *Critique* is called the understanding (the faculty of understanding or cognizing—of applying concepts to—percepts)?

Kant's solution comes via the faculty of judgment, which mediates between imagination and understanding. Suppose we have a percept (of a rose, as it happens) in the imagination. Before we can make the empirical or "determinate" judgment "This is a rose," we have to engage in what Kant called "reflective judgment," which is a search for a concept to fit the percept at hand. To solve the big-picture problem, Kant thought "judgment" must make the assumption—in Kant's language, judgment takes as a transcendental or synthetic *a priori* principle—that the world is receptive to the cognitive activities of the mind.[5] Reflective judgment is to view nature as if designed for human cognition, as if purposive; though since such purposiveness cannot be objectively established, it is called by Kant "purposiveness without purpose" or, sometimes, "the form of purposiveness."

The mental mechanics problem now takes on another dimension. We begin with a percept *a* and then search for a concept, perhaps *F*, with which to understand *a*. The process of reflectively judging, which is the search for a concept adequate for the percept at hand, cannot itself be rule-governed, for rules are given in concepts and *ex hypothesi* we do not yet have a concept to apply to anything. Hence the pure reflective judgment must be "aesthetic"; that is, it must be grounded in feeling.[6] Such feeling will turn out to be pleasure. The general idea is that the purposiveness of nature is shown (really, experienced only as a felt pleasure) through the harmony of the imagination and the understanding: that is, through the harmonious working of a faculty which presents intuitions of the world (not quite raw

5. This is the substance of the (second, or published) introduction: "Now this [transcendental principle of reflective judgment] can only be the following: since universal natural laws have their basis in our understanding, which prescribes them to nature... the particular empirical laws must... be viewed in terms of such a unity as [they would have] if they too had been given by an understanding (even though not ours) so as to assist our cognitive powers by making possible a system of experience in terms of particular natural laws.... In other words, through this concept we present nature as if an understanding contained the basis of the unity of what is diverse in nature's empirical laws" (§IV, 180–81).

6. See especially the (published) introduction, §VII.

intuitions, for they must already be organized by the categories of space and time) and a faculty which seems to grasp them. The imagination and understanding are, as Kant sometimes says, in free play, a free play that is productive of (and signaled by) pleasure. It is here, at this juncture in the process of reflectively judging *a,* that the judgment that *a* is beautiful is occasioned. In fact, "*a* is beautiful" is an expression of this felt pleasure, though we need not have yet grasped that *a* is *F* (that *a* is a rose, say). What Kant will do in the theory of beauty proper—I mean what he writes after the transcendental *mise-en-scène* of the introduction(s)—is to elaborate on the nature of the pleasure, what should *not* be involved in judging the beautiful, and so on.

2

In generating his theory of the beautiful, Kant does a sort of back-and-forth between delivering up deep intuitions about the beautiful—describing what Wittgenstein might have called the grammar of judgments of the beautiful—and bringing his transcendental epistemology to bear on explaining or justifying those deep intuitions. So, for example, Kant thinks, apparently independently of his transcendental epistemology, that *beauty* is not a concept, by which he means that to say of something, *a,* that it is beautiful does not express a way of understanding *a*—does not express, we might say more bluntly, a fact about the object *a.* He will explain/justify this intuition with the claim that a judgment of the beauty of *a* is made during the process of pure reflective judging in which the search for a concept *F* to apply to *a* is conducted precisely in the absence of an understanding of the character of *a.*

The formalism that dominates Kant's theory initially derives not so much from considerations about the beautiful, though Kant is apparently quite happy to accept some kind of formalism with respect to beauty, but from the way he solves the epistemological problems of the introductions. The character or nature or "content" of an item of perception, *a,* cannot be known until the conclusion of the pure reflective judgment; that is, the point at which the mind has come to a determinate judgment (that *a* is *F*). So, if we cannot know the character or nature or "content" of *a,* what can we know or at least be acquainted with? Kant's initial suggestion cannot be that we are acquainted with *nothing* about *a,* for that would entail that we have no motive to begin to engage in any kind of judging at all. Thus Kant adopts the idea that the judgment of the beautiful is triggered by the *form* of *a*. This idea in itself hardly says anything at all, for the concept of form is notoriously elusive. It is not that it cannot be unpacked at all, though the way Kant unpacks it pre–§43 is in large part the source of the difficulties he and his commentators encounter later in trying to explain how it is that aesthetic ideas can be beautiful.

The difficulties begin when the pre–§43 exposition understands the form of an item of perception *a* to be an arrangement that obtains among the parts of *a*, either spatial arrangements or shape (if *a* is a visual object) or temporal arrangements or "play over time" (if *a* is an auditory object). It is not that this is wrong right from the start. It is, if anything, *right* right from the start, if we start with the ordinary instances of beautiful things—birds and their song, flowers, wallpaper, and so on. These precisely are items of perception (in the ordinary way of understanding perception), and it is entirely appropriate that form be introduced as roughly equivalent to shape or play over time. And indeed, when specifying just what it is that we judge beautiful, Kant has recourse to such formalistic terms as "form," "shape," "design," and "composition." For example, "When we judge free beauty (according to mere form) . . . our imagination is playing, as it were, while it contemplates the shape" (§16, 230). One of the consequences of this view is that we need not have a concept of the object—need not know what the object is apart from how it appears—to judge it as beautiful. "Flowers are free natural beauties. Hardly anyone apart from the botanist knows what sort of thing a flower is [meant] to be; and even he . . . pays no attention to this natural purpose when he judges the flower by taste" (§16, 229). And if, in reflecting on *a*, we need not know that *a* is a rose (or even what a rose is) to find *a* beautiful, what else could we know except how the item appears in perception, and what else could this be except its shape?

Intermingled with the examples of birds and wallpaper are formalistic art-critical remarks. Some of these are straightforward applications of form-as-shape to art forms: "In painting, in sculpture, indeed in all the visual arts . . . *design* is what is essential; in design the basis for any involvement of taste is not what gratifies us in sensation, but merely what we like because of its form" (§14, 225). Others derive from another of Kant's deep intuitions about the beautiful, according to which what is beautiful appears to be objective or factlike, yet to say of *a* that it is beautiful cannot itself express a fact about *a* (for *beauty* is, recall, not a concept). Yet there is an appearance of objectivity or facticity in the judgment of the beautiful that has to be accounted for, and Kant tries to account for it in his claim that judgments of the beautiful are as if objective in that they "demand universal assent." What cannot be shared universally (what cannot be considered part of *common* sense), then, cannot properly be part of the judgment of beauty. Thus in §§13–14, emotion, color, and tone are excised from the pure judgment of the beautiful.[7]

This recitation of some aspects of Kant's theory of beauty—*beauty* is not a concept; we need not have a concept of a thing to judge it as beautiful; judgments of the beautiful concern form which seems to be identified as shape; the paradigms of beauty are things such as flowers in nature that do not express or communicate anything—explains why the theory of fine art that starts with §43 seems almost to begin another work, and why Kant's remark at §51 that beauty in general is the expression of aesthetic ideas astonishes us. In what follows I will outline my understanding of Kant's theory of fine art. I will then explore one solution to the §51 perplex as given by D. W. Gotshalk, according to which Kant has *two* theories of the beautiful. Ultimately I will argue that Kant has but one theory and that it can accommodate the beauty of natural objects, the beauty of pure design, and the beauty of aesthetic ideas.

To prefigure my argument a bit: Kant misleads us (and perhaps himself) into thinking, initially, that physical form is the sole ground for the judgment of the beautiful. Suppose I judge that *a* is beautiful. It is easy enough to venture into considering just what it is about *a* that occasions the judgment that it is beautiful, and to identify that aspect or those aspects as the ground for the judgment that *a* is beautiful. Kant flirts with this once in a while. "Everything that [shows] stiff regularity (close to mathematical regularity)"—Kant's rather charming example is a pepper garden with its regular rows and parallel lines—"runs counter to taste because it does not allow us to be entertained for long by our contemplation of it" (general comment after §22, 242–43). It may begin to seem as if it is the unvaried regularity that is unbeautiful, thus that beauty applies to things in virtue of an objective property such as variety in shape. Once one does this, it is

7. Kant is confusing (and, I think, confused) on the role of color. At §14, 224 Kant considers whether a color considered in itself could be beautiful. His answer seems to be that if color consists of "vibrations of the aether in uniform temporal sequence, as in the case of sound," then a color could be beautiful because it would then have parts in "regular play"—an odd view, as it equates the beauty of color to the beauty of music; that is, color as a kind of temporal art. A bare *Akademie* page later we find Kant saying that "charm is a vulgar error that is very prejudicial to genuine, uncorrupted, solid taste." For instance in painting: "The colors that illuminate the outline belong to charm. Though they can indeed make the object itself vivid to sense, they cannot make it beautiful and worthy of being beheld."

natural to think that Kant simply glues a formalistic theory of beauty onto the expression of aesthetic ideas where it cannot possibly remain stuck. But, I will argue, this is to confuse what often occasions a certain mental activity (the free play of the cognitive faculties) with that mental activity itself. The pleasure of free play is *often* occasioned by pure design, but it is not *necessarily* occasioned by pure design and pure design alone. The entertaining of aesthetic ideas, I argue, stimulates (as far as we can tell) the same mental activity as a judgment of the beauty of wallpaper. Thus, the grasping of aesthetic ideas can itself be beautiful.

3

We can divide Kant's theory of fine art into three parts. In the first part (A–G) Kant describes the purpose of art, summarized below (omitting mainly Kant's thoughts on rules and his comparisons between art and science):

A. Artworks are made by rational agents ("through a power of choice that bases its acts on reason"). Such agents have in mind "a purpose to which {an artwork}[8] owes its form." Works of nature, honeycombs for example, are products of "instinct" and not "rational deliberation." (§43, 303)
B. The purpose of the agreeable arts (e.g., setting a table) is "that the pleasure should accompany presentations {of possible or actual objects} that are mere *sensations.*" The purpose of the fine arts (e.g., poetry) is "that the pleasure should accompany presentations that are *ways of cognizing.*" (§44, 305)
C. "Fine art . . . is a way of presenting" possible or actual objects that has as its purpose "social communication." (§44, 306)
D. The pleasure engendered by fine art, if it is to be universally communicable, requires "that this pleasure . . . be a pleasure of reflection rather than one of enjoyment arising from mere sensation." (§44, 306)
E. Fine arts "must necessarily be considered arts of *genius*" (§46, 307), which provides "rich *material* for products of fine art; processing this material and giving it *form* requires a talent that is academically trained." (§47, 310)

8. Remarks within braces are my glosses on the text.

F. One of the "powers of the mind which constitute genius" is "spirit" [*Geist*]. The artist, by dint of spirit (and other talents), having created an artwork, is thereby able to animate the minds of those who view, hear, or read his artwork.[9] (§49, 313)

G. The artist animates the minds of his audience by his "ability to exhibit aesthetic *ideas.*" (§49, 314)

This is a theory of art, grounded in plausible intuitions and plausible reasoning from those intuitions. Art is made by rational beings with a purpose, and the purpose of fine art has to do with communicating a way of cognizing the world. The pleasure of fine art, therefore, must have something to do with cognizing broadly construed. (So far, this would be agreeable to Aristotle or Nelson Goodman.) The artist has a special power, genius, by which he produces these special cognitions, which are here termed "aesthetic ideas." (This is distinctively Kantian.) Therefore, art is the expression of aesthetic ideas.[10]

I might mention that Kant is not entirely clear or consistent about how this theory of art applies to music. Consider, for example, his mention of "fantasias in music (namely, music without a topic)" in §16 as an instance, along with flowers and birds, of free beauties. We might naturally interpret "music without a topic" to mean "nonprogrammatic (or pure) music," but does this mean that much music does not express aesthetic ideas? If so, then Berlioz's *Symphonie fantastique* is art (since it is programmatic) but Beethoven's First Symphony is not art (since it is not). Odd. Did Kant mean something else by "music without a topic"? Or was this a just a careless remark at §16? I shall take it that Kant's final view is that all (and only) artworks are expressions of aesthetic ideas, without thereby foisting a philosophy of music on him.

9. In Pluhar's translation, Kant wrote this: "Spirit [*Geist*] in an aesthetic sense is the animating principle in the mind. But what this principle uses to animate [or quicken] the soul, the material it employs for this, is what imparts to the mental powers a purposive momentum, i.e., imparts to them a play which is such that it sustains itself on its own and even strengthens the powers for such play."

10. This theory prefigures some modern views according to which a necessary condition for being a work of art is to have a meaning. See Arthur Danto, *The Transfiguration of the Commonplace* (Cambridge: Harvard University Press, 1981) or Richard Wollheim, *Painting as an Art* (Princeton: Princeton University Press, for the Bollingen Foundation, 1987).

4

What are aesthetic ideas? In what I call the second part of Kant's theory of art, the explanation of how fine art accomplishes its purpose, Kant defines and discusses aesthetic ideas:

H. An aesthetic idea is "a presentation of the imagination which prompts much thought, but to which no determinate thought whatsoever, i.e., no [determinate] *concept,* can be adequate, so that no language can express it completely and allow us to grasp it." (§49, 314)
I. "It is easy to see that an aesthetic idea is the counterpart (pendant) of a *rational idea,* which is, conversely, a concept to which no *intuition* (presentation of the imagination) can be adequate." (§49, 314)
J. Aesthetic ideas result from an imagination that uses association and analogy to "process" material from nature into something that "surpasses nature." (§49, 314)
K. The reason these are called "ideas" is to indicate "that they at least strive toward something that lies beyond the bounds of experience." (§49, 314)
L. A presentation of an aesthetic idea in an artwork quickens the mind by prompting "so much thought as can never be comprehended within a determinate concept," and prompts such thought by "opening up for it {the mind} a view into an immense realm of kindred presentations." (§49, 315)

In Tolstoy's well-known theory of expression in *What Is Art?* the artist begins by experiencing an emotion which he wants to share, and he prepares an external object—a poem, for example—designed to cause its readers to experience that emotion. The artwork is successful—and counts as art—only if the poem's readers are subsequently "infected" with the artist's emotion. Kant shares what we might call the form of Tolstoy's theory, though Kant's candidate for artistic communication is not emotion but aesthetic ideas. What he tells us is that aesthetic ideas are products of the artist's genius and "prompt much thought" in his audience. Now (H) and (J) are as close as Kant comes to describing the formation of aesthetic ideas in the artist's mind (and since Kant thinks that aesthetic ideas are the product of genius and that genius cannot be explained, one is grateful for the little he says here). And remark (L) seems to be a description of the reception of aesthetic ideas by the spectator of the artwork. There are strong similarities between the formulation of aesthetic ideas (by the artist) and the reception of them by the spectator: imagination is essentially involved, mainly since no determinate thought is involved (and a determinate thought is the product of the application of a concept by the understanding to an item in the imagination). The mind is "quickened," though not because it has made some exciting determinate judgment but because it has *entertained* something indeterminate, something that is rightly called an "idea" because it is more propositional than shapely. It is in this sense that artworks *express* aesthetic ideas: thoughts on the part of the artist, an artwork created in order to "prompt" those thoughts, and finally thoughts on the part of the audience prompted by the artwork.

Kant, of course, did not mean that aesthetic ideas are any old thoughts on the part of the artist that led him to make an artwork which could then prompt any old thoughts on the part of the spectator. Kant conjures up an example of a painting. "Jupiter's eagle with the lightning in its claws is an attribute of the mighty king of heaven" which does not "present the content of our concepts of the sublimity and majesty of creation" but presents "something that prompts the imagination to spread over a multitude of kindred presentations that arouse more thought than can be expressed in a concept determined by words" (§49, 315). In another example, "a certain poet, in describing a beautiful morning, says: 'The sun flowed forth, as serenity flows from virtue.' The consciousness of virtue . . . spreads in the mind a multitude of sublime and calming feelings and a boundless outlook toward a joyful future, such as no expression commensurate with a determinate concept completely attains" (§49, 315).

These examples (the eagle as an expression of majesty, the sun as an expression of virtue) and Kant's remarks, (I) that aesthetic ideas result from an imagination that used association and analogy and (K) that artworks generated from such a use of the imagination open up to the mind "a view into an immense realm of kindred presentations" which (H) no determinate concept can express completely, suggest that Kant thought every artwork was a metaphor.[11] More specifically, Kant thought that every artwork is the result of an imaginative process of making a metaphor, and every artwork is to be understood in the way that metaphors are interpreted. For what "ideas" other than metaphor proceed by analogy and are indeterminate in content?

11. I am not the first to interpret Kant's notion of aesthetic ideas as a theory of metaphor. See Francis X. Coleman, *The Harmony of Reason* (Pittsburgh: University of Pittsburgh Press, 1974), pp. 158–67.

Kant's theory, in fact, approaches an account of metaphor by Max Black.[12] According to Black's theory, in Romeo's exhaltation "Juliet is the sun" there are two "subjects," one being used literally (Juliet) and the other metaphorically (the sun). Black considers a metaphor to be "an instrument for drawing implications grounded in perceived analogies of structure between two subjects belonging to different domains."[13] More specifically, Black writes,

> Although I speak figuratively here of the *subjects* interacting, such an outcome is of course produced in the minds of the speaker and hearer: it is they who are led to engage in selecting, organising, and "projecting." I think of a metaphorical statement (even a weak one) as a verbal action essentially demanding "uptake," a creative response from a competent reader.[14]

We can call Black's an "uptake" view of metaphor which, in essence, holds that metaphorical meaning is not, as it were, in the sentence but in the thoughts provoked by the metaphor. Since Romeo cannot mean that Juliet *is* the sun, and since the terms "Juliet" or "the sun" do not grow a special metaphorical sense or reference for just this occasion, we the hearers produce one: Juliet is the center of Romeo's life, she is his warmth, without her he cannot live, and so on. As Donald Davidson, another defender of "uptake" views, puts it: "A metaphor makes us attend to some likeness, often a novel or surprising likeness, between two or more things."[15] This is a virtual reading of Kant's remark about "an immense realm of *kindred* presentations" (emphasis added) that are "prompted" by the artwork. Kant's theory of aesthetic ideas, if indeed it is a theory of metaphor, is an "uptake" theory.

There is some agreement by contemporary philosophers that the meaning of metaphor is, as Kant says, "immense" and "indeterminate" (i.e., inadequately definable by any determinate concept). Black says: "There is an inescapable indeterminacy in the notion of a *given* metaphorical statement."[16] Stanley Cavell speaks of "the burgeoning of meaning" in metaphor, mentioning the fact that most attempts to paraphrase metaphor

12. The theory as cited here is from Max Black's paper "More About Metaphor," *Dialectica* 31 (1977): 431–57, which is a later reworking of the "interaction" theory of a better-known essay by Black, entitled simply "Metaphor," in his *Models and Metaphors* (Ithaca: Cornell University Press, 1962).

13. Black, "More About Metaphor," p. 446.

14. Ibid., p. 442.

15. Donald Davidson, "What Metaphors Mean," in *On Metaphor,* ed. Sheldon Sacks (Chicago: University of Chicago Press, 1978), p. 31.

16. Black, "More About Metaphor," p. 438.

end with "and so on."[17] Davidson states that "there is no limit to what a metaphor calls to our attention, and much of what we are caused to notice is not propositional in character."[18]

Kant, like Black but unlike Cavell, offers a brief explanation of why it is we need metaphors. Kant's claim that aesthetic ideas are a "way of cognizing" is so blunt as to discourage further analysis, and it is complicated by a remark at §57: "An *aesthetic idea* cannot become cognition because it is an *intuition* (of the imagination) for which an adequate concept can never be found." Is Kant saying, for example, that metaphors are a way of cognizing that is never statable or that is not, really, cognizing proper at all?[19] That no answer is forthcoming from Kant is unfortunate. Davidson opens his paper on metaphor with "Metaphor is the dreamwork of language." Now my inclination is to say that his metaphor is beautiful and enlightening. Metaphors seem at the same time to delight and enlighten. We shall, however, have to forgo the enlightening in treating Kant's theory.

We are on firmer ground in rejecting a kind of interpretation that at least one commentator has made.[20] This is to take Kant as holding that we need metaphors only to express the supersensible. This interpretation is not entirely unfounded. In remarks (J) and (K), aesthetic ideas are said to "surpass nature" and "the bounds of experience." While it is plausible to maintain that we cannot portray something supersensible such as the power of heaven except metaphorically (this recalls the running Scholastic dispute about literal versus nonliteral descriptions of God), there is no reason to think that metaphors *must* be about the supersensible. The fact is that aesthetic ideas—if indeed they are metaphors—could be of mundane, empirical things. To borrow an example from Black (who borrows it from Ezra Pound), a metaphor of education as sheepherding does not seem to involve the supersensible at

17. Stanley Cavell, "Aesthetic Problems of Modern Philosophy," in his book of essays *Must We Mean What We Say?* (New York: Charles Scribner's Sons, 1969), p. 79.

18. Davidson, "What Metaphors Mean," p. 44.

19. Perhaps Kant is verging on a view recently expressed by Rorty, according to which "there are three ways in which a new belief can be added to our previous beliefs, thereby forcing us to reweave the fabric of our beliefs and desires—viz., perception, inference, and metaphor. . . . A metaphor is, so to speak, a voice from outside logical space, rather than an empirical filling-up of a portion of that space, or a logical-philosophical clarification of the structure of that space. It is a call to change one's language and one's life, rather than a proposal about how to systematize either." Richard Rorty, "Philosophy as Science, as Metaphor, and as Politics," in his *Essays on Heidegger and Others* (New York: Cambridge University Press, 1991), pp. 12–13.

20. See Donald W. Crawford, *Kant's Aesthetic Theory* (Madison: University of Wisconsin Press, 1974), p. 134ff, whose discussion of aesthetic ideas is a springboard into sections on the "supersensible" and aesthetics and morality.

all. It is perhaps wrongly thought that inexpressibility by determinate concepts entails supersensibility (it of course does not); or perhaps commentators are enchanted by Kant's pietistic examples, which mention paintings and poems of "the mighty king of heaven" and "the sublimity and majesty of creation."

We should not forget that Kant gives aesthetic ideas as the counterpart of rational ideas. Aesthetic ideas are intuitions that cannot be adequately captured by determinate concepts, while rational ideas are concepts that cannot be adequately illustrated by intuitions. So Kantian aesthetic ideas are attempts to illustrate rational ideas:

> A poet ventures to give sensible expression to rational ideas of invisible beings, the realm of the blessed, the realm of hell, eternity, creation, and so on. Or, again, he takes [things] that are indeed exemplified in experience, such as death, envy, and all the other vices, as well as love, fame, and so on; but then, by means of an imagination that emulates the example of reason in reaching [for] a maximum, he ventures to give these sensible expression in a way that goes beyond the limits of experience, namely, with a completeness for which no example can be found in nature. (§49, 314)

This remark, too, needs clarification; but Kant is of no further help. Maybe the realm of the blessed "goes beyond the limits of experience" and can therefore be only metaphorically illuminated, but envy, love, and fame are hardly in the same category. Instances of these are, in a perfectly ordinary sense, found in experience. Of course, what Kant says is that the artist wants to give "sensible expression" to, say, envy "with a *completeness* for which no example can be found in nature," though it is hard to know what is meant here by "completeness." This remark is suggestive of Aristotle's famous claim that the poet differs from the historian in being more "philosophical," by which he meant "expressing the universal," though both poet and historian are in a way recounting the same set of facts.[21] There are problems here as to how the poet can rise to the universal, but it is uncertain whether Kant has anything like this in mind. Indeed, we wonder how Kant could explain how "completeness" can (or must) be conveyed metaphorically—that is, indeterminately, through association and analogy—for one would think "completeness" and "indeterminacy" to be in conflict with one another.

21. See chap. 9 of Aristotle's *Poetics*. On how the poet might achieve the universal, see Robert J. Yanal, "Aristotle's Definition of Poetry," *Noûs* 16 (1982): 499–525.

5

In the third part of Kant's theory of art, he attempts to combine his theory of art and aesthetic ideas with his earlier account of the beautiful:

M. "Whenever we convey our thoughts, there are two ways (*modi*) of arranging them, and one of these is called *manner* (*modus aestheticus*), the other *method* (*modus logicus*); the difference between these two is that the first has no standard other than the *feeling* that there is unity in the exhibition [of the thoughts], whereas the second follows in [all of] this determinate *principles;* hence only the first applies to fine art." (§49, 318–19)
N. In art "a product is called *mannered* only if the way the artist conveys his idea *aims* at singularity and is not adequate to the idea." The pretentious and stilted is "without spirit." (§49, 318–19)
O. If art shows genius it is called inspired, "but it deserves to be called *fine* art only insofar as it shows taste." (§50, 319)
P. "In order [for a work] to be beautiful, it is not strictly necessary that [it] be rich and original in ideas, but it is necessary that the imagination in its freedom be commensurate with the lawfulness of the understanding." (§50, 319)
Q. "We may in general call beauty (whether natural or artistic) the *expression* of aesthetic ideas; the difference is that in the case of beautiful [*schön*] art the aesthetic idea must be prompted by a concept of the object, whereas in the case of beautiful nature, mere reflection on a given intuition, without a concept of what the object is [meant] to be, is sufficient for arousing and communicating the idea of which that object is regarded as the *expression.*" (§51, 320)
R. "Now although the two cognitive powers, sensibility and understanding, are indispensable to one another, still it is difficult to combine them without [using] constraint and without their impairing one another; and yet their combination and harmony must appear unintentional and spontaneous if the art is to be *fine* art." (§51, 321)

The preceding remarks start off with hardly a strain on the earlier exposition of beauty. The artist, according to (M), has a certain way of proceeding which essentially involves feeling (as opposed to the scientist, who proceeds "logically"). The artist should avoid what is stilted (N) and should certainly show taste (O). Remark (Q) seems to point out the difficulties of being in artistic control ("using constraint") yet producing an object that appears as "spontaneous." (Kant has nothing more to say about how to ease these difficulties.) So far, these remarks could be addressed to the wallpaper designer as well as to a painter of landscapes, for they raise no problems against the formalism of the theory of beauty to that point.

The difficulty begins with (P), for here Kant seems to require that a work of fine art be "rich and original" in ideas in order for it to be beautiful. And all bets seem to be off with (Q), which all but identifies beauty with the expression of aesthetic ideas.

I should add that this is not, as it were, a blunder that Kant should have avoided—I mean, a blunder in even raising the issue of the beauty of aesthetic ideas. Kant rightly sees that he cannot just parenthesize expression when addressing the formal beauty of an artwork (as in: *The design of this artwork is beautiful; and, by the way, the artwork expresses a certain aesthetic idea*); nor can he ignore formal beauty when addressing its expression (as in: *This artwork expresses a certain aesthetic idea, though we will pass over in silence the issue of the beauty of the artwork*). That is to say, Kant acknowledges that the beauty of artworks is complex in a way that the beauty of flowers and wallpaper is not. Whether he adequately accounts for the complexity remains to be seen.

6

Our first question is, How can beauty be applied in any way to aesthetic ideas? In a famous paper on Kant's theory of art, D. W. Gotshalk claims that Kant cannot consistently allow aesthetic ideas to be beautiful. "In Kant's conception of Beauty in Art . . . the emphasis shifts from form to expression. Above all the natural source of Beauty in Art is identified with expressive power rather than with formal excellence."[22] But not only does the "emphasis" shift; in Gotshalk's view, Kant advances a different, post–§43, theory of beauty:

> Kant holds a *formalist* theory of Natural Beauty and an *expressionist* theory of Fine Art. . . . To a purely disinterested observer there is

22. D. W. Gotshalk, "Form and Expression in Kant's Aesthetics," *British Journal of Aesthetics* 7 (1967): 253.

> considerable difference between a formalist and an expressionist aesthetical theory, and in Kant's third *Critique* there is clearly a change from the first type to the second when we proceed after some delay (over the Sublime) from his theory of Natural Beauty to his theory of Fine Art.[23]

Gotshalk's concern is to explain why Kant made this shift. Kant, in Gotshalk's view, is seeking "*a priori* evidence for a harmony between Nature and moral aspiration"[24] or, as we might also put it, between the realm of natural causality and the realm of human freedom. Such evidence is eventually provided by the concept of genius, which "is the innate mental predisposition (*ingenium*) *through which* nature gives the rule to art" (§46, 307). Natural beauty is then—guilelessly—redefined to accommodate genius.[25]

Before we entertain an explanation of why Kant held two theories of beauty, we should be convinced that he did in fact hold two different theories. Gotshalk's evidence that Kant held two theories rests on little more than the supposed *obviousness* of a "considerable difference" between the theory of pure beauty and the theory of aesthetic ideas. It is undeniable that there *appears* to be a difference. This largely has to do with the earlier remarks emphasizing form-as-shape. But might there not be a deeper interpretation that demonstrates a unity? It makes Kant into quite a muddler if he has *inadvertently* abandoned what on Gotshalk's view must be thought of as the pre–§43 theory of beauty—and it would have to be inadvertently abandoned, since Kant does not *say* that he is summoning up a different theory of beauty post–§43. He does not, for example, claim a distinction between "formal" and "expressive" beauty, in the way that he distinguished (in §§15–16) "free" from "accessory" beauty. In fact, the so-called "Dialectic of Aesthetic Judgment" (§§55–60) which follows the theory of fine art is a near restatement of the pre–§43 remarks.

Most tellingly against Gotshalk, there seems to be no second theory of beauty adumbrated in the *Critique of Judgment.* One does not present a *theory* of beauty by the mere implication that a judgment of the beauty of an artwork is grounded in something different from a judgment of the beauty of a flower. So even if Kant's pre–§43 remarks cannot, ultimately, be

23. Ibid., p. 260.

24. Ibid., p. 258.

25. I do not deny that Kant's larger project involves seeking such evidence. Nonetheless I think it fair to say that if Kant is just surreptitiously redefining a concept, he is not discovering evidence; he is cheating.

held to apply to the expression of aesthetic ideas, we should conclude not that Kant had two theories of beauty, but that he has one theory of beauty which cannot accommodate his theory of fine art.

In a paper partly written as a response to Gotshalk, Paul Guyer says that "Kant's formalism and expressionism may be seen as aspects of a complex but non-contradictory theory of the pleasures which we take in beautiful objects."[26] The crucial aspect of Guyer's view is this:

> Nothing in [Kant's formalism] need be seen as excluding concepts, or representations of concepts, symbols, and the like, from being *part of the manifold of imagination* which the mind ranges over in its free play. Nothing in what I have argued to follow so far from the theory of cognitive harmony need exclude the meaning or significance, the suggestiveness or symbolic aptness, of a given representation, work of art or of nature, from being among that which disposes the mind to the state which grounds an aesthetic judgment.[27]

But this is only half the solution. If nothing *excludes* expression from being beautiful, what *enables* expression to be beautiful?

I think the answer is that an expression of aesthetic ideas—a metaphor—can be found beautiful because entertaining one mimics the same mental processes and acts as the judging of natural beauty. Kant's remarks suggest that he found a deep similarity, which he did not fully spell out, between the grasping of aesthetic ideas and the perception of beautiful form. Remark (M) says that when we "arrange" our thoughts "in the aesthetic mode" (which we can take to mean "when we think metaphorically"), then they can have a unity signaled by a feeling, a feeling, we might assume, of pleasure. Remarks (Q) and (R) suggest that the grasping of aesthetic ideas involves "reflection" with the possibility of the "harmony" of sensibility and understanding.

This is as far as Kant goes. We might continue speculatively along the following lines. Consider a painting, *Jupiter's Eagle,* which depicts an eagle with lightning in its claws, flying through ominous clouds, and so on. It provokes aesthetic ideas by prompting us to discover a meaning for it. This is like the search for an adequate concept for an item of perception; in other words, the search for metaphorical meaning is a kind of reflective judgment.

26. Paul D. Guyer, "Formalism and the Theory of Expression in Kant's Aesthetics," *Kant-Studien* 68 (1977): 48.

27. Ibid., p. 55. Guyer has not modified this view in his more recent book; see *Kant and the Claims of Taste* (Cambridge: Harvard University Press, 1979), pp. 233–34.

In the case of "ordinary" reflective judgment, the understanding is presented with percepts and tries to find an adequate concept. In discovering metaphorical meaning, we are not exactly trying to recognize the subject in a painting. At least we know it is an eagle with lightning in its claws. (As Kant says, "In the case of beautiful art the aesthetic idea must be prompted by a concept of the object.") What we have to discover are concepts adequate to express the meaning of the painting. So we run through concepts such as "sublimity," "majesty," "might," and so on, none of which is entirely adequate, though each feels like it fits. This feeling of fit might be what Kant calls the "unity" in an expression of aesthetic ideas, and might therefore be the source of the (pleasurable) feeling he takes to be part of the grasping of aesthetic ideas.

This line of reasoning entitles Kant to say that an expression of aesthetic ideas by a work of fine art, such expression being considered by itself, can be found beautiful. It does not, exactly, substantiate the notorious remark at §51, quoted as (Q) above. That remark simply seems overstated—a mistake on Kant's part. If beauty were "in general" the expression of aesthetic ideas, then it would follow that all beautiful things are expressions of aesthetic ideas. But this is simply false: we have the simple counterexample of beautiful flowers and birds. True, there is a passage in which Kant writes about "the charms in beautiful nature" which "contain, as it were, a language in which nature speaks to us and which seems to have a higher meaning. Thus a lily's white color seems to attune the mind to ideas of innocence . . . " and so on through other colors (§42, 302). Yet these colors, while perhaps calling to mind certain ideas and therefore "as it were" expressing aesthetic ideas, do not *actually* express such ideas since only the work of human *Geist* can do this.

7

I have established that Kant, without switching theories, can say both that an object that does not express aesthetic ideas (e.g., a rose) and that an object that does express aesthetic ideas (e.g., a poem) can be freely or purely beautiful. Beauty is therefore not limited to pure form (of the spatial or temporal sort). This is a kind of reconciliation of the pre–§43 natural beauty portion of the theory with the post–§43 fine-art segment. However, not all questions are answered.

Is it possible to arrive at what we might think of as an all-things-considered judgment regarding the beauty of an artwork? This is a question that Kant did not seem to raise explicitly, though one or two proposals may be teased out of some of his remarks. The problem is that many works of art offer *both* form and aesthetic ideas—painting and kinds of visual art for sure; less certainly music (Does music express aesthetic ideas?) or poetry (Is there any way in which a poem exhibits spatio-temporal form?). It apparently does not follow that if an artwork is beautiful in aesthetic ideas, then it will be beautiful in form. Nor vice versa. Beauty of form and beauty of aesthetic ideas seem on first glance to be logically independent. (And they will prove to be logically independent; see the discussion of the "equivalence proposal" below.)

Consider four visual artworks—Alpha, Beta, Gamma, and Delta. A spectator renders certain judgments about each: that Alpha's form and expression of aesthetic ideas are beautiful, that Beta's form but not its expression of aesthetic ideas is beautiful, and so on. Let us tabulate this spectator's verdicts:

Artwork	**Form**	**Expression of Aesthetic Ideas**
Alpha	Beautiful	Beautiful
Beta	Beautiful	Not beautiful
Gamma	Not beautiful	Beautiful
Delta	Not beautiful	Not beautiful

These seem to be possible verdicts. That is, there is no obvious inconsistency about them. In that case, we need some additional proposal to get a univocal answer to the question "Is artwork Beta or Gamma beautiful?" since the answer thus far seems to be yes and no. Here are three proposals concerning any artwork, *A:*

The Disjunctive Proposal: *A* is beautiful iff *A*'s expression of aesthetic ideas is beautiful or *A*'s form (design, composition) is beautiful.

The Conjunctive Proposal: *A* is beautiful iff *A*'s expression of aesthetic ideas is beautiful and *A*'s form is beautiful.

The Equivalence Proposal: *A*'s form is beautiful iff *A*'s expression of aesthetic ideas is beautiful.

Kant, vaguely, inclines toward the conjunctive proposal here, toward the equivalence proposal there; though we shall see that he is probably entitled only to the relatively uninteresting disjunctive proposal.

The conjunctive proposal is suggested by (N), (O), and (P). Remarks (N) and (P) seem to say that an artwork lacking beauty of expression simply fails to be beautiful. Remark (O) says that a work of art needs "taste" in addition to genius to be beautiful, which hints that a work of art needs formal beauty—its design or composition must be beautiful—in order to be beautiful. Thus (adding it up) it appears Kant held that a work of art needs both formal and expressive beauty in order to be beautiful (all things considered). On the conjunctive proposal, Alpha alone would be properly speaking beautiful.

What sort of position is this? If Kant thinks he is describing our intuitions (or what almost amounts to the same thing, our word usage), he is not being entirely accurate, for we are comfortable in "splitting" our verdicts. We might say that the expression of aesthetic ideas but not the design of Marcel Duchamp's notorious *Fontaine* (the urinal-as-artwork) is beautiful. Alternatively, a person could judge the idea-less, purely sensuous, aspect of an artwork to be beautiful, yet judge its aesthetic ideas to be ugly. This, in fact, could be said to describe the initial critical reception of such works as Manet's *Déjeuner sur l'herbe* or the recent reception of Robert Mapplethorpe's dicier photographs: beautifully composed works with off-putting subject matter. It could be argued that "interest" has intruded—our spectator just does not like nudes or he is homophobic or some such thing. Hence he is not delivering himself of a pure judgment of beauty.

Well, then, consider the general possibility of weak metaphors. Consider a painting that expresses aesthetic ideas about the nature of heavenly bliss. This painting depicts people in white robes sitting on clouds strumming harps. It is not necessarily evidence of the intrusion of "interest" if a spectator fails to find its expression of aesthetic ideas beautiful. This painting is the fine-art counterpart of the dull and regular pepper garden: its ideas simply do not "play." Nonetheless, the spectator may find the design of the painting beautiful.

If the conjunctive interpretation is supposed to reform our intuitions, Kant gives no reason why we should withhold a pronouncement that thus-and-such work of art is beautiful unless we judge *both* its form and expression to be beautiful. So the conjunctive proposal, even if Kant intended it, is not justified.

The equivalence proposal might be suggested by (Q), which does tell us that "we may *in general* call beauty (whether natural or artistic) the *expression* of aesthetic ideas" (emphasis added). In effect, the equivalence proposal denies the possibility that a work of fine art could be beautiful in form and fail to be beautiful in its expression of aesthetic ideas. The equivalence proposal entails that the spectator's verdict regarding artwork Beta or Gamma is not just false but incoherent. On the other hand, if the equivalence proposal could be argued for successfully, Kant would have a way of *fully* integrating his theory of fine art with his theory of beauty.

Suppose an observer pronounces the painting *Jupiter's Eagle* to be beautiful. Could Kant argue for an equivalence between form and expression by alleging an inseparability of form and expression—alleging that *that* very form, *that* pictorial design and no other, could express the aesthetic ideas it in fact expresses? No. Even granting that those ideas could be expressed only by that pictorial design, we still could judge the painting's design ugly and the ideas it expresses beautiful (or vice versa).

Alternatively, Kant may claim that it is indistinguishable to internal sense whether we judge beauty of expression or beauty of form: reflective judgment operates in so similar a way in each. We may find an artwork to be beautiful, yet be uncertain as to whether the source of its beauty is its expression of aesthetic ideas or its composition. Yet what follows from this? Surely not that beauty of expression is equivalent to beauty of form, for examples such as Duchamp's *Fontaine* or Manet's *Déjeuner* demonstrate not only that there *is* a difference but that we can, at least in these cases, *tell* the difference. There is, then, no reason to think the verdicts regarding Beta or Gamma to be anything but consistent.

In the end, then, we are left with the disjunctive proposal. This is disappointing, for it does not really integrate Kant's theory of fine art into his theory of pure or formal beauty. It merely says that an artwork can be beautiful in either or both of two aspects. While this may be hardly unsettling in itself—we often say of an artwork, a movie for example, that its script was interesting but its acting was not, which is a perfectly acceptable way of answering the question "Is it a good movie?"—our conclusion about Kant reveals that the only thing which the beauty of spatio-temporal pure form and the beauty of aesthetic ideas have in common is that each elicits a condition of free play in its perceivers. But, of course, that may be the only thing the beauty of a nautilus shell and the beauty of a rose have in common.

8

I would like to attempt a correction to the reputation of Kant's theory of beauty in modern aesthetics, in particular as Kant and his theory are understood in George Dickie's recent book *Evaluating Art.* I will close with some comments on the vexed question of the aesthetic versus the cognitive.

The correction: Kant is usually seen as the progenitor of the modern apparatus of the aesthetic. The ideas of disinterestedness, of a special mode of attention that later is called the aesthetic attitude, and of formalism in art criticism are traceable to Kant who, if not quite the first to formulate them, is credibly held to have installed them firmly into modern thought. I do not wish to counter this view. However, some writers insist that art be valued for its aesthetic merit alone, others that cognitive import be included as well. The mistake comes, I think, in finding Kant on the side of aesthetic merit alone. Mary Mothersill recently wrote: "Kant seems to think that it is *just* their lack of 'meaning'... that qualifies conventionalized design motifs or unfamiliar botanical specimens for being paradigms of beauty. This is why people who care about the arts think that Kant's aesthetic theory ends by trivializing what is important."[28] But Mothersill simply ignores the theory of aesthetic ideas.

The problem is that Kant's theory of aesthetic ideas is not part of the canonical history of aesthetics. George Dickie in *Evaluating Art,* for example, traces a line of ancestry from Kant's disinterestedness through Schopenhauer's account of aesthetic consciousness and culminating in Monroe Beardsley's theory of art evaluation.[29] It is not that there is no such line, but we must remember that an idea moving through history, like a passenger on a long train trip, may well lose some baggage along the way. In getting from Kant to Beardsley, we should not forget that Kant's theory was processed by Clive Bell, whose 1914 book, *Art,* portions of which still appear in nearly all introductory anthologies, is a virtual Kant-made-simple, and whose central concept of "significant form" strips Kantian aesthetic judgment of anything except a preoccupation with design and composition. "Significant form" is "the one quality common to all works of visual art." It is "lines and colours

28. Mary Mothersill, *Beauty Restored* (Oxford: Clarendon Press, 1984), p. 225.

29. George Dickie, *Evaluating Art* (Philadelphia: Temple University Press, 1988), pp. 27–37, 53–54. See also Monroe C. Beardsley, *Aesthetics: Problems in the Philosophy of Criticism* (New York: Harcourt, Brace & World, 1958), pp. 454–556; and "In Defense of Aesthetic Value," in *Proceedings and Addresses of the American Philosophical Association* (Newark, Del.: American Philosophical Association, 1979), pp. 723–49.

combined in a particular way, certain forms and relations of form, [which] stir our aesthetic emotions." Of a certain "descriptive" painting, Frith's *Paddington Station,* Bell says: "In it line and colour are used to recount anecdotes, suggest ideas, and indicate the manners and customs of an age: they are not used to provoke aesthetic emotion. Forms and the relations of forms were for Frith not objects of emotion, but means of suggesting emotion and conveying ideas."[30] This is a good synopsis of the way the later twentieth century understood Kant, and hence why Beardsley and Kant *seem* to stand in the same line of thought.

Beardsley, for example, clearly opposes aesthetic appreciation to the expression of ideas. In a late essay, he offered the definition that "an artwork is something produced with the intention of giving it the capacity to satisfy the aesthetic interest," where aesthetic interest is specified as standing in opposition to such things as an interest in the cognitive (which presumably includes not just what might count as knowledge but also what is clearly presented as mere opinion). "The fuss that has been made about Duchamp's *Fountain* has long amazed me," Beardsley wrote. "It does not seem that in submitting that object to the art show and getting it more or less hidden from view, Duchamp or anyone else [!] thought of it either as art or as having an aesthetic capacity. . . . Many objects exhibited today by the avant-garde evidently do make comments of some kind on art itself, but these objects may or may not be artworks."[31] But this would not be Kant's view. Were Kant to be resurrected and confronted with Duchamp's artwork-urinal, he would probably faint. When revived and stuffed with a hundred and fifty years of art history, however, he *could* say that the form (design, composition) of *Fountain* was not especially beautiful, yet, still, the work not only expressed aesthetic ideas (among which is the idea that art need not be especially pleasing in design), hence its expression of aesthetic ideas was beautiful—a comment in clear opposition to Beardsley. I do not mean to pit a hypothetical and speculative Kant against an actual Beardsley. The fact is that Beardsley's theory does not allow him to appreciate ideas aesthetically, while Kant's does.

It is a near-standard feature of contemporary discussions of the value of art that "aesthetic value" is other than "cognitive value." For example, the two major modern theorists of the value of art in Dickie's *Evaluating Art* are Beardsley (on behalf of aesthetic value) and Nelson Goodman (for cognitive

30. Clive Bell, *Art* (1914), as reprinted in *Aesthetics: A Critical Anthology,* ed. George Dickie and Richard Sclafani (New York: St. Martin's Press, 1977), pp. 40–41.

31. Monroe C. Beardsley, "An Aesthetic Definition of Art," in *What Is Art?* ed. Hugh Curtler (New York: Haven Publications, 1983), pp. 21, 25.

value). Dickie tries to effect a kind of synthesis by ascribing *artistic* value to artworks, where artistic value is a kind of composite of the aesthetic and the cognitive. He holds "that Beardsley is right to hold that aesthetic, non-referential characteristics of works of art are important for the evaluating of art and that Goodman is right to hold that cognitive characteristics of works of art are important for the evaluation of art."[32]

By calling Dickie's view a kind of synthesis, I do not mean that he *blends* Beardsleyan-formalist and Goodman-cognitivist assessments of a work of art into one all-things-considered judgment of that work. Dickie adopts the notion of "independently valued properties," which are properties valued (positively or negatively) independently of their relations to other aspects of the work.[33] The discussion of independent properties, unfortunately for my purposes, occurs in the context of comparing works of art, so that Dickie's examples of independent properties are, in his first illustration, a poem's subtle meter against a painting's brilliant color. "Meter and color are such different things that it does not appear to make sense to try to compare and rank them."[34] Probably, but what of cognitive and aesthetic qualities? While Dickie does not come right out and say this, it seems to be implied in his discussion of *The Adventures of Huckleberry Finn* that Twain's work could be valued *independently* for its aesthetic properties (its beautiful writing and plot construction, say) and for its cognitive import (its confrontation with racial attitudes).[35] If so then Dickie, I think, should agree a) that the matrix above regarding artworks Alpha, Beta, Gamma, and Delta represents independent value judgments, and b) that the conclusion I have drawn with respect to Kant—namely, that Kant seems to be entitled only to what I have called the disjunctive reading (a work of art is beautiful in either or both of two aspects: its form or its expression of aesthetic ideas)—is not a bad position to be in, is, in fact, the *correct* position.

There is an exception to be noted: Dickie would not describe the judgments regarding the four artworks in terms of the beauty of their form versus the beauty of their expression of aesthetic ideas, but rather as aesthetic value versus cognitive value. I think there is more at stake here than a difference in terminology.

32. Dickie, *Evaluating Art,* pp. 115–16.

33. Ibid., p. 164. Dickie muddies the waters, however, when he tells us (p. 173) that independently valued properties sometimes "interact"—which seems to be prohibited by the very definition of independent properties.

34. Ibid., p. 165.

35. Ibid., p. 174ff.

Dickie plays out aesthetic value by and large via Beardsleyan formalism, which is, in its simplest formulation, to look at or listen to or read the artwork itself and notice the degree of unity, intensity, and complexity it embodies. The greater the unity (etc.) the more aesthetically valuable the artwork, for its unity contributes to a heightened aesthetic experience. When cognitive value is addressed by Nelson Goodman, it seems we have to back off from pure Beardsleyan formalism. We must begin to notice the reference of the artwork; and reference, whatever else it is, is a relation between aspects of the artwork and something else.

In contrast, the expression of aesthetic ideas is or appeals to something we can rightly call "cognitive," though the motivation to *oppose* the cognitive to the aesthetic is absent in Kant's case. The cognitive, not only in *Evaluating Art* but also in Goodman's *Languages of Art*, revolves around the ability of works of art to make reference to something outside themselves—to "say something about the world." However, the expression of aesthetic ideas does not involve reference, except indirectly, insofar as artworks stimulate the mind to thoughts of things. If the cognitive/aesthetic distinction is drawn along the lines of attending to the reference of a work versus attending to its unity, complexity, and intensity, then the cognitive is opposed to the aesthetic: we either see what the artwork says about the external world, or we look toward how its parts are arranged. Or both. But the point is that these seem to be activities of differing kinds, which lends support to the common view that cognitive valuation is different enough from aesthetic valuation to force us to speak of different values.

If, on the other hand, we take Kant's route, the cognitive in art will not necessarily aim at stating truths or at standing as samples of reality but will be that which stimulates metaphorical thinking, which lays claim to being a cognitive activity. (I do not mean that the cognitive in art *cannot* aim at truths or exemplification, only that the cognitive in art need not be *limited* to reference.) More important, on Kant's view the appreciation of aesthetic ideas is not an activity different in kind from the appreciation of design and composition. There is no contemplation/verification split of the sort that motivates an aesthetic/cognitive value distinction. In fact, Kant shows how Duchamp's *Fountain*—of all things—is susceptible to aesthetic appreciation without falling into the trap of "mooning over the gleaming surfaces of the porcelain object [Duchamp] had manhandled into exhibition space."[36] And

36. Danto, *The Transfiguration of the Commonplace,* p. 94.

we may have a kind of reconciliation in the offing: perhaps Duchamp's *Fountain* and a work like Michelangelo's *Moses* are not so *radically* different as some think.

George Dickie:
A Biography and Bibliography

George Dickie was born in Palmetto, Florida, in 1926. After serving (and boxing) with the Marines, he graduated from Florida State University and went on to earn a Ph.D. at UCLA in 1959. Having taught at the University of Houston and Washington State University, he was persuaded in 1965 by Ruth Barcan Marcus to move to the University of Illinois at Chicago (then called "Chicago Circle"), where he is currently Professor of Philosophy. George has received a number of fellowships and grants, including an NEH Senior Fellowship and a Guggenheim Fellowship. He was also a Fellow of the Institute for Advanced Studies in the Humanities at the University of Edinburgh (Scotland). He is serving a term (1992–94) as President of the American Society for Aesthetics. George is married to Suzanne Cunningham, herself Professor of Philosophy at Loyola University in Chicago, and has two sons, Garrick and Blake.

BOOKS

Evaluating Art. Philadelphia: Temple University Press, 1988.

The Art Circle: A Theory of Art. New York: Haven Publications, 1984.

Aesthetics: A Critical Anthology (co-edited with R. Sclafani). New York: St. Martin's Press, 1977. Second edition (with R. Roblin), 1989.

Art and the Aesthetic. Ithaca: Cornell University Press, 1974. Korean translation 1982. Material from this book has been reprinted in Lars Aagaard-Mogensen (ed.),

Culture and Art; W. Kennick (ed.), *Art and Philosophy;* M. Rader (ed.), *A Modern Book of Esthetics;* and P. Alperson (ed.), *The Philosophy of the Visual Arts.*
Aesthetics: An Introduction. Indianapolis: Pegasus, 1971. Korean translation 1980. Finnish translation 1981.

ARTICLES

"A Tale of Two Artworlds." In Mark Rollins (ed.), *Arthur Danto and His Critics.* London: Blackwell, 1993.
"Kant, Mothersill, and Principles of Taste." *Journal of Aesthetics and Art Criticism,* 1989: 375–76.
"Beardsley, Sibley, and Critical Principles." *Journal of Aesthetics and Art Criticism,* Winter 1987: 229–37.
"Experiencing Art." In T. Anderberg *et al* (eds.), *Aesthetic Distinction: Essays Presented to Göran Hermerén on His 50th Birthday.* Lund: Lund University Press, 1988.
"Radical Disinterest." In Doug Bolling (ed.), *Philosophy and Literature.* New York: Haven Publications, 1987.
"Hume's Way: The Path Not Taken." In Peter McCormick (ed.), *The Reasons of Art.* Ottawa: University of Ottawa Press, 1985.
"The New Institutional Theory of Art." *Proceedings of the 8th International Wittgenstein Symposium,* Vienna, 1984. Reprinted in Dickie *et al* (eds.), *Aesthetics: A Critical Anthology.*
"Evaluating Art." *British Journal of Aesthetics,* 1985: 3–16.
"Stolnitz's Attitude: Taste and Perception." *Journal of Aesthetics and Art Criticism,* Winter 1984: 195–203.
"Instrumental Inference." *Journal of Aesthetics and Art Criticism,* 1983: 151–54.
"The Return to Art Theory." In *Modern Trends in Philosophy,* vol. 2. Tel Aviv: Yachdav Publishers, 1983. Reprinted in P. Werhane (ed.), *Philosophical Issues in Art,* 1984.
"Art and the Romantic Artist." In J. Fisher (ed.), *Essays on Aesthetics: Perspectives on the Work of Monroe C. Beardsley.* Philadelphia: Temple University Press, 1983.
"Art and Actuality: A Reply to Professor Cohen." *The Personalist,* 1977: 169–72.
"What Is Anti-Art?" *Journal of Aesthetics and Art Criticism,* 1975: 419–21.
"Beardsley's Theory of Aesthetic Experience." *Journal of Aesthetic Education,* 1974: 14–23.
"Taste and Attitude: The Origin of the Aesthetic." *Theoria,* 1973: 153–70.
"Psychical Distance: In a Fog at Sea." *British Journal of Aesthetics,* 1973: 17–29. Reprinted in P. Werhane (ed.), *Philosophical Issues in Art,* 1984.
"The Institutional Concept of Art." In B. Tilghman (ed.), *Language and Aesthetics.* Lawrence: Kansas University Press, 1973.
"Defining Art II." In Matthew Lipman (ed.), *Contemporary Aesthetics.* Boston: Allyn and Bacon, 1973. Reprinted in translation in G. Genette (ed.), *Esthétique et Poétique,* 1992.
"Bullough and Casebier: Disappearing in the Distance." *The Personalist,* 1972: 127–31.
"Defining Art." *American Philosophical Quarterly,* 1969: 252–58. Reprinted in P. Werhane (ed.), *Philosophical Issues in Art,* and J. Fisher (ed.), *Reflecting on Art.*

"Art Narrowly and Broadly Speaking." *American Philosophical Quarterly,* 1968: 71–77.
"I. A. Richards' Phantom Double." *British Journal of Aesthetics,* 1968: 54–59.
"Meaning and Intention." *Genre,* 1968: 182–89.
"Beardsley's Phantom Aesthetic Experience." *Journal of Philosophy,* 1965: 129–36. Reprinted in translation in D. Lories (ed.), *Philosophie analytique esthétique.*
"The Myth of the Aesthetic Attitude." *American Philosophical Quarterly,* 1964: 56–65. Reprinted in the Bobbs-Merrill Reprints Series; J. Hospers (ed.), *Introductory Readings in Aesthetics;* W. Kennick (ed.), *Art and Philosophy;* Dickie *et al* (eds.), *Aesthetics: A Critical Anthology;* D. Lories (ed.), *Philosophie analytique esthétique;* J. Margolis (ed.), *Philosophy Looks at the Arts;* P. Alperson (ed.), *The Philosophy of the Visual Arts.*
"Is Psychology Relevant to Aesthetics?" *Philosophical Review,* 1962: 285–302. Reprinted in the Bobbs-Merrill Reprint Series; F. Coleman (ed.), *Contemporary Readings in Aesthetics;* and in translation in *Il Verri,* December 1963.
"Design and Subject Matter: Fusion and Confusion." *Journal of Philosophy,* 1961: 233–38.
Plus many discussion notes and book reviews, including reviews of E. D. Hirsch's *Validity in Interpretation,* D. W. Prall's *Aesthetic Judgment,* and M. Weitz's *Hamlet and the Philosophy of Criticism* (for *Journal of Aesthetics*); of M. Weitz's *The Opening Mind* (for *Journal of Philosophy*); of N. Wolterstorff's *Works and Worlds of Art* and J.J.C. Smart's *Philosophy and Scientific Realism* (for *Philosophy and Phenomenological Research*); and of C. Wright Mills's *Images of Man* and Charles Darwin's *The Problem of World Population* (for *Philosophy of Science*).

Index